The Mission of Mysticism

The Mission of Mysticism

Richard Kirby

LONDON
SPCK

First published 1979
SPCK
Holy Trinity Church
Marylebone Road
London NW1 4DU

Printed and bound in Great Britain at
The Camelot Press Ltd, Southampton

ISBN 0 281 03690 X

For my
three mystical companions
Best of friends
Apostles of love

Sister Rosslyn, Dss. C.S.A.
The Revd Dr Martin Israel
The Revd W. G. D. Sykes

Contents

Tables

Acknowledgements

Thanks are due to Turnstone Books for permission to reproduce the table of contents of *The Many Ways of Being* by S. Annett (Abacus: London).

Quotation of 1 Cor. 15.51–5 on page 170 has been taken from the New English Bible, Second Edition © 1970 by permission of Oxford and Cambridge University Presses.

Foreword

The interest in mysticism grows strongly as the churches become ever emptier and the religious festivals become mere periods of recreation amid a boisterous, heedless world. It is evident that contemporary society, if it is at all interested in spiritual things, demands direct experience and not merely teaching that comes from ancient texts, nor is it impressed with traditional doctrine that does not have the savour of a living force behind it.

The strength of this book is its powerful contemporary note and its concern with current mystical and occult practices. The more staid, conventional reader who prides himself on his knowledge of mysticism may be slightly put out as he reads name after name of which he has never previously heard, for Richard Kirby has not written a standard text on mysticism in which the various religious traditions are examined in turn and an overall synthesis is attempted. He has, instead, very wisely concentrated on the present scene. The result is a very interesting analysis of many current trends, ranging from unidentified flying objects and science fiction, on which subject he has a great knowledge, to the literature and teaching of the Theosophical Society and the practice of meditation, all of which have a lesser or greater contact with mysticism. The author has had a thorough training in academic psychology, and speaks with authority against the traditional critique of behaviouristic and psychodynamic circles on the subject of mystical experience. To be sure, the more recent school of humanistic psychology takes a much more positive view of what it calls 'peak experiences', but even here there is insufficient recognition of the radically transforming quality of real mysticism.

This book breathes an ardent love of mysticism. In the mystical life the author sees the way of evolution of the human species from mere *Homo sapiens* to what he calls *Homo christus*. The whole being of the author flows out in response to the high destiny of the christed man who lives and works in full communion with the Spirit of God. This is the work of a youthful spirit, and it embodies the aspirations of all spiritually aware members of the younger generations. I can only hope that its message reaches as many minds as possible.

MARTIN ISRAEL

Preface

Mysticism is an affirmation of the perfectibility of man. It is the apostle of perfection and love, and its mission to individual men and to the human race is to awaken them to the ideal expression of those virtues.

This is a book about the nature of mankind, and thus it is a theory of human nature. But it is concerned with man's future and destiny as well as with those essential components of man with which theories of human nature are normally concerned. The distinguishing feature of the theory outlined here is its extreme modernity. It incorporates not only the classical corpus of mystical thought, but also all modern art forms, with special reference to music and science fiction, in connection with which it develops a theory of mystical aesthetics, and in fact it surveys the entire field of modern culture for clues to the modern purpose of mysticism. This leads to a special consideration of the relationship between science and mysticism, and the presentation of a theory of science-mysticism in which it is shown how the common aims of these two enterprises, as regards the inspiration and sustenance of mankind, leads to a rapprochement of them at the highest point of science. The great value of science fiction is shown here: as the evolutionary conscience of mankind it is the servant of mysticism, while as the principal student of the future and potential of science it plays an indispensable part in the wise growth of that endeavour.

Because this is a study of human perfection, it must be a book about Jesus Christ, who is the prototype of all mystics, and therefore it is a contribution to the literature of Christianity, and indeed to both theology and Christology. The literature of mysticism is the record of the experiences of those men and women who have followed Jesus Christ's call to perfection; it is time for the whole human race to follow him, becoming in the end not *Homo sapiens* but *Homo christus*, the race built at last in his image.

Several of the features of contemporary humanity suggest that this 'divinization' of the species, as Pierre Teilhard de Chardin described it, is imminent. These include the developing 'whole-earth' outlook consequent upon the astronauts' view of the earth as a whole; the widespread realization that natural selection has come to an end because science and technology enable man to redesign not only his environment but also his own nature; the great danger of the extinction of the race through nuclear war, ecological disaster, the exhaustion of supplies; and the onset of the so-called Aquarian Age, in which it is said that all mankind will awaken to spirituality and mysticism.

But these unifying influences may come too late. The Way of Jesus Christ passes through the Cross of Calvary, and the Path of Mysticism entails one or more sojourns in the Dark Night of the Soul. For this reason the mystic will not be rashly swept away in a tide of millenarian enthusiasm; he will be able to contemplate peacefully the present plight of *Homo sapiens* without being surprised or cripplingly dismayed. Perhaps, like Jesus himself, mankind will have not only to be crucified, as is happening at present, but to suffer unto death. But in that case the imitation of Christ will have been all the more perfect, and the reward will be commensurate.

Ealing, London   R. S. K.
October 1978

PART ONE

The Nature of Mysticism

1

An Introduction to some Key Issues

Perfection

Mysticism is concerned with the perfection of men and man. This is its ineradicable core, which should be at the centre of every discussion of it.

Perfectionism is unfashionable at the present time. It is commonly said that man now regards himself as intrinsically flawed, incapable of perfection. It is said that after Copernicus showed that the earth is not the centre of the universe, Darwin asserted that man is only an animal, and Freud declared that he is governed by reprehensible subconscious motives, man gave up hope of progressing to a better state, believing that his very nature made perfection impossible.

Some critics of religion have also argued that it will be time enough to worry about perfection when the mere survival of the human race is ensured: in the meantime, they urge, it is irrelevant to seek perfection.

Such views apply only to man's material nature. He has a spiritual nature also, and it is divine. If we recall the wonderful teaching that the Kingdom of God is within us, that it is a part, and the most central part, of each and every man, we will have more confidence in our capacity to become perfect. For the fact is that man is already, for the most part, perfect! It is only the tiny part of ourselves which we call our mind and body that is imperfect; and when they learn to obey the dictates of the divine Self of which each man has a share, it will be seen how natural it is to pursue that perfection which is our atavistic right.

It is true that material man is selfish and unregenerate, but it is open to any man to put on his Christ-nature and rule benevolently over his lower, material, nature. The reality and feasibility of this spiritual revolution is attested in the literature of many traditions, and many names have been assigned to the process and to the result: nirvana, liberation, independence, kaivalya, God-realization, self-realization, perfection, heaven,

3

mystical union, the spiritual marriage, the unitive life, yoga. Any human being can attain this mystical perfection (which is irreversible and permanent), and he need not wait for death. It can be achieved in this mortal life, and indeed its attainment is the purpose of incarnate life. Many have been blessed with this culmination of life while still on earth; Evelyn Underhill's classic work *Mysticism* enumerates several hundred of the most famous. And there are many alive today who reside in those mystic heights. They are found not only in monasteries but in the full range of secular occupations, for God-realization does not entail retreating from the world; on the contrary, the mystic has a sacred duty, with the Christ who is risen within him, to minister to the suffering world, and his duty may require him to practise a secular career. He will be none the less perfect for that, for he worships God in all that he encounters, and his every deed is a hymn of praise to the Almighty who lives unfettered within him. Indeed, the idea of perfection, in the Christian tradition, is at the heart of its doctrine. And perfectionism is the language of mysticism. Jesus Christ, in his incarnate life, showed us what we must do, and he laid it upon us as a duty to become as perfect as God himself! This is such an incredible command, so sublime a destiny, that for the most part we forget it, or repress it. But it is a truth which should be the subject of every morning's meditation.

The Christian way of perfection is amazingly simple. It is simply to be absolutely self-surrendered to God, to be his perfectly willing instrument. Perfection for any person consists in doing perfectly God's will for himself, and, as God's will covers everything that a person will think, say, or do, he will thereby merge imperceptibly with God, thereby being granted perfection. In other religious traditions this self-surrender is also a commandment, but sometimes it is expressed differently, such as 'consecrating everything to the Spirit'. This is the way to perfection, the way with a million million corridors, each person having his own road to the goal for which he is destined.

To know that one is to be perfect as one's destiny, it is necessary only to pray and meditate as commanded by our Lord and his great saints and mystics. The materialist whose view of human nature is confined to the body can easily learn of the inevitability of perfection by looking within in patience and humility, for there he will find the Kingdom of God, and when he has made that discovery all other things, including perfection, will be given to him (Matt. 6.33).

Grace

One of the most important issues which arise in the discussion of mysticism is grace. Mysticism, it is true, is concerned with perfection, and perhaps this is its greatest single attribute; but the instrument of mysticism is God's grace, and there is no real mysticism without it. However, to understand exactly what this doctrine means in practical terms is an extremely demanding task, and one which must almost always be costly to a man's pride, for to understand it entails the realization of the absolute impotence of self, and the absoluteness with which God creates all that is good in a man. Moreover, the spiritual life contains another paradox, which is that although grace cannot be earned in any way, the aspirant must none the less strive as fervently as if he could in that way cause grace to descend upon him.

Grace is the most central paradox of the mystical life, and the paradox can be shown to be the root cause of the disagreement which orthodox Christian spirituality has with three enterprises which seemingly have the same aim of mystical perfection: occultism, esotericism, and theosophy. Christian mystics find themselves agreeing with this trio that man's destiny is mystical perfection, but they differ from these three schools as regards the means by which that perfection is to be obtained. In this connection, however, orthodox Christians share with the general public certain false assumptions. Since the three ways do have an important part to play in the mystical future of mankind, it is essential to set the record straight as early as possible in this book.

Occultism

To begin with, a very clear distinction must be made between 'occultism' and its adjective 'occultist', and the popular term 'the occult', whose adjective is the same as the noun, 'occult'. Of course, the original denotation or meaning of these words is simply 'hidden'. But other shades of meaning have now accrued. 'The occult' now largely refers to anything which is sensational, mysterious, and commonly frankly satanic too, and the connotation of 'occult' is simply unsavoury. But this has nothing to do with 'occultism', which is an extremely devout and painstakingly scholarly tradition of thought and practice whose sole purpose is to promote the progress, along the spiritual path to perfection, of all who have awakened to their mystical destiny, for the sake of all mankind. And occultism is defined as the science of mystical evolution; it is 'the employment of the hidden (i.e. occult) mystical faculties of man to discern the hidden reality of nature, i.e. to see God as the all in all'. Occultism differs from religious mysticism only in the self-consciousness with which the spiritual path is trodden. The mystic is the intuitive, the occultist is the mapmaker. The oft-quoted dictum is that the occultist is the practical mystic, but this is misleading, for the vision of true mysticism is intensely practical. Perhaps a better image is given in the parable of the elevator. It is said that on the way to the beatific vision the occultist plods up the stairs, but the mystic takes the lift. However, the occultist takes the lift down, while the mystic has to walk. Perhaps the fact that mystics tend to despise occultists is due to the feeling of superiority which mystics have as a result of having gravity on their side during their pedestrian period. Anyhow, the best definition of the occultist is that which simply calls him the intellectual mystic. He codifies the path and sets up landmarks, but is none the less devout and God-fearing for all that. In this sense Jesus was the prince of occultists; the Sermon on the Mount is an exposition of occultism.

Christian critics of occultism argue that the practitioners of the latter deny the necessity of grace; they contend that occultists make a terrible error in supposing that they can achieve spiritual perfection through their own efforts. To Christians this is impossible by definition! But the conflict is again more apparent than real. For the fact is that the occultist urges that man can do nothing spiritually of his own power: only the higher Self is potent in that respect. And that higher Self is the God within, or the Christ within, or the Christ-principle in the soul, or many other names by which it is known. Thus the occultist is saying above all else, 'Seek ye first the Kingdom of God (within)', and he also commands that the aspirant must 'die unto self daily' before he can progress. In essence this is identical with the practice and doctrine of the religious mystic.

Christians also point out that occultism is doomed if it substitutes impersonal meditation for prayer to the Person of God, but this too is a misconception. The 'meditation' of advanced occultists is identical with the prayer of advanced mystics: it is no accident that both traditions use the same word for the highest reaches of their respective activities: contemplation (*samadhi* in yoga), which is the temporary unity of God and the worshipper or meditator. Moreover, the final destination of all, the unitive life, is identical with the liberation sought by occultists. It must also be borne in mind that many occultists do pray as well as meditate; for occultism is the pursuit of mystical perfection, and is consonant with any other tradition which shares that aim. And such are the riches of occultism that mysticism cannot afford to neglect them.

For those unfamiliar with the literature of occultism, it may be helpful to mention the names of some of its most well-known advocates. In this century the most famous names have probably been Rudolf Steiner (1861–1925), who founded the now worldwide Anthroposophical Society, and Annie Besant (1847–1933), World President of the Theosophical Society. Both were extremely prolific authors, great leaders, and, in general, remarkable forces for good. Ernest Wood (1883–1965), who will be mentioned several times in the course of this book, was an English author who spent a lifetime working for the Theosophical Society and supervising education at every level in schools, colleges, and universities. He wrote more than thirty books, most of them concerned with practical mysticism, i.e. occultism, which in his rendering was concerned with self-culture towards spiritual realization, in the service of the community of man.

All three repudiated 'the occult' and lived lives that were, by any standards in human history, outstanding in moral integrity; though they will never be canonized by the Roman Catholic Church, their lofty, inspiring compassionate behaviour was truly saintly.

There are several other misunderstandings surrounding 'occultist' practices. Probably the most damaging is the idea that occultism is 'selfish', concerned with self-inflation, if not with frankly exploitative intentions towards other people. This belief has confused magic with occultism. Evelyn Underhill gave us the

7

excellent distinction, that magic wants to get, mysticism wants to give. By this criterion occultism undoubtedly falls into the latter camp, although there are always enough renegades to help the press announce the avarice of (the) occult(ism). The belief that occultism is selfish is usually partnered by the idea that it is 'separatist' and hence contrary to mysticism, which engenders and preaches and enacts non-separateness, the brotherhood of man.

There is a poignant irony in this accusation. Occultism, especially in its theosophical expressions, has stood for universal brotherhood as no religion except Christianity. The Theosophical Society, which we will consider in its own right presently, has as its first object 'the establishment of a universal brotherhood of man, regardless of colour, race, creed, or sex'. And Ernest Wood laboured mightily for this cause. He wrote the only great book on the subject, *The Science of Brotherhood* (1931); and in every book he exhorted his readers to understand that they were literally one with all their brethren, and must act accordingly. Some brief excerpts from his books give the flavour of this: the following quotation from *Concentration* (1913) absolutely epitomizes the way in which occultism combines the urgent quest of self-culture for spiritual development with the mystic love of all men:

> You can no longer regard life as a battle with others or for a few others; if your aim is gradual mastery of self and the full development of your powers, your only possible attitude to others, to all and all the time, is that of a benevolent intention to share with them the freedom and power that you are winning for yourselves.

In *The Intuition of the Will* (1926), a mere 40,000 words which contain one of this century's most brilliant expositions of the mystic truth of the one life uniting all men to each other and to nature, he wrote:

> He now sees that all souls are dwelling in one being, that they are parts of that one over-soul, and each is in its rightful place, as so many hands and feet. And each is in its rightful place not only in space, but also time. In the earlier stage we discovered that one position in space is as good as another,

one set of circumstances as acceptable for our purposes as another; now we see clearly that one position in time is as good as another, that it does not matter where anyone stands in the long procession of souls in evolution. (pp. 126–7)

There Ernest Wood's mystical perception has not only matched that of many religious sages, he has transcended it, and gone on to show how the supremely enlightened mystic can, while loving his fellow-man perfectly, not grieve over his complaints, for he has seen that the evolution of all, no matter how appalling their exterior fortune, is perfectly assured of its divine destiny, oneness with God, in due season. And as Ernest Wood shows, the alleged love of neighbour, coupled with immaturity and mistrust of God's omnipotence, leads to 'selfishness at second hand' – and to worse travesties of religious compassion, such as the Spanish Inquisition. He remarks in *The Seven Rays* (1925), in this connection: 'It is all right to lift a lame dog over a stile, but it may be foolish and unkind to carry it all the way home.'

However, the unique genius of occultism, the quality which distinguishes it from mysticism, religion, and theosophy, is its insistence upon the Kingdom of God within every man at all times. Occultism preaches to every man: The Kingdom of God, the Christ himself, are within you *now*! Their divine powers are powers of *your soul*! And it is not only your right and capability, it is your duty to begin realizing them (in both senses of that phrase) *now*! Religion is for most people a very tepid experience – if it can truly be described as an experience at all. Sometimes one hears people saying, 'I go to church on Sundays, and I say my prayers, but I haven't had any religious experience.' It is a pathetic lament. And if one points to the great mystics and saints, the same person will sadly shake his head, and say, 'No, I know my limitations. I could never be like them.' But occultism is the affirmation of the potential sainthood of *every* man. And it is not an affirmation of the potential saintly behaviour of everyone, but also of the saintly *experiences*, i.e. the mystical experiences, of the greatest saints and mystics. Religion and occultism thus serve parallel purposes: religion's tendency to deal with generalities is supplemented by the frantic insistence of occultism that the pearl of great price is truly within the reach of everyone. Occultism specializes in two endeavours: describing the religious and spiritual potential each person has, and providing very practical methods whereby they may begin to awaken their dormant faculties, and become, as Ernest Wood says, 'free from material desires, and free from resentment, anger, pride, fear, impatience, and all their brood; such binding emotions have been blown out like so many candles. The man is free on earth. He has reached nirvana in the lower world.' (There are two other, even more blessed, nirvanas.)

To make the point still clearer, it is worthwhile considering another work of occultism, *Golden Precepts* by G. de Purucker, partly because it has the interesting sub-title, 'A handbook for mystics, written by an occultist', and partly because the author has succeeded in capturing vividly the occultist's constant, gnawing, exhilarating vision that the higher consciousness, the mystical 'peak experiences', the revelation of God as the all in all, the profoundest spiritual perception, can be ours *now*, since Christ is the true self of each of us. The book describes itself as a 'guide to enlightened living', which informs us further about occultism, and in the light of the campaign to hold occultism guilty of selfishness and separateness, it is amusing to note that there is a whole section of the book which is called 'The Great Heresy of Separateness'! On the first page of this section it states, with an explicitness and maturity present in few comparable writings in religion:

> The Law of Laws of the universe is self-forgetfulness, not concentration of attention upon one's personal freedom, not even upon one's individuality. The primal law of the universe is living unto all things, not the doctrine that each must live for himself in order to develop for himself the spiritual powers within.

The book is full of equally penetrating, mystically impeccable insights. We must quote this author on the subject which it is the special skill of occultism to teach, the mission of each man to unfold and realize the divine powers immanent in him, and to do so *now*:

> Divinity is at the heart of you. It is the root of you. It is the core of the core of your being; and you can ascend along the pathway of the spiritual self, passing veil after veil of

obscuring selfhood, until you obtain unity with that inner divinity. That is the most sublime adventure known to man – the study of the Self of man. . . . You will, in time, by following this inner pathway of self-knowledge, grow so greatly in understanding and in inner vision, that your eyes will take in ranges and sweeps of inner light, unveiling to you the most awful, because the holiest and the most beautiful, mysteries of the boundless universe. . . . The inmost of the inmost of you is a god, a living divinity; and from this there flows downwards into your human mentality all the things that make men great, all the things that give rise to love and mighty hope and inspiration and aspiration, and, noblest of all, self-sacrifice.

In yourself lie all the mysteries of the universe. Through your inner self, your spiritual nature, you have a road reaching to the very Heart of the Universe.

This is the vision which nourishes religion, when it is permitted to do so.

Similarly, it is the work of occultism to affirm man's free will, and, more than this, his duty to use it for spiritual development. Just as certain forms of the heresy of quietism insensibly appear as a consequence of certain forms of mysticism, so a comparable heresy, which might be called omnipotence, or the notion of total helplessness, occurs when the practice of 'self-abandonment to divine providence' is used wrongly. Passivity is not man's true nature; God, by making man in his own image, has given each man a share of his divinity, and he surely expects each man to act upon this privilege. Occultism warns religion that an excess of self-abasement will be simply inhibiting; each man must stand up and express the Christ who is within him. Then it will be seen that the use of the will as prescribed by occultism is not selfish or bumptious, but an abdication of one's throne to him who will rule wisely, purposefully, and forcefully. And he is one's truest self; the little personal ego has no real part to play in any human endeavour involving the will.

Occultism, it can thus be seen, is the equivalent of the Minister for Self-improvement in every soul. It is its duty to provide the inspiration and the practices that will encourage a man to put into practice his religious beliefs, and so seize the destiny which is rightfully his. A Christian would say that the Blood of Christ bought each man eternal life; the occultist agrees, and adds that occultism offers each man that eternal life at once. The mystic and the religionist may exclaim that they do too, but the occultist points silently at the long lines of disappointed people queueing to leave the churches and try elsewhere, and he says to his brethren among mystics and religionists: 'If through you those people come to the spiritual awakening, I shall be very happy to bow out and watch with pleasure. But you have failed, and I must try my method of communicating the perennial truths, in my way, because, if I do not, there is a fearful price which we all have to share, the possibility of large numbers of ex-church people falling into the hands of people and groups and movements who have nothing to do with religion at all. I know you think that I am vulgar, grandiose, and assertive, just as I think you timid, superstitious, and spiritually superficial; but I contend that even you must admit that for people to come to religion via occultism and thence mysticism, through me, is better than to have them leave religion altogether.' Of course, what is required is an alliance between Church and occultism; the charismatic movement is a gesture in that direction, but so much remains to be done.

It is no accident that the topic of occultism has merited considerable space so early in this book; it is one of the leading contemporary embodiments of the mystical impulse, and has a great part to play in the mission of mysticism both to individuals and to the species. But, as we have seen, it is a matter of bitter disputation between many religious-minded people and occultists, and with good reason, since the name of occultism has been besmirched by undesirable practices conducted under its name. The Church performs a very useful service to occultism by insisting that it respect religious virtues; and occultism, it has been shown, claims to stimulate the Church in a way conducive to the growth of religion in self-realization. A definitive judgement between the two cannot be made in the space available here. But the subject is so central that the debate will break out again and again throughout the rest of this book.

Esotericism

The tradition known as esotericism has also had a bad press from Christians, who mostly regard it as élitist and fascist: and they are fond of saying that Christianity is for everybody. So is esotericism. The word does not mean for a few but by a few. That is to say, esotericism is the embodiment of knowledge which is sometimes called the Perennial Philosophy, and which is known to a few only because it is sought by only a few. Esotericists are those who followed the instruction of Jesus to seek, ask, and knock; the esoteric wisdom or secret doctrine is the reply which is ever-present. This knowledge is always available when the aspirant wants what; it is never withheld from those who seek it. It is secret only in the sense that people build within themselves walls which block their perception of the wisdom. When by spiritual aspiration they demolish those walls, the knowledge is instantly perceptible. Perhaps this is why there is an esoteric saying to the effect that 'when the pupil is ready, the Master is there – because he is always there'.

Theosophy

The third school with which Christianity has picked quarrels is theosophy. Christians denounce this as pseudo-religion, while theosophy claims simply to be the house of the secret doctrine, the wisdom which is the Perennial Philosophy, which is common to all religions. Christians deny the possibility of such a phenomenon, since they proclaim the uniqueness of the one incarnation. Theosophists counter that if Christians studied esotericism and comparative religion more they would be less convinced of such a thing.

So great a debate cannot be resolved here. But it must be noted that the literature of theosophy, and its own tradition, is especially valuable for this volume, because it perfectly embodies the aims of occultism and the content of esotericism. And as these constitute a mystical tradition which, though overlapping with Christianity a good deal, also provides a parallel and separate argument, the outlook and data which we shall henceforward call theosophical must have their place in the rest of this book, even if it is under protest from Christians, and even if the theosophical data are regarded as hypothetical. For only thus can an intellectually honest argument be developed. Theosophy is the embodiment of even more mystical literature than is Christianity, especially with reference to the mystical constitution and destiny of mankind. Moreover, the theosophical tradition has always closely championed yoga and Buddhism, so the presentation of the theosophical account will ensure that eastern religions join Christianity in the discussion.

The disagreement between the theosophical and the narrower Christian formulations is not always a trifling matter. Theosophists take as their 'Bible' the gigantic work *The Secret Doctrine*, published in 1888 and written allegedly at the direction of Adepts by H. P. Blavatsky. At once some differences emerge. Theosophists believe, and with good evidential backing, in the existence of perfected men, whom they call Adepts, Mahatmas, Masters of the Wisdom, and who, they believe, intercede in man's development. This may sound outrageous to a Catholic, but actually a moment's reflection will show how close it is to the doctrine of the saints and their intercession for us in heaven. The theosophical tradition endorses the doctrine of reincarnation, and in spiritual progression as successive lives occur, and it is very natural that perfected beings must occur in the procession somewhere. And the Adepts have shown their miracles as have the saints. The former have precipitated whole books on to media – such as rice-paper – that could not be written upon, and their wisdom is profound.

Another major disagreement occurs in connection with the age of mankind. Theosophists state that we are the fifth race of mankind, and that the species is some eighteen million years old. This is naturally somewhat shocking to Christian ears, but it does not really affect issues of fundamental belief; all are agreed that God is Love, that Christ is as God to us, and that we are all pilgrims. However may be the disagreements, one indisputable fact is that this modern trio – occultism, esotericism, and theosophy – have contributed so much to mystical thought and are so vital a force today that no account of modern mysticism can deny their right to be included in the discussion and given generous space.

The jigsaw theory of truth

Yet another major issue which arises in connection with mysticism is the nature of truth. The problem of the nature of truth has many aspects, and it has been much discussed by philosophers over the last 2000 years. Deep in the roots of the philosophy of truth and knowledge, technically known as epistemology, are premises which are partly inspired by the ancient and primeval logic of Aristotle. One of his most well-known logical principles asserts that nothing can be both A and not-A. But this has had a disastrous consequence in epistemology, as only the God-realized mystic with his generosity of mind can see. Aristotle's principle, employed in our world of infinitely diverse minds, leads to our view that if two men disagree, both cannot be right. It is so obvious to us that if this is so, either one man is wrong, or both are. The mystic disagrees. His enlightenment, as the Holy Spirit led him into 'all truth', has shown him that truth in our universe is organized according to a different principle, which may be called 'the mystic's jigsaw theory of truth'. It is a remarkably convivial philosophical theory. The mystic is aware that the divine spark in each man gives him a private and unique piece of the truth. The mystic sees truth not as a slowly increasing empire to which mankind adds bit by bit from the common effort. Rather, no man can ever see the actual totality of truth (only God can do that), but each man has his own piece of the jigsaw, his own contribution to truth. And this is despite the fact that some men – some parts of the jigsaw – look blank when the jigsaw is incomplete. An important part of the theory is that a man attests his piece of the truth not necessarily by writing or speaking, but with his whole personality. Indeed, each human life *is* the contribution to truth of the man who lived it.

Another major aspect of the theory is that it recognizes that the multiplicity of human temperaments, characters, personalities, and intellects *all* have a role, and an equal one, in the quest for truth. Philosophy, therefore, is not a competitive enterprise. Human diversity is thus not an obstacle to truth but our greatest asset in finding it. The mystic is indeed constantly aware of, and giving praise to, the phenomenon of individual differences between human beings and all the created entities. He sees each person as a unique song, divinely sung by his Creator, with a very special mission in life, with much to offer his fellow-men, and with a charm, grace, and splendour all his own. To offer contempt to another person, even if he appears to be what the world calls contemptible, is a great sin and a foolish oversight. Even the down-and-out on Skid Row evokes awe in the mystic's heart, and the unitive knowledge of non-separateness causes the mystic to know that he is one with all creation. It is ignorance of the jigsaw nature of truth that causes disputes between religions and between sects of a religion. Dogmatists try to fit all types of religion on to the bed of Procrustes, not knowing that they are *all* right. Similarly there is no literature, be it fiction or non-fiction, poetry or prose, drama or philosophy which the mystic dislikes. He is deeply grateful to every literary work for the insights it bears.

The mystic's perfection as a thinker

Another issue in the study of mysticism is the view that mysticism is mental woolliness, vagueness, and (in consequence) based on confusion. The opposite is true. The mystic is the man with the perfected mind. He alone has the passion and perception of the poet, the patience of the saint, the perseverance of the scientist, the razor-sharpness of the mathematician, the penetration of the philosopher, the intelligence of the logician, and he combines these with calmness and peace born of long years of meditation, and with creativity that follows the Holy Spirit into all truth. The mystic is, in fact, the Black Belt of thinking men, and he is master of every branch of thought while being mastered by none. He has every style and technique of thought in his repertoire, and his is the style of no styles, as he responds with perfect fluidity to each cognitive situation, according to the response it merits. The mystic is, in fact, the only complete thinker, for only he has developed the mental, personal, and spiritual faculties to their limits. Indeed, this is hardly surprising, since the perfected mystic is the perfected person, one who has trodden every inch of the way to Calvary with Christ, and reaped the corresponding reward.

The extinction of Homo sapiens

In the context of eternity mankind is saved already; in Christian terms Christ's harrowing of hell extended to all time and space: he is perpetually harrowing hell (which is why eternal damnation is an impossibility). But perhaps the most contentious issue introduced in this chapter is the matter of the possible extinction of the human race. Christianity has a genius for turning defeat into victory, and all its talents are going to be necessary if the human race is going to have a future at all.

Nobody wants to see the human race devastated or destroyed, through internal or external agencies. Yet it is an event which is probable, and only the Christian mystic who has the courage to think through to its conclusion the likely fate of his species can be prepared for that awful event. For as Pierre Teilhard de Chardin has so brilliantly pointed out,[1] death is the means of reconstituting that which has lived out its usefulness, served its purpose: and the Christian mystic has to be prepared to follow his faith to the point where he can look at the possible imminent end of *Homo sapiens* as an event of joy. If mankind must die painfully, through nuclear war or starvation and civil struggle, the Christian will rejoice with the martyrs that he is being allowed to share Christ's crucifixion; and he will look with faith to the inevitable beyond of the crucifixion: to the resurrection which mystical certitude assures us must follow. Just what will be the resurrection body of mankind is a mystery: but it is a mystery which is open to investigation, and, in a sense, this book is that investigation. For the mission of mysticism is, perhaps metaphorically speaking, to build a resurrection body for the entire human species. We must have the courage to see *Homo sapiens* as merely the caterpillar who will become the butterfly, and we must put on the armour of Christ to steel ourselves so that we may look upon the possible end of mankind with suitable dispassion. As noted in the Preface, in recent years, as the astronautical ventures of the superpowers produced photographs of the whole earth for the first time, a 'whole-earth' perspective has developed, especially in America, and especially among the younger people. The mission of mysticism is to teach mankind to build upon this whole-earth outlook, to learn to study and love the human race as a whole, to teach each person to be a citizen of mankind. Only then will it be possible to move to the next task of our mystical evolution, which is for all mankind to discuss the nature of the species and its future as a whole. It is in this context that science fiction assumes its great mystical significance, as the only other tradition which has explored in breadth and depth the future of mankind in relation to his nature, in the light of likely or possible developments in science and technology. To emphasize this point it is helpful to

[1] *On Suffering* (a Teilhard anthology). Collins 1975.

consider the aphorism: science fiction is the science of the future of science.

If man's future is destined to end very soon, the mystics will stand up and lead the world in the development of the appropriate outlook, and in the loving contribution to the nature of the creature which is destined to succeed our race. And the mystic will teach that we ourselves will, in some form or other, be present and active in that new race.

The mission of mysticism

It can be no coincidence that in this fateful twentieth century man's science has developed with his mysticism so that the one gives the resources to re-create the very species, and the other provides the wisdom to supervise that task. For the shattering truth is that the real mission of mysticism is for mankind to design his successor, in whom science and mysticism will have combined to create a being purged of original sin, citizens indeed of the New Jerusalem which they will inhabit. It is God's awesome intention that that most modern and materialistic entity, science (with its perpetual offshoot, technology), should be a major contributor to the efforts made by man to bring into created reality his very own future. In other words, just as in the mystical doctrine of the East men make, quite literally make, their own future and destiny by their karma, so the vision of western science-mysticism is that destiny of man to create, literally, the mystical future which he will inherit. In God's universe nothing is without purpose, and it is the destiny of science to achieve perfect unity with mysticism in the creation of our mystical descendants, who, after *Homo sapiens* has gradually been replaced by *Homo christus*, will be nothing other than ourselves, mystical-scientific architects of the new human nature which first walked the earth in the person of Jesus Christ, who is our gateway and our bridgehead to our inexpressibly glorious metamorphosis.

2

A Survey of Mystical Thought

One of the major discoveries of mystical thought is that change is an illusion. In ancient Greece, two of the earliest philosophers contemplated the nature of reality and came to diametrically opposed conclusions. Parmenides argued that change is an illusion, because being not only is, but can never cease to be. The opposite opinion came from Heraclitus, whose philosophy is best known in two famous fragments of his thought, 'Everything is flux', and 'You cannot step in the same river twice' (because the second time it will have changed and become different).

The mystics have respected the insight of Heraclitus, but they have observed that Parmenides had attained the deeper perception. Mysticism affirms that God alone is real, and that his attributes include changelessness and eternal life. That which we call change is only part of a secondary type of 'reality', one which in Vedanta is known as maya or illusion. Beneath the diversity, a joyous, timeless, perfect unity sustains and inspires the entire manifest universe. In chapter 4 we shall see how Wittgenstein's linguistic philosophy reconciles on the intellectual level the Parmenides-Heraclitus dispute.

This perspective is one which can be applied to mysticism itself. Throughout recorded history the mystical consciousness has manifested itself in many ways, some of which seem to be in direct opposition; at the least, there appears to be a vast range of mystical ideas, and this has led critics of mystical thought to conviction that there is no common theme, no monolithic structure of mystical thought – only semi-chaotic diversity. This is a sincere theory with obvious evidential support, and it deserves respect from mystics and mystical philosophers. Anyone who has actually studied the varieties of mystical thought deserves a hearing, and if so learned a person is convinced by his study that mysticism is so heterogeneous that no firm conclusions, concerning its implications for action, can be drawn, he should receive considered attention. Actually, this conception of mysticism is very interesting, in that it is an echo of the ancient dispute. The critic is the modern descendant of Heraclitus: he argues that mysticism is not one but many, and has no unchanging essence. But although this view is undoubtedly valid at its own level, it is evident that it too is addressing itself to the lower reality. The mystic, descended from Parmenides, accepts the lower reality, but knows that it is the product of a lower level of perception, a less advanced philosophical vision, than the Parmenidean metaphysic.

Nevertheless, the Heraclitean philosophy is a very cogent and compelling one, and it offers a framework for the quest of the present chapter and the next – the identification of the essential nature of mysticism. Thus, in this chapter we will survey the multitude of types of mystical thought, concentrating on their diversity; and in the next chapter we will employ the Parmenidean outlook and identify the essence of mysticism.

The varieties of mysticism

The view that everything is flux, though an arresting idea, can lead to chaos if used indiscriminately, and it is prudent to preface the survey of the multiplicity of mysticisms with a brief attempt at defining mysticism sufficiently for the guidance of this chapter.

Mysticism is the name given to the long process by which an individual discovers the Kingdom of God within himself, and to the state which that realization engenders. It is also a term used to refer to the metaphysic which mystics subsequently enunciate to embody the philosophical consequences of their discovery that love is the supreme governor of the universe.

HISTORICAL PERSPECTIVES

The view that mystical thought is a Heraclitean flux receives *prima facie* support from an inspection of history. The history of mysticism reveals no cumulative pattern or revelation or research. Its character is more akin to that of the alleged appearances of the Loch Ness 'monster': it appears at intermittent, irregular intervals, and on any one occasion only a part is seen. The onlookers have the difficult task of piecing together the whole from the parts which they have seen. It is partly for this reason that mysticism is sometimes known as the Perennial Philosophy. This phrase was made popular by Aldous Huxley in a book of that name, in which he showed how the one mystical wisdom has recurred throughout history, and in all parts of the world. There is a suggestion that mysticism, or the Perennial Philosophy, has the character of revelation. It is not the product of sustained philosophical research, but is the expression of God's grace in man. As such, it obeys no man-made timetable. This is, of course, a corroboration of the doctrine of grace in chapter 1. God alone is the author of all mystical experience, behaviour, and understanding.

The idea of mysticism as divine philosophy and experience revealed through grace is corroborated by a famous passage in the Hindu equivalent of the Bible, namely the Bhagavad Gita or Song of God. This indescribably profound and beautiful treatise, whose author is unknown, takes the form of a series of sermons which God, incarnate as Shri Krishna, the charioteer of a great warrior-prince, Arjuna, delivers on the battlefield where Arjuna loses his nerve after seeing his own relatives among the enemy ranks. The character of the perennial mysticism is revealed when Shri Krishna, the Supreme Being, tells his disciple that:

> This deathless Yoga, this deep union, I taught Vivaswata, the Lord of Light; Vivaswata to Manu gave it; he to Ikshwaku; so passed it down the line of all my noble Rishis. Then, with years, the truth grew dim and perished, noble Prince! Now once again it is declared – this ancient lore, this mystery supreme – seeing I find thee votary and friend.

Arjuna replies with considerable puzzlement: 'Thy birth, dear Lord, was in these later times, and bright Vivaswata's preceded time! How shall I comprehend this thing thou sayest, "From the beginning it was I who taught"'?

Krishna, the Supreme Being, infinitely compassionate, replies in incomparable language with what must be one of the most concise statements of mysticism ever to find a place in literature:

> Manifold the renewals of my birth have been, Arjuna! and of thy births too! But mine I know, and thine thou knowest not, O Slayer of thy Foes! Albeit I be unborn, undying,

21

indestructible, the Lord of all things living; not the less – By Maya, by my magic which I stamp on floating Nature-forms, the primal vast – I come, and go, and come. When Righteousness declines, O Bharata! when Wickedness is strong, I rise, from age to age, and take visible shape, and move a man with men, succouring the good, thrusting the evil back, and setting Virtue on her seat again. Who knows the truth touching my births on earth, and my divine work, when he quits the flesh puts on its load no more, falls no more down to earthly birth: to Me he comes, dear Prince! (chapter iv, trans. Sir Edwin Arnold).

The statement is quite explicit here that mysticism *is* revealed religion, given not earned, gift of God's grace to his people. It is also a very mystical doctrine, since it suggests that, true to type, the history of mysticism is highly mystical: Arjuna points out that Vivaswata (the Sun) was not born in time (i.e. was of eternal life, not mortality), yet Shri Krishna taught him too. And he comes in human form when he is most needed. But his revelations, being of the essence of mysticism, have no beginning and will have no end: they are born of eternity and have no place within mortal histories.

Christians, of course, have agreed that the doctrine of many births is in error: they preach the one incarnation, and the one earthly life for men. In contemporary spirituality there is a growing disposition among Christians to share the doctrine of reincarnation with eastern religion, without compromising the integrity of their own religion. There is indeed a growing number of evidential phenomena which support the theory. But in any case it is not critically important whether, in the 'many mansions' of which Jesus spoke in connection with after-life, there are embodiments on this or some other earth. Catholics accept at least two transitions after death, and the Pauline teaching of the resurrection body shows that, in a sense, post-mortem life does entail reincarnation of a sort. The exact nature of this and possible other bodies which post-mortem life contains can be known to living people, if at all, only by clairvoyants, but their research, though articulate and cogent, is not accepted by many Christians; so for the moment the matter must rest there.

Given the revelatory character of mystical philosophy, an historical reconstruction of the course of its development can add little of fundamental importance to our understanding. It remains to consider the geographical diversity of mysticism, and its many modern forms.

Mysticism is international. In ancient times it is seen emerging from an esotericist background in Egypt, whence we are familiar with the legends of Isis, Osiris, and Horus, with the mystery-religion, initiation, and the hierophant, with the pyramids and the sphinx, mystical numerology and related beliefs and practices. In ancient Greece, which derived its mysticism from Egypt, the mysteries were again taught, by the semi-historical figure of Orpheus, and then by Pythagoras and later by Plato (it is claimed that these three were all Egyptian initiates). The Middle East nurtured the mystical aspects of Judaism, including the kabbalah, and of course Christianity. India is the source of yoga, the Bhagavad Gita, the Upanishads, the Vedas, Vedanta, and Sankhya, and also Buddhism, exoteric and esoteric, mystical and religious. China yielded Taoism from Lao-tsze and Japan contributed Shinto and Zen. Arabia was the womb of Sufism, the mystical aspect of Islam.

In modern history, too, mysticism has been cosmopolitan, as a glance at the mystical dramatis personae of the Renaissance and after, clearly shows. Throughout the whole Christian era great mystics have been present – indeed, possibly all of the 2000 saints whose biographies are given in Butler's *Lives of the Saints* could be called Christian mystics. But we normally call them mystics as well if they have left some written account of their philosophy. By this criterion we call the following mystics: The thirteenth century saw the great lives of St Francis of Assisi and St Thomas Aquinas, and far-away Sadi and Jalalu'd Din (Rumi). The fourteenth century, which had many *anni mirabiles*, boasted, to name a few, Richard Rolle, Walter Hilton in England; while the great Meister Eckhart in Germany and equally important Dante Alighieri in Italy composed their monumental works, as did the continental trio Tauler, Suso, and Ruysbroeck, and the Persian Hafiz. Moreover, anonymous hands composed the enormously influential treatise on the *via negativa*, the mystical path of negation, *The Cloud of Unknowing*; and the two other great unknown authors published *The Mirror of Simple Souls* and *The*

Book of the Perfect Life. The fifteenth-century mystics included Julian of Norwich, Thomas à Kempis, and Jami; while the sixteenth century bore St Ignatius Loyola, who founded the Society of Jesus, and two inestimably great Spanish mystics, St John of the Cross and St Teresa of Avila.

It should not be thought that this brief catalogue is intended to be encylopaedic. It is not the intention, nor the capability of this chapter, to act encyclopaedically. Rather, its purpose is to illustrate with well-known and representative names the distribution of great mystics across time and space. However, the catalogue so far has concentrated on what might be called 'Establishmentarian mystics'. There is another side to the story. Throughout the Middle Ages esotericism continued to flourish, albeit secretly. Again, the esotericists were not trying to hoard their precious knowledge, nor were they trying to keep special wisdom solely within their grasp. True mystical wisdom could never coexist with such selfishness, for the invariable and necessary consequences of mystical illumination are always (and will always be) universal compassion, love of neighbour and God, and a dissolution of the illusion of separateness. The purpose of esotericism was simply to preserve the Perennial Philosophy from persecution and extinction. Esotericists gave freely to those who wanted the knowledge and could receive it, and they talked and wrote in an esoteric code to preserve the knowledge from those who would misunderstand it and try to persecute it. One of the esotericist maxims is the saying of Jesus, 'Neither cast ye your pearls before swine.' And the esotericists had good reason to fear that not only the pearls but they themselves would be trampled underfoot – as indeed many mystics were in many countries.

It may thus be seen that there are two types of mystical knowledge. One concerns the overt religious truths of love for God and neighbour, and the mystical life of piety and devotion. This is what is preached by the 'exoteric mystics', especially the orthodox Christians such as St Teresa. But there is a second kind of wisdom, with which occultism and esotericism (and their embodiment, theosophy) has been especially concerned, and this is the knowledge of the occult constitution of man and the universe. This is the mysticism which speaks of the seven principles of man, and of the constitution of the universe, the after-life, and the like.

Throughout history this tradition has been preserved, and during the Middle Ages a number of schools of esoteric mysticism flourished in a guarded way. The most famous include the Rosicrucians, the Alchemists, and many astrological schools, together with the tarot and the Knights Templars. The esoteric pursuit of the Holy Grail (i.e. the Christ within) is a clear example of intermingling esoteric and exoteric mysticism. This esotericism is the constant counterpoint to the religious mysticism: both schools strove for perfection, but the religious mystic subordinated all his efforts to direct knowledge of God, whereas the occultist took the intellectual path of perfection, what Hindus call the yoga of knowledge or jnana-yoga.

To resume the exoteric catalogue, the seventeenth century saw the works of Fox, Boehme, and Traherne, Pascal, and others of similar stature, while the eighteenth century was graced by the mysticism of Blake, Law, and Mme Guyon. The nineteenth-century mystics included Emerson and Thoreau, Eliphas Levi and A. E. Waite, Hegel, Sir Edwin Arnold, H. P. Blavatsky, and A. P. Sinnett.

3
Twentieth-century Mysticism

More changes have occurred in the twentieth century than in the previous nineteen put together, and this book is largely concerned with twentieth-century mysticism. It is science which has wrought these changes, but there has simultaneously occurred a remarkable and still-growing avalanche of mystical activity, whose volume and scope matches that of science and technology. It is said that this is the mystical age, the Age of Aquarius, and it is certainly living up to that description. While technology systematically changes every aspect of physical life, mysticism is doing the same with the psyche. It is the interaction of these two that will yield the true perfection of mankind. Nevertheless, following the Heraclitean principle stated earlier, it is proper to survey the twentieth-century manifestations of mysticism; they are exceedingly numerous and diverse, and they demand a chapter to themselves. At least fifteen groups of twentieth-century mysticism must be distinguished.

First, esoteric mysticism. This is, in effect, synonymous with theosophy. The modern theosophy dates to 1875, when the Theosophical Society was founded in America by H. P. Blavatsky and H. S. Olcott. In the twentieth century its work was carried on by a remarkable group of mystics and occultists, of whom the most famous were Annie Besant, C. W. Leadbeater, Ernest Wood, Jiddu Krishnamurti, and at least three leading occultists who defected from the Society: Rudolf Steiner, who founded his own society, the Anthroposophical Society; Dion Fortune (who founded her own esoteric school); and Alice Bailey (who went to preach the gospel of the imminent second coming of the Christ, and founded the Arcane School). And of course Krishnamurti was also an apostate from the Theosophical Society, and has a large independent following of his own. Nor were these gifted individuals alone in their quest: according to the Society, it was in reality founded by a group of Adepts or Masters, who resided in the Himalayas and guided the affairs of the Society on the subtle planes. In the British Museum are the original 'Mahatma Letters' to the occultist A. P. Sinnett; also still in print as a book, they contain the Adepts' teaching on many mystical and occultist matters. The Society thrives internationally to this day, and it will be discussed further in a later chapter, as will the Anthroposophical Society.

Much theosophical teaching is derived from, or identical with, traditional Hindu-spiritual metaphysics, but the theosophical societies are not the only ones to bring Indian mysticism to the West; there has been a veritable industry of it in the twentieth century, some of it profoundly welcome, other parts of it mere muddled journalism.

Both Buddhism and yoga are represented in this transmission of eastern wisdom. And the mystical element of each is often taught only as part of the wider religious framework. This is perhaps as good a time as any to describe the relationship between religion and mysticism. In this book the position adopted maintains that mysticism is the quintessence of religion: it is the real heart and purpose of religion, and the non-mystical parts of religion are but the suits and trappings. Shri Ramakrishna affirmed this truth when he declared, 'Realization (i.e. mystical experience) is real religion, all the rest is only preparation – hearing lectures, or reading books, or reasoning, is merely preparing the ground; it is not religion. Intellectual assent and intellectual dissent are not religion.' And he might have added that rules of observance are not mysticism. Mysticism, in fact, does not belong to the plane of matter nor even to the plane of intellect. It is solely communication between the higher self and the lower, and that communication is always in one direction, the former to the latter. It takes place only on the higher planes – the spiritual, Buddhic, nirvanic, atmanic, and many other names such as have been identified by mystics and clairvoyants; it is God, by whatever name he may be called (such as the higher self, the Christ-principle, the Voice of the Silence, the Light on the Path, the Intuition of the Will, etc.), talking to man. Thus, true mysticism is always an experience, and it is indescribable on the plane of language. Most of what we call mysticism is only verbalization about the experience, and it is always at best only suggestive. The only way to corroborate mystical utterances is to fulfil in oneself the requirement of moral purification which all mystical schools demand of the aspirant.

In the second group, the westernized Hindus and Buddhists, the Buddhist popularizers include Christmas Humphreys, who has specialized in the religious aspect, and his pupil, Alan Watts, who was more concerned with mysticism. We may mention again Aldous Huxley's anthology, *The Perennial Philosophy*, which introduced many Westerners to mystical thought; and Douglas Harding of England and Richard Alpert (Bab Rama Dass) of America have also popularized Hinduism. Another Englishman, Paul Brunton, has presented the world with a series of books mainly about Indian mysticism, and Mouni Sadhu has written many similar books, most of which centre upon the example of his guru, Shri Ramana Maharshi. Three Indian gurus have spent much of their lives in the western world, teaching yoga: the best-known is Maharishi Mahesh Yogi, friend of the Beatles pop group and famed exponent of transcendental meditation. A more profound teaching was brought by Paramahansa Yogananda (1893–1952), who established the Self-realization Fellowship in California and wrote many books; in his autobiography giving an enthralling account of Indian mysticism as seen by one of its products, he introduced many other yogis, including the line of gurus which included his own, Shri Yukteswar. Lahiri Mahasaya, guru of Shri Yukteswar, was portrayed along with his own guru, the semi-fabulous Shri Babaji. The third Indian was the brilliant and charismatic Brahmin scholar, Hari Prasad Shastri (1881–1956), also a prolific author, whose greatest writings include *The Heart of the Eastern Mystical Teaching* and the very practical *A Path to God-realization*. The especial genius of these three authors was to introduce to the West the doctrine that God-realization, or the peace of God, is a very realistic goal for this life – indeed, they argue that nowhere else can it be attained.

Robert Ornstein and Claudio Naranjo in America have popularized the psychology of eastern mysticism, as has William Johnston. And the Christian mystic Fr Herbert Slade, of the Society of St John the Evangelist, has courageously incorporated Indian and Chinese mysticism into his Christian Rule of Life: the community which he directs practises many eastern techniques as well as those typical of the Christian contemplative life. He has also written with penetration on the subject, and his recent book *Contemplative Intimacy* is a *tour de force* in its discussion of the integration of *eros* and *agape*.

A third group of modern mystics could be described as 'popular occultist'. It contains such authors as Gurdjieff and his disciples Ouspensky, J. G. Bennett, and Kenneth Walker, and Colin Wilson and like-minded semi-mystics such as William Arkle. The practitioners of high magic, such as the Hermetic Order of the Golden Dawn, and some imitative groups, also belong here. The common denominator of these authors is a rather shallow grasp of mysticism, with a particular lack of moral stature, coupled with a desire to speak to the masses, from an occultist platform, holding out sensational claims to the supposedly ignorant public. Another designation for this group is half-baked mysticism.

A fourth group, of comparable undesirability, may be termed 'instant-mysticism peddlers'. The most famous examples of this distinctly modern and not wholly un-American activity are John Lilly and Oschar Ichazo. Actually the latter taught the former, but they have gone their own ways. John Lilly has experimented with every modern technique for instant mysticism, and in his book *The Centre of the Cyclone* he describes his experiences with psychedelic drugs, sensory deprivation, all the main humanistic psychology therapeutic techniques from encounter groups to massage, along with the 'Arica' exercises taught by Oscar Ichazo, who came from Arica, South America, to teach the psychospiritual callisthenics which are the principal bidder in the instant-mysticism stakes. There is a considerable overlap between this school of thought and action and the American human potential movement led by Abraham Maslow. This also concentrated on the potentiality of a human being to experience joy and other peak experiences, and this movement has developed a host of highly practical, American-pragmatist techniques and practices with which to 'open up' the joy centres. This has led to some overlap with the Indian Kundalini yoga whose purpose is to activate the seven occult centres or *chakras* through which the life-force or *prana* travels in the spiritual evolution of a person. But it has led to its own techniques, of which the most well-developed include the many types of encounter group, the equally multifarious methods of enlightenment or sensitivity training awareness, and many new types of psychotherapy, such as gestalt therapy. One should, however, beware of glib dismissals of this movement (to which further space is devoted in chapter 6); it is now a vast industry, with much fine conceptual and original psychological work being done. The techniques whose general purpose is self-actualization now number several hundred, and the movement which is devoted to them has much to offer to religion and mysticism. At the same time, it is without doubt badly flawed as mysticism – though to be fair it has not *always* claimed for itself more than to be enlightened self-help. As mysticism it badly lacks the moral dimension. Mysticism, as the Christian mystics have so forcefully shown, is based on the moral or ethical equivalent within an individual of the Copernican revolution, by which the earth was displaced from the centre by the sun, and the former was shown to rotate around the latter, rather than vice versa. Mysticism puts God at the centre, and makes the little self follow his command. The American humanistic pseudo-mysticism keeps the pragmatic American personality at the centre, and, in this latest movement, tries to sell God in commercial systems. As mysticism, it is therefore doomed to failure. If it added the ethical dimension it would be a veritable new religion, and a very welcome one.

At the opposite extreme of seriousness and respectability is our fifth group, the *evolutionary mystics*. These are the thinkers whose argument tallies with the one at the basis of the present book – that mysticism is tied up with the evolution of *Homo sapiens* into a better species. The most famous name in this list is that of Père Pierre Teilhard de Chardin, s.j. (1881–1955), the Jesuit scientist, archaeologist, and palaeontologist whose importance for mystical thought can hardly be overestimated. In a series of great books, ironically forbidden publication in his lifetime (as a Roman Catholic he had to submit his manuscripts for the Catholic *imprimatur*, which was denied), he brought Christianity into the twentieth century with his doctrine of the cosmic Christ, and created a whole new metaphysic concerning mankind, his meaning and future as a psychological, biological, mystical, and cosmological creature. We will give him due attention later. His friend Julian Huxley, writing as a practical and theoretical biologist, came to similar conclusions in respect of the possible evolution of mankind. He has not written as a religious person, but has tried to make evolutionary humanism the true religion of mankind. His works, especially *Religion without Revelation*, have been impressive attestations of this thesis.

Colin Wilson, in a long series of books, has coupled evolutionary mysticism with phenomenological existentialism and romanticism, to produce a very stimulating theory as to the direction in which human evolution must go. All these thinkers, and the present writer, agree that evolution is a fundamental phenomenon in the universe. They also agree that on this planet life has evolved through natural selection hitherto, but that man represents a unique biological case, so far as we can say. Man has, with science, reached the point of superseding *natural* selection; henceforward he is master of his own fate. He has to redesign his own nature: and to do so science must collaborate with mysticism. This is the fundamental thesis of the present volume, and accordingly these evolutionary thinkers are held in the highest esteem.

It is a good omen that evolutionary mystics of a scientific bent have appeared this century. Sri Aurobindo is one: his book *The Future of Man: the Divine Life on Earth*, in which he predicts the evolution of the human mind to a state in which it enjoys perpetual mystical illumination, is invaluable in this respect. Lesser work, though still important, has been undertaken by P. D. Ouspensky, pupil and apologist of George Gurdjieff. Ouspensky's little book *The Psychology of Man's Possible Evolution* also argues that human evolution must be in the control and potency of mind. This suggests that the new *Homo sapiens* will have ethical, as well as intellectual, improvements. None of the evolutionary authors is particularly interested in the human body; they know that the growth of consciousness has made it superfluous.

A sixth group of mystics must be mentioned briefly: they are the *philosophical mystics*. Mention need only be made of Ludwig Wittgenstein, whose *Tractatus Logico-Philosophicus*, written during the First World War, tried to wed logic and mysticism. It is not a doctrine which has inspired many followers. Alfred North Whitehead included certain mystical elements in his popular writings such as *Adventures of Ideas*, and the existentialist philosopher Søren Kierkegaard showed the possibilities of wedding existentialist thought to the mysticism which, *prima facie*, it contradicts. However, philosophical mysticism is unfashionable and unlikely to become popular. This is not only because it is out of harmony with the *zeitgeist*, but because mysticism is intrinsically a supraphilosophical entity.

A seventh group is constituted by the *science-fiction mystics*. By this is meant the thinkers who have employed the medium of science fiction (mostly about man's future and possible evolution) to embody their ideas about human nature and the universe. A chapter is devoted to this medium, but here mention must be made of the three English intellectual giants who have dominated science fiction this century. There is considerable agreement among the three about evolutionary issues.

W. Olaf Stapledon (1886–1950) wrote the books which have been acclaimed as the ultimate science fiction, the finest ever: *Star Maker* is the story of the history of the future of the entire universe; *Last and First Men* is the history of *Homo sapiens* and his nineteen successor species over the next 2000 million years. These books are indeed sublime beyond description and they awaken, as nothing else has, the sense of awe but also of duty that has come upon our troubled species as we begin to take our destiny into our own hands. A clear descendant of Stapledon is Arthur C. Clarke, doyen of living science-fiction writers, whose *2001* is world-famous. But in all his novels, especially *Childhood's End* and *The City and the Stars*, he has painstakingly explored the possible evolution of man, and the role of artificial intelligence therein. Last of the three is the most famous: H. G. Wells (1866–1946), intellectual giant on a colossal scale, novelist, and encyclopaedist. Wells explored in more detail than any predecessor had done, the 'amphibian' nature of man – half animal, half god. His non-fiction and his fiction alike relentlessly probed the ways in which this amphibian could evolve into a creature no longer having to return to the water of animality from time to time, but able to walk with glorious permanence and comfort on the dry land of spirit.

No self-respecting intellectual can afford to neglect these authors, and many other science-fiction writers of only marginally lesser stature. Science fiction is the true modern language of the intellect. In it man's intellectual business is done, and its stock of concepts and parts of speech is now at the centre of intellectual life. Science fiction is the voice of the higher Self, and its language must be learned by all those who aspire to make a balanced contribution to intellectual life. Science fiction has taken over the baton for this stretch of man's relay race to perfection, and it is nothing less than an intellectual disgrace that there exist large numbers of philosophers, mystics and scientists, politicians, sociologists and psychologists, who are completely ignorant of it. Quite apart from the duty to be aware of its content, the best science fiction has a literary quality equal to that of Shakespeare, Goethe, or Dante. To be unread in science fiction is a mark of bigotry and laziness which is rewarded with an exclusion from the greatest literature of the day, and from the main intellectual debating hall of this era. No living intellectual can afford to ignore science fiction any longer.

Our eighth group is rather heterogeneous, and it is hard to assign a single title to it. Perhaps the nearest is 'science-mysticism'. By this is meant the belief that natural science can be and should be expanded to incorporate occult and mystical phenomena. The most vocal champion of this view, who argues that ordinary scientists are blinkered (a view which he shares, perhaps unwittingly, with Erich von Däniken), is the physicist and mathematician Professor John G. Taylor, whose hectic intellectual life includes playwriting and investigating supernormal powers: he is a member of the Uri Geller fan club, and believes that ESP is present in some children whom he has tested. But he has written in a semi-mystical way in his books on minds to come and on black holes. He has developed a semi-mythical theory with a distinctly mystical flavour about the implications of black holes for human experience, and although he has hitherto rigidly shunned religious mysticism, it would not be at all surprising to find that he declared his work to be compatible with the latter. An American scientist, Fritjof Capra, has already argued, in the well-known book *The Tao of Physics*, that modern quantum mechanics and cosmology are highly compatible with ancient Indian metaphysics. It is perhaps worth mentioning at this point that H. P. Blavatsky, in *The Secret Doctrine*, stated categorically that there was no actual or even possible disagreement between occult science and natural science. Another trained scientist who believes that science can and must embrace mystical, or at least occult, phenomena, is Andrija Puharich, friend and biographer of Uri Geller. He has gone on record as believing in science but also in ESP, artificial intelligence, and extraterrestrial interference in human affairs. This is a theme shared by our thirteenth group.

There are two other species of science-mysticism. The first is represented by the group of brilliant physicists who, earlier in this century, tried to relate modern physics and cosmology to the metaphysics of their time. Sir Arthur Eddington, Sir James Jeans, Alfred North Whitehead (who was primarily a mathematician), and Albert Einstein were prompted by their awe at the world revealed by physics to make mystical statements about reality. This group is obviously the forerunner, if not the progenitor, of the modern physics-mysticism of Capra and others.

The other science mystic is the contemporary English philosopher of science, A. Nicholas Maxwell (born 1937). In a remarkable recent book, *What's Wrong with Science?*, he demonstrates that the alleged objectivity of science is absent and impossible, since scientific theories are never objective but answerable to some anterior aim, which itself is selected for evaluative, not objective, reasons. His philosophy is a striking confirmation of the cry of the great ancient Greek philosopher Protagoras, that 'man is the measure of all things'. The mysticism of Maxwell's thesis is a very subtle one. It consists partly in the fact that he undermines the whole distinction commonly made between science and mysticism: he denies the pure/applied dichotomy in science, and in fact proves it an illusion. With this collapses the subjective/objective distinction and Bertrand Russell's mysticism or logic dichotomy. Maxwell's work is only in its early stages, but its importance is immense.

Our ninth group is a literary one. It contains the various authors who have written on mystical themes or in a mystical way, and we can only mention the names of some representative authors: Bulwer Lytton, John Cowper Powys, W. B. Yeats, Bernard Shaw, Hermann Hesse, and D. H. Lawrence – the latter is particularly interesting in that his sex-mysticism constitutes an interesting opposition to the evolutionary theorists who postulate a supraphysical humanity. It is interesting too to recall Olaf Stapledon's idea, in *Last and First Men*, that mankind builds huge brains as the new *Homo sapiens*, but that these in the end fail because 'they lacked the bowels of mercy'. Perhaps D. H. Lawrence should be remembered by the planners of the new species.

The tenth group consists of psychologists and psychiatrists who have interested themselves in mysticism. The most famous is of course C. G. Jung (1875–1961), who won an enormous following with his studies of a huge range of occult and mystical phenomena, from flying saucers to alchemy, even though thereby losing his friendship with Freud. In this relationship the matter of sex rears its head again. It is a wryly comic recollection that Freud accused Jung of sublimating his sex into religion, and Jung charged Freud with the opposite – fleeing his religious responsibility into an obsession with sex. On a more sober note, in mainstream psychology, a number of authors, especially Gordon Allport, Leslie Hearnshaw, and R. M. Bucke, argued for the inclusion of religious experience, including mysticism, in the syllabi and research programmes of academic psychology.

The traditional home of western mysticism – Christianity itself – has been equally productive in this century, and its innumerable mystics constitute the eleventh contingent.

Christianity has itself become increasingly diversified this century, and the major Christian sects and branches number a score or more, ranging from Quakerism to Christian Science, Catholicism to Methodism. It is thus not easy to pinpoint the essence of twentieth-century Christian mysticism (and of course some authors, such as Teilhard de Chardin, appear above in other groupings). But it may certainly be said that it is flourishing. The London Ecumenical Centre, led by Mark Collier, published in November 1975 a directory of groups concerned with the development of spirituality. Its list for England ran to thirty-eight groups, and some of these, such as the Association for Promoting Retreats, are groups of groups. The flavour of contemporary Christian spirituality may be gleaned from the names of some of the groups: Christian Contemplative Meditation; Houses of Prayer Ecumenical (HOPE); Institute of Christ Studies; Pax Christi; Liturgical Dance Group.

Evidently the spirituality (equals mystic-ality) of contemporary Christianity is undiminished. This is seen in literature as well as in associations. In recent decades Thomas Merton (1915–68) has made a deep impression with his sublime ecumenical writings on spirituality, and Herbert Slade (born 1912) has striven to effect a genuine union of Christianity and yoga, as has Déchanet in France.

The implication of the continuation of Christian mysticism (admittedly under the guise of spirituality, with which it is none the less almost synonymous) is simply that Christianity cannot be thought, despite the predictions of hostile critics, to be redundant in the face of the proliferation of modern mysticism. Far from it: Christianity has always been the womb and the cradle of western mysticism, and it welcomes rather than fears modern mysticism. As will appear later in this book, all modern mysticism is bound to return, in due course, to Christianity, which alone is capable of redeeming aberrant speculation in any language or currency.

In the context of the vast expansion of mysticism this century, a need has arisen for mystical scholarship, and a number of mystical scholars form a twelfth group. The most well-known include Evelyn Underhill, who wrote a series of books on mysticism following the success of her still-definitive treatise, *Mysticism* (1911: 500 pages). More modest contributions have been made by Professor Geoffrey Parrinder, who still holds the Chair of the Comparative Study of Religions in the University of London, and is the author of such works as *Mysticism in the World Religions*. From another direction a remarkable contribution came from the pen of Hari Prasad Shastri, the Brahmin professor referred to earlier in this chapter. Scholars such as W. Y. Evans-Wentz have contributed studies of Tibetan mysticism, and Paramahansa Yogananda also published a series of volumes on Indian religion and mysticism, in addition to his well-known autobiography mentioned earlier.

Scholars have also been responsible for the promulgation of ideas originating in middle-eastern mysticism. Z'ev Ben Shimon Halevi has disseminated the basic principles of kabbalistic mysticism in an excellent series of books such as *The Way of Kabbalah* and *A Kabbalistic Universe*. And for Sufism, the mysticism of Islam, Sayed Idries Shah has, for his part, written a series of books on Sufism, including *The Way of the Sufi* and *Thinkers of the East*.

Science-fiction mysticism has another branch, which we may call our thirteenth group of twentieth-century mysticism, in the *flying-saucer mystics*. George King, founder of the Aetherius Society, leads a gallant band who claim to be in touch with Jesus, who is, according to them, living on Venus. Moreover, their world is one peopled by flying saucers and aliens, against whose hostile efforts they must unite to practise spiritual 'pushes'. George King has invented a prayer-power box. In what one may suppose to be a representative exercise, he was shown with his disciples on top of a hill. They were chanting with incredible rapidity the Buddhist mantram 'Om Mani Padme Hum' ('Hail to the Jewel in the Lotus'), apparently doing callisthenics simultaneously, while their leader collected in his box the spiritual power thus generated .

An even more egregious member of this group is the notorious L. Ron Hubbard, a science-fiction writer who, according to Sam Moskowitz, decided that it would be more lucrative to found a religion. So he did, and scientology, the first science-fiction religion, is the result. This indubitably mystical creature reads like a cross between science fiction and esotericism, with much mysticism stitched in for good measure.

A more serious contribution has been made by the British theosophist Rex Dutta. He is a noted commentator on Blavatsky's *Secret Doctrine*, and, being committed to belief in the reality of flying saucers, has woven the ingredients into a mystical metaphysic which he calls Viewpoint Aquarius.[1] His idea is that flying saucers are real enough, but in a mystical sense.

John Michell is an author who has won great popularity for his brand of science-fiction mysticism. He has stirred together the ingredients of UFOs, numerology, occult history, and biblical hermeneutics, to produce an indigestible mixture with indeterminate implications for action.

But undoubtedly the most successful – at least, in material terms – and famous of these authors is Erich von Däniken, a Swiss hotelier with no scientific qualifications but, according to John

[1] He published a journal with this name, with much documentation of 'sightings', and regular diatribes against the British Government for its refusal to admit the reality of UFOs. He is also the author of several abrasive books on UFOs.

Allan, convictions for embezzlement, fraud, and forgery. The absolutely central place that the science-fiction outlook has in the modern mind is emphatically indicated by the public response to his writings. His few books have sold, to a worldwide audience, over thirty million copies in a very few years; and he has had full-length feature films devoted to his work, and even a long-playing record. His thesis is well known: extraterrestrial aliens, mistaken by primitive men for gods, interfered in human development in prehistoric times. For some reason this idea seems to have struck a nerve, or in Jung's terms an archetype, in modern man's psyche. The idea is at the very heart of the most successful science-fiction film ever: *2001, a space Odyssey*, in which the aliens are shown educating an ape who becomes, as a result, a sapient homo. In both that film and von Däniken's work, there is a now well-understood formula present: a mixture of science-fiction ideas, about extra-terrestrial aliens and flying saucers, together with mystical notions of the divine, the eternal archetype of the god, and the clear hope that man may himself evolve into a god. So many of the basic ideas of religion are present there: of course man can grow godlike – Jesus laid it down as a duty for man to do so. And of course there are supernatural elements; and of course Jesus 'came down from heaven' to save us: it is apparent that what is now going on is not a flight from religion or mysticism, but a greater and more desperate, intense flight to it, away from materialism, than history has ever seen. All that has happened is that modern authors are not only demythologizing the Bible, as Bultmann has done; they are *re*mythologizing religion, using the metaphysic of today.

Some important conclusions emerge from a consideration of this thirteenth group:

1   Christians should be aware that something very near to Christianity is being practised all around them today, in bigger numbers than ever before. It is their duty to bridge the narrow gap that separates them from the modern incarnation of Christianity. Obviously this has implications for evangelism, church attendance, preaching, and the like, but it involves both vicars and parishioners. It is a fatal mistake for Christians to shun the science-fiction faction who are in reality close enough to touch.

2   Christian theologians and all Christian authors must realize that modern science fiction and its tendrils contain great quantities of lay theology, from which they have much to learn.

So important is the science-fiction influence on modern mysticism that a whole chapter will be devoted to it.

A fourteenth group of modern mystics includes those who cannot easily be classified elsewhere. One of them is Carlos Castaneda, whose four volumes on the Mexican sorcery and mysticism taught by the Yaqui Indian Don Juan have also achieved worldwide fame. And in another tradition Benjamin Creme leads the ranks of a growing number of modern prophets who are proclaiming the second coming of the Lord. This event is said to have happened at last.

Benjamin Creme is one of a number of modern theosophical authors who have based themselves on the writings of Alice A. Bailey (1880–1945), another lapsed theosophist who broke away to form the Arcane School. Claiming to be the mouthpiece of a Tibetan Adept, she gave to the world an impressive series of occultist treatises, such as *A Treatise on Cosmic Fire* and *A Treatise on White Magic*. She subscribed to the theosophical doctrine of the Masters, and in fact declared that Jesus of Nazareth was a Master who had been 'used' by a mighty cosmic being, the Christ, 2000 years ago. And she foretold, somewhat like John the Baptist in his time, that Christ would come again this century.

In November 1977, it was announced that the Christ's second coming had occurred. He was incarnate in an invulnerable body, and the new age had begun.

Time will give more evidence for believers or unbelievers, for the theosophical disciples of the Christ claim that he will soon reveal himself to the world. Unbiased people would no doubt welcome his return, but, although openminded, they will nevertheless require a good deal of evidential validation of his presence. The expectation of the Lord's imminent return has been a feature of every era, from the first century to the twentieth, and Norman Cohn showed, in his study *The Pursuit of the Millennium*, how the millenarian sects of the Middle Ages confidently expected the second coming. But it must be admitted that the state of metaphysical unrest, or massive influx of the ancient wisdom, is greater in this age than ever before.

Perhaps, as occultists claim, this is the action of the Age of Aquarius in opening the Third Eye of mankind (see Vera Stanley Alder's book *The Initiation of the World*); perhaps, as Alice Bailey declared in her book *The Externalisation of the Hierarchy*, not only the Christ but all the Masters of the Wisdom are going to externalize, i.e. reveal themselves to the world. If this is so, doubtless there will be millions of grateful human beings to welcome them.

The fifteenth and last group is actually only an individual, but one whose contribution to mysticism and occultism is greater than that of many groups. Ernest E. Wood (1883-1965) was among the greatest English philosophers of this century, although he has no reputation in academic circles, for he was primarily a mystical occultist and theosophist. He was a prolific author of some thirty-eight books, an educationalist, and a scientist. He spent over thirty years in India, where he held nearly every major post in the Theosophical Society, and worked closely with the great theosophists Annie Besant and C. W. Leadbeater. He became headmaster of a congress high school, preparing students for the University of Madras. After that he became managing secretary of a group of thirty-seven schools and colleges, and was also principal and president of the Sind National College and the Madanapalle College, of the Universities of Bombay and Madras. All along he was deeply interested in the yoga and Vedanta philosophies of India, and learned to read them in the original Sanskrit language, while associating closely with indigenous scholars and accomplished yogis. He travelled round the world, and was active in America, where he was president and dean of the American Academy of Asian Studies, and founder of the Woods School. His many books are on yoga, theosophy, and education, but his great personal contribution to mysticism and occultism lies in his series of books in the tradition of raja yoga, showing how mystical enlightenment can be attained through strict self-cultivation. He had a gift of language of Shakespearean stature, and his books radiate the noblest heroism of character of the kind associated with Gautama the Buddha – the highest possible integrity and deepest compassion, combined with perfect self-mastery and an exemplary depth of spiritual insight. The essence of his thought can be seen in four of his books:

Concentration, an Approach to Meditation; *Character-building*; *The Intuition of the Will*; and *The Seven Rays*. The special philosophy of his mysticism is a truly westernized raja yoga, based firmly in character-building and self-training, and with a unique teaching about the way in which self-knowledge can be attained and employed in spiritual development. His genius was to show the reality of spiritual development, and its cumulativeness. To illustrate his style (which can also be seen in chapters 1 and 13), the following quotation is ideal:

> Later than and additional to the love which considers others and their pleasures and pains, is the will which knows the purpose of our being, which has predestined a triumphant goal as the end of human life.
>
> One may be as full of love as of thought; the love may convert our trackless and dangerous forest of thought into a land of beautiful meadows and gardens. It is not enough. We may wander for ages in those pleasant parks, but the Voice of the Silence, the Intuition of the Will, will ultimately sow these lands with discontent, for we must become lords of lightning, masters of the world, homeless, triumphant. *The Intuition of the Will* polarises every particle of our lives like a great magnet, and puts an end to purposeless wandering – bodily, emotional, or mental (*The Intuition of the Will*, pp. 33–4).

In dealing with the mysticism of this century, it is worthwhile to acknowledge the contribution made by the American character. America, in its youthfulness, has not been a great home for church mystics; but the American character embodies many of the best qualities of mankind, and in a mysticism concerned with the redesigning of humanity Americans have much to tell us. So many of their fundamental character qualities are conducive to modern mysticism: courage, strength, flexibility, and vitality, the freedom from religious persecution, and the right to pursue happiness; the closeness to nature, the backwoodsmanship and self-sufficiency, the humanism and openmindedness, and the generosity. Europeans often call Americans culturally backward and gauche, but they forget that all vital culture now tends to originate in America. The American contribution to just one form of culture – music – is astonishing: jazz alone is the sign of a wonderful spirit at work, and pop music, rhythm and blues, rock and folk are superb contributions to the growth of the human spirit. And it is American science and technology which yields the hope of planning a new species. There is no specific American mysticism but the warm and noble American character permeates, sustains, and uplifts all contemporary mysticism. It deserves greater recognition in this connection.

4
The Essence of Mysticism

Heraclitus and Parmenides disagreed as to whether the One was Many or vice versa. At about the same time Plato's Socrates is seen to be trying to obtain 'essence' definitions of fundamental word-concepts such as 'justice', 'virtue', and 'beauty'. Recently Sir Karl Popper published his 'anti-essentialist exhortation', in which he begs intellectuals never to argue about the meaning of words, and never to ask questions about what something 'really' is, i.e. its essence. The ancient debate is thus very much alive, and, apparently, unsolved. In seeking to know the 'essence' of mysticism we may be inviting mere confusion. If we consider the survey of the many types of mysticism, the question now is whether all those types had anything in common with each and every other – that is, did they have anything in common other than that they shared the title 'mysticism'? Philosophy has been very active this century on problems of language, especially definition, and the technical answer to the question was that so-called realists argued that there *is* something other than the name in common, whereas nominalists denied this, and declared that only the name was common to all the exemplars.

The contribution of ordinary-language philosophy
The deadlock was broken by the genius of Ludwig Wittgenstein (1889-1951), the Cambridge German philosophy professor and student of Bertrand Russell. Wittgenstein's philosophy has dominated the years since the First World War. In his *Philosophical Investigations* (published posthumously in 1953),[1] Wittgenstein particularly addressed himself to the question of 'essence' definitions. In this book, which was one of the founding volumes of what became known as 'ordinary-language philosophy', Wittgenstein pioneered a new, empirical approach to philosophy, in which one examined the behaviour

[1] The ideas in the book had been circulating much earlier.

43

of the words in question. Wittgenstein's genius lay in his ability to do what no one else had dared to do, simple though it was: he studied what the language actually was like, and disregarded assumptions about it. His brilliant solution, to the problem of defining complex concepts whose essence seems impossible to pin down, is stated in several publications. In his *Blue Book* (a record of his lectures preparatory to the larger work) he speaks of our 'craving for generalities', and he traces it to its sources, which he suggests are connected with particular philosophical confusions, including the nominalist/realist debate.

In the following passage from the *Philosophical Investigations* (the odd punctuation is entirely Wittgenstein's) he is speaking of the word 'game' in its highly multifarious usages, but his remarks apply equally well to mysticism in all *its* usages, for it too is a complex multi-componential conceptual word:

Instead of producing something common to all that we call language, I am saying that these phenomena have no one thing in common which makes us the same word for all, – but that they are *related* to one another in many different ways. And it is because of this relationship, these relationships, that we call them all language. I will try to explain this.

Consider for example the proceedings that we call 'games'. I mean board-games, card-games, ball-games, Olympic games, and so on. What is common to them all? Don't say: 'There *must* be something common, or they would not be called "games" – but *look and see* whether there is anything common to all. – For if you look at them you will not see something that is common to *all*, but similarities, relationships, and a whole series of them at that. To repeat: don't think, but look! – Look for example at board-games, with their multifarious relationships. Now pass to card-games; here you find many correspondences with the first group, but many common features drop out, and others appear. When we pass next to ball-games, much that is common is retained, but much is lost. – Are they all 'amusing'? Compare chess with noughts and crosses. Or is there always winning and losing, or competition between players? Think of patience. In ball-games there is winning and losing; but when a child throws his ball at the wall and catches it again, this feature has disappeared. Look at the parts played by skill and luck; and at the difference between skill in chess and skill in tennis. Think now of games like ring-a-ring-a-roses; here is the element of amusement, but how many other characteristic features have disappeared! And we can go through the many, many other groups of games in the same way; can see how similarities crop up and disappear.

And the result of this examination is: we see a complicated network of similarities overlapping and criss-crossing: sometimes overall similarities, sometimes similarities of detail.

I can think of no better expression to characterize these similarities than 'family resemblances'; for the various resemblances between members of a family: build, features, colour of eyes, gait, temperament, etc., etc. overlap and criss-cross in the same way. – And I shall say: 'Games' form a family. (Sections 65–7)

The mystic's credo

The matter is made blindingly clear by Wittgenstein: and we will follow him and say that the particular types of mysticism also *form a family*: and in that lies the reconciliation of the Parmenides-Heraclitus dispute, for mysticism is both One *and* Many. In mystical metaphysics it is, however, asserted that the Parmenidean view is higher: for the One is the generator of the Many, not vice versa. It remains to work out the full solution in this particular instance – to detail the 'family traits' that run through and bind together the many types of mysticism. A constructive way of doing this is to tie it into a presentation of the common traits as the mystic's credo. This credo will not be that of the 'average mystic', for such an entity is impossible. It will rather be based on what in statistical inference is called the mode: the commonest occurring item. But here we are dealing with many items, so the mystic's credo is a sort of ideal-type, containing the idealized network of beliefs that mystics share. This has the slightly perverse effect of making the credo exactly descriptive of very few actual mystics; but it is the best compromise.

Readers who desire greater exactitude can easily provide it themselves, by drawing up a two-dimensional matrix in which mystical beliefs are plotted against individual mystics. That matrix would itself, in Wittgenstein's philosophy, actually *be* the best possible definition, indeed the perfectly accurate one; for he proved that in complex words 'meaning' lies in complex patterns and relationships. But for our purpose the mystic's credo suffices. It is in two parts: the general credo, which is shared by most mystics, and the remaining beliefs, which are a prominent part of some mystical philosophies, but not the majority.

THE MYSTIC'S CREDO: General

(The individual affirmations correspond to the 'resemblances' in the 'family' which the types of mysticism comprise.)

Table 1
The mystic's credo

I MAINLY METAPHYSICAL

1 The only reality in the universe is spirit. Material events are insignificant except in so far as they conduce to spiritual development.

2 Despite all appearance to the contrary, suffering is illusory, merely appearance; the reality underlying appearances is perfect and of the character of infinite bliss.

3 The Supreme Object of Worship, by whatever name he may be called, is the mainstay of the entire manifest universe. And he pervades where he possesses, so he is in all and all is in him. He is present in the soul of every human being.

4 The supreme goal of mysticism, which is accessible to all, is total union with the Ground of Being (who is known by many other names).

5 Love conquers all, and governs the universe; God is love.

6 The universe is One. All are connected to all, everything to every thing. Harmony, oneness, non-separativeness, union are the fruits of the realization of this truth.

II MAINLY CONCERNING HUMAN BEINGS

7 There is no death. The immortal soul takes many forms, but it cannot be slain; for 'birthless and deathless and changeless remaineth the Spirit for ever' (The Bhagavad Gita, trans. Sir Edwin Arnold).

8 All creatures are ensouled; all shall tread the one mystic path to the Absolute. All are immortal; all shall triumph eventually.

9 In mysticism lies the pinnacle of human fulfiment, and the total conquest of death.

10 Mysticism is the heritage of the species, *Homo sapiens*.

11 Eternal life is possible even now by right thinking and spiritual effort; indeed God-realization, nirvana, enlightenment, supreme bliss: these are all possible for devotees of the spiritual path even while they are incarnate.

12 Mysticism is the perfect fruit of man's quest for God; it is the final banishment of man's 'divine discontent'.

III THE SUPREME MYSTICAL VISION

13 The pain and destruction of the manifest world are illusory.

14 Despite all appearance to the contrary, this is the best of all possible worlds. 'And pain, sin, evil, and death are "behovely"; and all shall be well, and all shall be well, and all manner of thing shall be well' (Julian of Norwich).

15 There are no problems in reality, only lifeless, timeless bliss; and this is available to everyone, as indeed all will discover in due season. Love and compassion are the powers supreme in the visible and invisible universe, all shall be well in the infinitely sensitive and loving hands of god, and in the fullness of time all the manifest universe will be redeemed and brought to final consummation; for evil has no substance and no sway in reality.

IV MAINLY CONCERNING COMPASSION

16 Hatred, strife, and evil can only be overcome by love; they must be redeemed, transmuted; neither they nor anything in God's creation can ever be destroyed. Nevertheless love and compassion *will* always triumph over dark forces.

17 *Ahimsa*, harmlessness, must be extended to all creatures whatsoever.

18 The growth of mystical consciousness is exactly paralleled by the growth in the individual consciousness of *compassion* – from the particular to the general to the universal.

V MAINLY CONCERNING SPIRITUAL DEVELOPMENT

19   The whole of an aspirant's life must be consecrated to mysticism, i.e. to God (Spirit) or the Good, if he is to succeed in his quest.

20   Those treading the moral path of mysticism are certain to be blessed with mystical experience in an ever-increasing degree.

21   Patience and perseverance in the face of apparent failure are necessary trials for every pilgrim; he can be reassured, not frightened, by them.

22   Self-abnegation is the key to spiritual progress and development: this entails a growth in humility, love, compassion, truth, and (above all) unselfish service of others; and a decrease in egocentricity, egotism, pride, and separatist individualistic thought. There is no such thing as separate or individual mystical or spiritual development. Such growth is only possible by a growth of one's compassion for, and service of, and identification with, all that is.

23   Prayer and meditation are, with the practices mentioned in article 22, the principal instruments of spiritual growth.

VI   IN PRAISE OF MYSTICISM

24   Mysticism represents and embodies the perfect flowering of human thought.

25   In mysticism reside the most joyful states of mind to which man can attain: truth, beauty, bliss, and peace, in unlimited abundance, are found within it.

26   The highest values revered by humanity find their most perfect expression in the aspirations, in the insights, and in the affirmations of mysticism.

27   Mystical experience is the apotheosis of human cognition.

VII   CONCERNING GRACE AND HUMILITY

28   Mysticism is God's work; he is the author of every mystical experience. Mystical development is accomplished entirely through the grace of God, which cannot be earned.

29   The only right response to mysticism is humility. There is a danger that mystical exaltation may lead to self-aggrandizement, which is deadly to true mysticism. The Sermon on the Mount is the best exposition of this precept: the meek shall indeed inherit the earth, and heaven too.

30   True mysticism expresses itself in a flow of selfless compassionate

concern for others: a true and deep love of one's neighbour[1] (for in mysticism one learns that to love one's neighbour is not hard, for one's neighbour *is* oneself. Non-separateness is the heart of mysticism, and a mystic cannot seek personal, separate development, even spiritual development. He can only work for all the world, and find himself growing in spiritual awareness which is indeed a greater oneness with all).

THE MYSTIC'S CREDO: MINORITY ELEMENTS
(not shared by the great majority)

(*a*) CHRISTIAN: (1) Jesus Christ is God.

(*b*) OTHER TRADITIONS: (1) Mysticism is common to all religions; (2) Mysticism is the advance guard of human scientific thinking.

(*c*) PECULIARLY MODERN AXIOMS: (1) Benevolent extra-terrestrial or extradimensional entities watch over us, often in UFOs; they watch our progress, and sometimes intervene to expedite our growth; (2) The aliens are godlike compared with us, yet we may grow to be like them; (3) Astrology, as a map of spiritual development, is valid; (4) We will soon create artificial intelligence (mainly 'computers'), which will not only be sentient but indeed of godlike power compared with us.

NOTE: The articles of the creeds are not all found in one particular mystic: they are a composite portrait of the creed of some fifty mystics studied for this purpose.

The articles are non-evaluative. They are not judged as right or correct simply because they are included: they are included simply because they have appeared in the writings of mystics. Attempts to evaluate them are found elsewhere in this book.

Other approaches to the essence of mysticism

Our investigation of the definition of mysticism has now reached an advanced stage, and the basic task has been completed. But in mysticism it is necessary to go beyond the

---

[1] This article, concerning compassion, in part repeats article 18 of the credo; but the repetition is deliberately made because of the importance of the issue. Likewise the repetition, in the parenthetical passage of article 30, of a point made in article 22 concerning separateness.

letter of the law of language if one is to get to the spirit beneath; accordingly, we now approach the problem from another direction that of the course of mystical development in the individual. There is nothing so instructive as human case histories or similar documents, in the development of an understanding of mysticism. Also, the present writer, in an effort to utilize every resource in our language in the impossible endeavour of communicating mystical truths – a task which bankrupts human language – has throughout the book resorted to aphoristic expression and actual aphorisms whenever it seemed helpful.

THE SEQUENCE OF MYSTICAL EVOLUTION IN INDIVIDUALS

Two mystics who have been prominent among those charting the geography of spiritual development, are Ernest Wood and Evelyn Underhill. The subject is vast, and will be returned to in a later chapter, but for the present we will concentrate on one book from each author: the former's *The Intuition of the Will* and the latter's *Mysticism*. One of the benefits of this study is that it broadens the understanding of the nature of mysticism. One of the most characteristic properties of mysticism is that it is a *process*: hence it can only be fully understood when a time-slice is added to a static perspective. The study of mystical development usefully rounds out the definition.

Evelyn Underhill's book is pellucid. The larger part of it is an essay on the Mystic Way; it is this that is so helpful here, since it is set out as a series of chapters, each of which discusses an important stage on the mystic path, copiously illustrated with case histories.

The course of mystical awakening, as described by Evelyn Underhill, begins with the 'awakening of the self'. From this fact two inferences may be made: one is that people – most people – are 'asleep' to mysticism until God awakens them, or 'calls' them: and the person is awakening to his own 'self' – evidently his higher self, or higher aspects, theretofore unknown, or what he thinks of his ordinary self. The awakening is effected by the Holy Spirit, and usually consists of some intimations of God's love. God brushes the soul with his love and power, and the soul is instantly awakened to the mystic truths that God is love, who rules the universe, that all are one, that all will triumph. In the wake of this experience the individual, who may until then have been a militant atheist, or a tepid, churchgoing Sunday Christian without religious realization, suddenly sees the absolute reality of religion. Until then his religion had been at best a matter of hope, or perhaps just of rules. Now it is a living entity, and he has become a mystic. Suddenly a whole new universe blossoms out before him. All the world's religious literature becomes his property and his joy; he devours any writings on mysticism – and perhaps undertakes such writings himself. Suddenly the biographies of mystics and saints become fascinating to him. He is filled with joy and gratitude at the wondrousness of the universe, at God's love and might, and he is filled for a while with deep compassion for his fellow-men, especially the suffering; for he has momentarily lost his sense of selfish separateness.

The awakening is not all unbroken joy, however. For the newly 'awakened' individual is, in the mystical scheme of things, by definition a deeply flawed character and personality. Indeed it is impossible for deep mystical illumination to coexist with a deeply flawed personality; one of the two has to go. Part of the awakening is the sense of self-disgust and inadequacy that the embryonic mystic has when, immediately after his initiatory mystical experience, he contemplates his own nature. Now he has seen reality, he has seen perfection, and he learns that the ethical requirements of all religions are right and necessary: for the faults which they aim to eradicate are so many fetters which bind the individual on the lower rungs of the ladder of perfection. The image of the ladder now epitomizes the experience of the soul. He has ceased to be a relatively aimless person, or one with secular ambitions. Instantaneously he has become an aspirant, a pilgrim. At the moment of his mystical illumination he became aware of the reality of God, and of the immense gulf between him and his Lord. But he learned that it is his privilege and his duty to traverse that gulf. He sees that there is a way: he has seen the reality of the spiritual path, has seen that he – and all others, did they but know it – are treading that one path to perfection. Now he wants nothing except to hasten along the path, and he begins to wonder how he may do so. He has reached the gateway of the second stage of mysticism.

The purification of the self must now occur. It consists of a long process of character-building (this is the watchword of the mystic, who knows what incredible depths lie in his character, which is the gateway to the Kingdom of God within), of self-improvement, correction, and, in a word, purification – mental, ethical, physical, behavioural. Every flaw is a distortion in the mystic vision, and must be removed. The process is, for ordinary persons, unending; it only ceases on the threshold of absolute perfection. Still, it is a joy, since the mystic knows that in character-building he is doing the best that he can do in striving to carry out God's will and thus come nearer to union with him: for the mystic has learned the shattering truth that he can achieve oneness with God – and that it is his duty so to do.

The other major activity in the purification of the self is the interior life. Perhaps for the first time, the aspirant learns that he must pray, and meditate. This serves several purposes. It provides the priceless opportunity to learn mind-control which is so essential in the quest; it opens the gateway to God, provides a channel for his intuitions; and it is building the vehicle in which the mystic will later travel, in the supramental realms of existence. Prayer and meditation are the most exacting and the richest of all human tasks. In them the aspirant is learning to seize his birthright and claim his destiny; he is learning for the first time, through prayer and meditation, just what being human really means; and he comes to understand that truly the realms of prayer and meditation are more worthy of the epithet 'real' than the so-called 'real' world'.

As the purification of the self proceeds, the next stage dawns. It is the illumination of the self, and in it the apprentice mystic begins to experience more and more frequently, and in ever deeper quality, the truths which he glimpsed in his awakening. He learns that in literal truth the Kingdom of God is within him. His personality has become softer but stronger, sharper but more loving, and his character has a superb strength and vitality.

It is at this point that many stop, this side of the grave. Very few are those whom God calls to higher stages; and as their privilege is greater, so must their sacrifice be. They pass on into the vale of darkness in the penultimate stage of the path.

'The Dark Night of the Soul' is the name now commonly given to the last but one stage. In the Sufi tradition it is known as 'seeing hell before one can see heaven'; but in any language it is purgation, and the author of the phrase, the great Spanish mystic St John of the Cross (1542–91) explicitly states that it is purgatory on earth, undergone by a very blessed few. In the Roman Catholic tradition, purgatory is the place or state or process in which souls are, after death, purged of their faults so that they see God. Mysticism is the story of those who see God before death; they have to undergo the same purging. In the Dark Night suffering and pain do the work of purging, and they appear in an infinite number of guises. However, certain pains *must* occur at this point: the soul has to feel abandoned by God. Only this will teach him his utter helplessness and dependence on his Maker; only this can show him that God, not he, is the author of his life, and thus wean him finally off his pride, especially the more subtle spiritual pride. Only when he is seemingly abandoned can he understand hell, and this gives him that holy fear which is the first gift of the spirit. This phase is the Dark Night of the Spirit. The other part of the Dark Night is called the Dark Night of the Senses, and it is the means whereby the mystic is weaned off his fleshly appetites and mental desires. This is more active in the sense that the mystic can, up to a point, choose which desires to mortify in self-selected mortification; the other Night is imposed from without: St John calls it strong cleansing.

The trials of the Dark Night are usually accompanied by a loss of perceived religious consolation. Only faith is left to sustain the mystic. He has forgotten his illumination, and cannot understand why he is suffering so much when he had been progressing so well.

The exact pattern of the Dark Night varies with each soul, but it is usual for the mystic to experience *some* consolation by God, during it; he is not utterly abandoned. And the movement into, and the exit from, the Dark Night are not usually sudden, but very gradual, like the slow movements of heavenly bodies along their preordained zodiacal path. As the Dark Night draws to a conclusion, the dawn begins, and gradually all that was dark becomes clear and beautiful as the mystic emerges with half-doubting joy from his last trial into the daylight of his apotheosis. For he is entering the last stage, of union with his God; he is absolutely free, and the veil within is lifting to reveal the land of bliss absolute which is to be his new and permanent home.

The three nirvanas

This last stage is the culmination of the mystic journey. It is, in Evelyn Underhill's terminology, the unitive life. It is the spiritual marriage, the beatific vision, and a host of other names bestowed by the delighted mystics who have been blessed with it. It is heaven on earth. We will obtain a better understanding of it by moving now to Ernest Wood's descriptions, since he has done what no other has done, and shown how the heaven-life, or nirvana, is not only not a vacuous joy, it is in fact a triplicity of complex initiations, through all of which the mystic must pass before he can understand how it is that all will be triumphant, and that all is bliss even now, despite apparent suffering.

Ernest Wood speaks first of the nirvana of earth, and describes this as truly inheriting the world. It is an initiation, a realization, beyond which the man can never again be unhappy. He has reached the level of insight at which he understands that 'the world is a perfect school for man': whatever happens, his spiritual intuition has learned, is for the best. Truly we live in the best of all possible worlds, and whatever happens to the man he will accept gratefully as a gift from God. He has to fight: then he enjoys the opportunity of growing stronger. He is imprisoned unjustly; he uses the time to meditate. He grows ill: he enjoys sharing in the crucifixion. He is to die soon: he knows there is no death. He is tortured: he knows that the real self, in which he is grounded by his mystical apprenticeship, is invulnerable: pleasure and pain alike can now be sources of happiness. And 'nothing can use this man as its slave, because he is free from material desires, and free from resentment, anger, pride, fear, impatience, and all their brood; such binding emotions have been blown out like so many candles. The man is free on earth. He has reached nirvana in the lower world.'

But this sublime, lofty state is in turn superseded by the nirvana of the soul. First, however, the Five Fetters of the delusion of self, doubt, superstition, taste, and prejudice must be removed by patient purification. Then the new nirvana is entered. In this the mystic obtains a direct vision of the immortality of life and the fact of rebirth. He learns that 'death' is simply the changing of uniforms. When others are appalled and upset by gory deaths, such as in war, he sees the life beyond the forms, and is aware that even in the most horrific disfigurement the life has gone on its way, unharmed, indestructible. And should such happen to him, he only asks, 'What use can I make of this for the purposes of the soul?' He has become one who sails on the waters of material existence, but is not submerged or buffeted by storms. Nor will he become so involved with others that he sinks when they sink. He is incapable of selfishness at second hand. Still, he does yearn to help his fellow-men, but they will not heed his call to perfection. He deals with them as souls but they do not so regard themselves. He tries to do their work for them, but the Law which governs the universe will not permit it.

When he steps upon the ladder's upper rung he will attain a new freedom, achieve the nirvana of the soul, enter the place of serenity and peace. And now he sees that each being, notwithstanding its outward circumstances, is in its rightful place. In the nirvana of earth it was learned that one position in space is as good as another; now he learns that one position in time is as good as another, that it does not matter where anyone stands in the long procession of souls in evolution. And no one's progress can be hastened beyond its due pace: others cannot intervene; God will not.

Now, too, the divine nature immanent in every form begins to reveal itself everywhere, as the disciple learns that where God pervades, he possesses:

> There is then not one small event in his life, not the picking up of a pin or the tying of a shoelace, which is not lighted with spiritual significance. Every incident in the newspaper becomes an epic; every dusty corner in a slum is a world filled with wonders. Every small thing, every small action has become divine, far-reaching, universe-shaking. All things have become new, and filled with light.

> And his consciousness is also new, as though it had gone through fire and come out burnished gold. . . . It has become perpetual light. . . . It is as though all the universe were within yourself.

But even this supreme mystic vision is short of the perfect

nirvana. Five more fetters must be broken: the first two are attachment to life, whether in form or formless, that is to say, attachment to any limiting form of love. But in the nirvana of the self the vision of the whole is attained; it is seen that there are no particulars, that truly all is one, and not just metaphorically. Leaves are not separate from a tree, because without a tree there can be no leaves. So with people. We are all one. The third and fourth fetters are pride in the power of consciousness and agitation from outside on account of love, and the fifth fetter is ignorance.

When ignorance of the Self is overcome, the man realizes that he is not only not his mortal body or his instrument the mind; he is not his consciousness either. He is that beyond of the consciousness. And Ernest Wood's magnificent vision concludes with these words:

> We can understand something of what the glory of life must be when all this is over, when the consciousness has its powers perfected. It is so complete, its strength is so magnificent, that there is no need for descent into camera in order to see. The man can live with all his windows open to the world, and take in great sweeps of reality without confusion. The goal of human existence, the Nirvana of the Self, is at hand (*The Intuition of the Will*, p. 144).

Such is the mystic realization; it is the mission of mysticism to convey all men to that third nirvana – and its beyond through Christ.

PART TWO

Modern Mysticism and its Simulacra

5
Mysticism and Pseudo-mysticism in Contemporary Culture

The need to distinguish real and pseudo-mysticism

The mission of mysticism has to be discharged by particular examples of the mystic consciousness. And it is today's mysticism that shoulders this responsibility, even when it uses the ideas of earlier mystics.

There is reason to count the post-Second World War period as among the most mystically awakened periods in recorded history; yet there is both real and spurious mysticism at work in our culture. The purpose of this chapter is to adapt the work which in our earlier chapters produced an understanding of the nature of true mysticism, so as to provide some rudimentary criteria by which the genuine mystical elements can be recognized, and the false eliminated from the discussion. This chapter will also add to the catalogue of fifteen twentieth-century schools of mystical thought as described in chapter 2. It will present a brief survey of all the mystical and allegedly mystical endeavours which are abroad at the time of writing: it is the totality of these which is subsumed under the head of this block of chapters, 'Modern Mysticism'. The remaining chapters in Part Two then take up particular aspects of modern mysticism, and each chapter examines one or more modern movements, investigating its authenticity in the light of the criteria enunciated in this chapter.

When this section is complete, a beachhead will have been established. We will have made a deep and solid definition of mysticism, and be familiar with its authentic and inauthentic offspring; we will be guided by a substantial intimation of the nature of the mission of mysticism (though this cannot be stated in full until the very end of the book, for it requires every other part of the book to support it, each in its own way), and, the special fruit of this section, we will have learned just what is the manpower and the instruments which will constitute the agents of that mission. Men, movements, societies, ideas, and philosophies: these are the building-blocks, the mortar and the clay, of the edifice whose construction is the mission of mysticism; these are the instruments of its creation.

In the wake of the frequent mention of the mission of mysticism, it is helpful to recall that this is none other than the Holy Spirit's mission; it is he who is God's agent in divine communication. And what is here called the 'mission' is in principle the same task as is referred to in the evangelical Christian's usage of the word. But here the scale is global, the intention racial, the method an interaction of science with religion in an unprecedented way.

Naturally, the feasibility of the mission of mysticism depends upon the truth of the articles of the mystic's credo. If those articles, as stated in chapter 4, are true descriptions of reality, then mysticism is the most important product of human (and superhuman) consciousness. If true, it is the most wonderful thing ever to befall the human race. If valid, the genuine article is the most precious possession of *Homo sapiens* – perhaps the only justification of the *sapiens* in his title.

The proliferation of paramystical enterprises in recent times

Whether or not mysticism is valid, it is the principal target of the hopes of modern man, especially among the younger generation. One of the most remarkable features of contemporary culture is the hunger of people of the most diverse backgrounds for some degrees of mystical illumination. This is expressing itself in an astonishing proliferation of occult, mystical, and religious groups and sects, which occultists attribute to the onset of the Age of Aquarius and the associated demise of materialism. Stephen Annett compiled a dictionary of these groups in England, under the title *The Many Ways of Being*: he mentioned 119 groups in England, and Table 2 presents their names (many of them well known), divided into the seven categories of Christian, eastern-oriented, esoteric, astrological, psychic and spiritualist, fringe medicine, and development groups.

Table 2
The many ways of being

1   CHRISTIAN GROUPS

Children of God, Lonesome Stone, Jesus Liberation Front, Musical Gospel Outreach, Unified Church, Pentecostal Church, The Quakers, Christian Community, The Mormons, Christian Science, Unity School, Science of Mind, Association for Promoting Retreats, The New Church.

2   EASTERN-ORIENTED GROUPS

Hinduism, Krishna Consciousness, Divine Light Mission, Sai Baba, Sri Chinmoy, Rajneesh Meditation, Transcendental Meditation, Meher Baba, Aurobindo Society, Self-realization Fellowship, Vedanta, Sikhism, 3HO Foundation, Subud, Baha'i, Sufism, Yoga, Martial Arts, Sati Society, Buddhism.

3   ESOTERIC SOCIETIES

Theosophy, Anthroposophy, Alice Bailey, Universal World Harmony, Gurdjieff, Teilhard Centre, Grail Foundation, Spiritual Inner Awareness, Findhorn, Scientology, Pyramid and Sphinx, Order of the Cross, Esoteric Society, Avatar, The Emin, Axminster Light Centre, Dartington Solar Quest, Aetherius Society, Viewpoint Aquarius, The Atlanteans, Pyramidology, The Druids, Torc, Glastonbury Zodiac; Intergroup catalysts: Wrekin Trust, Human Development Trust, Holonomics, World Congress of Faiths.

4   ASTROLOGICAL

Astrological Lodge, Faculty of Astrological Studies, Astrological Association, Jeff Mayo, John Iwan, White Eagle Lodge, Astroscope.

5   PSYCHIC AND SPIRITUALIST

Society for Psychical Research, College of Psychic Studies, Spiritualism, Spiritualist Association, Spiritualists' National Union, The League, White Eagle Lodge, Psychic Press, The Confraternity.

6 FRINGE MEDICINE

Homeopathy, Herbalism, Bach Centre, Nature Cure Clinic, Tyringham, Acupuncture Association, Veganism, Vegetarianism, Psychic Diagnosis, Radionics, Psionic Medicine, Somatography, Spiritual Healing, Burrswood, Churches' Council, World Healing Crusade, Foundation for Wholeness, Health for the New Age Hygeia.

7 DEVELOPMENT GROUPS

Arica, Quaesitor, Community, Bristol Centre, Atma, Centre House, Sempervivum, Centre for Group Work, Entrophy, London School of Bodymind Health, Centre for Human Communication, Psychosynthesis, Hallam Centre, Transactional Analysis, Human Cybernetics, Therapeutic Communications, Franklin School, Organizational Research, Churchill Centre, Human Potential Research, Humanistic Psychology, Science Fiction.

From Stephen Annett, ed., *Many Ways of Being* (London 1976).

It is helpful to have this study, but it should be borne in mind that it is far from being a complete study of modern mysticism; it is really a list of the many 'alternative' ways of being – the ways frequented by young people seeking religion but 'turned off' the traditional religions. John Allan, in a remarkable little book called *The Gospel According to Science Fiction*, made a study of modern semi-religious groups and reported that, from the point of view of many young modern people, a desirable religion was one which had five characteristics: it will be *'scientific'* (UFOs rather than angels), *esoteric* (equals oneupmanship over the poor deluded 'ordinary' Christian), *mind-expanding, simplifying,* and *undemanding.* In chapter 6 this analysis will be pursued further. For the moment it is sufficient to recognize that Annett's 119 groups are only the 'alternative' schools of modern mysticism; the traditional ones are by no means moribund. In Christianity alone, a comparable study of Christian spirituality, conducted for the London Ecumenical Centre by Mark Collier, enumerated thirty-eight active groups concerned with spirituality. It is perhaps not entirely coincidental that this study appeared under the similar title, *Ways of the Spirit.*

These two studies, reporting the healthy existence of 157 mystical or semi-mystical groups, shows the populousness of mystical aspirants; but it is still far short of showing the whole picture, even in this country. It does not include the millions of Protestants and Catholics who do not affiliate themselves to esoteric or spectacular mystical or spiritual groups, or even to Christian spiritual groups. These are the backbone of the Church, the people for whom the Mass or Holy Communion is so powerful and numinous an experience that they have no need for extra-church spirituality. And perhaps an equally large number of 'private Christians' obtain what they feel to be their ration of mystical experience in their private prayers. Nor is there any evidence to suppose that the Christian monastic tradition is less flourishing, less popular, or less far-reaching in its effects upon the community than in times past.

Still, even taking into account all the 'alternative' and 'traditional' outlets for spiritual-mystical aspirations, we are far short of having a complete picture of modern mysticism in contemporary culture; next must be considered the crypto-mystical.

Science fiction has a strong mystical component – it provides the imagery and the concepts, as well as some particular metaphysics and scientific theories – and it has a massive following all round the world. Many hundreds of millions of people consume science fiction in the several media in which it appears, and the fervour of the devotees is legendary. There can be no doubt that science fiction is the breeding-ground and the tertiary education for most modern mystics. Christopher Evans has pointed out that a whole institutional religion – scientology – has sprung fully-formed from the arm of a science-fiction writer, L. Ron Hubbard.

Television

Even science fiction is not absolutely universal, and there is another influence that is more nearly so: television. It has been said, in a commentary on the Japanese love of modern technology, and especially photography, that where other people have their hearts, Japanese have a Nikon camera. But really modern industrial man all over the world has a television set as the centre of his being. It is the shaper of his thought and opinion, and for many its programming sets the pattern of the day. It comes closer than any government dictatorship has ever come to perfectly subjecting the populace. The cynical cartoonist Feiffer showed this in an excellent cartoon strip: a man is alone in a room watching the television, and he says to it, 'I'm becoming too dependent on you, I can't do anything any more.' The TV replies, 'Nonsense. Watch – ' and the programme changes to an Open University programme. 'You understood that, didn't you? Well, there's nothing wrong with your mind.' 'But my emotions are deadening – ' 'Nonsense,' says the TV, and turns to a tragic film, when the man weeps, and then to a comedy, and he laughs. With an imperious flick of the programme selector, the TV concludes with a sports programme, and commands, 'Enjoy!' Emotionally wrung out, sprawled in his chair, the man cries in joy, 'No one understands me like you do!'

With the moral of that story in mind, it is not so easy to underestimate the power of the television. It is an alarming thought that a high percentage of marriages contain arrangements in which the husband or wife listens to the television more than to his or her partner. If, then, mysticism was found to have a foothold in television, it would necessarily entail a further increment in the mystical consciousness of modern culture. And, of course, there is a substantial mystical component in television. For though television is so powerful, it must be remembered that it is impotent *per se*; it can only reflect the wider culture, or perhaps amplify it. The mysticism of television contains, therefore, roughly the same things as the wider cultural environment, except that its visual nature invites more mystical presentation. But since television is the main source of culture to millions of illiterate, semi-illiterate, and pragmatically illiterate people, it follows that even those who escape the mystical consciousness in literature will meet it in the mass media. And it is not just a matter of documentary programmes, about such as von Däniken; the peak-viewing slots are filled with, among other programmes, ones about more evolved human or semi-human beings (a favourite theme of science fiction and religion), such as *The Man from Atlantis*, *The Bionic Woman*, and *The Six Million Dollar Man*, to say nothing of such blatantly science-fiction mysticism regulars as *Dr Who*

(who, in the last fifteen or so years, has graduated from Dalek opponents to an ever-increasing cavalcade of black magician foes who must be defeated by a combination of science and mysticism), and *Space 1999*.

It may thus be taken as read that, in contemporary culture, the modern mystical consciousness has permeated almost everywhere – certainly among younger people, and to an increasing extent among the older.

It should not be thought that this explosion of mystical consciousness is confined to Britain, or even to the English-speaking world. It is common knowledge that America has been the principal origin of the modern mysticism, and the state of California alone is probably the home of more new sects than all the British ones put together. But it is less well known that in Japan too there has been a comparable expansion of mysticism. In the century leading up to the Second World War, religion had been used by the state as a binding force for political purposes: the national religion of Shinto had been the mainstay, bound up with worship of the emperor as a descendant of the sun god; the only other religion allowed was Buddhism, and temples had to be registered with the government. After the war, the conquering Americans forced the emperor to renounce his divinity publicly, and since that time, it is now estimated, several hundred new sects or religions have been formed. It has been, as one observer put it, 'the rush hour of the gods'.

Such are the far-reaching and manifold expressions of modern mysticism. Regrettably, a great deal of what passes as genuinely mystical in contemporary culture, and thereby attracts many votaries, is pseudo-mysticism, a more or less aberrant distortion of the genuine article. And the question which every contemporary human, especially those born since about 1945, must face, is: Of all these hundreds of apparently competing schools of thought, all these apparently conflicting world views, which are true? And if true, which are valuable? And some will ask which of these have that highest purity, and confer that peace of God, which is the hallmark of man's supreme body of wisdom: mysticism?

To answer this last question is the task of this whole section. The answer can only be found by examining each main school of thought systematically and individually, and the remaining five chapters of Part Two are devoted to this task. In each case the policy adopted is to delineate the general nature of the group or belief-system or technique or institution concerned, then to enunciate its beliefs and practices, and in conclusion to say a little about the size and nature of the membership or subscribing body of people. Then the 'mystical candidacy' of the entity will be discussed. The purpose of each discussion is to disentangle the elements of genuine mysticism and pseudo-mysticism.

How can mysticism and pseudo-mysticism be distinguished?

The short answer to this question is that mysticism is that which accords with the mystic's credo, which was democratically constructed in accordance with modern philosophy of language, in chapter 4. But that solution is inadequate. Cases will certainly arise where some articles of the creed are subscribed to, but others rejected. What is to be done in this case? It is here that the weakness of Wittgenstein's method emerges. It is true that by his method it was possible to isolate what may in a technical, philosophical sense be called the 'essence' of mysticism, but the drawback is that it is necessary to treat all articles of the creed as being of the same importance, which they manifestly are not. What is needed, therefore, is a further analysis of the credo, determining the rank importance of the articles. A method for this task is not to be found in philosophy, but in inferential statistics: the technique of factor analysis provides a way of obtaining the information needed.

Factor analysis is a mathematical method of analysing sets of scores to determine which scores cause the variation in numbers and which are the cause. For example, in psychology the technique is used to study many scores of personality variables, in order to determine whether one cardinal trait or many specific traits are causing variations in behaviour. Greatly simplified, the method can be used here to decide whether the articles are really equally important as the essence of mysticism, or whether they are mostly governed by a few. If the latter is the case, we will have advanced in the definition of mysticism to a new point, which, being of a precision and depth beyond that which was called the 'essence', can only be called 'the quintessence of mysticism', the final point on this particular definitional route. There are several senses in which some articles of the creed could be 'more important' than others. Not every sense entails election to the 'quintessence', so they must be clearly distinguished.

In some multicomponential words, of which 'mysticism' is in fact one, some of the 'traits', components, or articles are actually nothing more than *implications* of logically more central propositions. For instance, the proposition 'Love conquers all' is more important than some of the propositions which it *entails* or *implies*: for example, 'All shall be well', 'Hatred and evil can be overcome by love', etc. A second type of importance is to be found in the cases where there are two articles of the creed, not connected by logical implication or entailment, but with one clearly semantically or philosophically more important. Such a case is to be found in articles 19–23. Important though these undoubtedly are, they are less important than articles 1–5; for the latter state the great religious and metaphysical truths from which all follows, and the former are merely *methods* by which the great truths can be exploited for personal advancement, *consequences* of the master axioms. Naturally, the articles selected as quintessential are those master mystical truths.

The quintessential mystic's credo, as it should be called, reduces the thirty articles of the main creed to five. (The minority elements are not included in this analysis, since it is by definition impossible for them to be quintessential.)

Quintessential article no. 1 states that God (Spirit) is love; he is omnipotent and omnipresent, and is indeed the only reality.

No. 2 states that every human being has a most glorious destiny of perfect fulfilment in and with God (Spirit).

No. 3 states that all men are on the route to God, the spiritual path, and they can verify the first two articles of this creed by diligently living the spiritual life.

The first three articles have been mostly concerned with belief, and are therefore inadequate as a test of mystical authenticity. Article 4 provides the missing element; it states: 'The true mysticism reveals itself at work by a steady growth of compassion, from the particular to the general to the universal, manifested in not only reported states of consciousness but in actual behaviour.'

Some amplifying comments are called for, since the burden of this article is potentially great.

We are proposing to examine modern culture to test for the authenticity of mystical-type movements. A study of beliefs is only one indicator; right actions are just as important an index. The ray of mysticism leaves very visible marks on a person and on organizations: it heals and soothes, inspires and energizes; and above all it enhances compassionate action. The following may therefore serve as a short commentary on quintessential article 4:

'The appearance of a compassionate impulse towards friend or family is the first infinitesimal step along the path of mysticism. The expansion of this into a universal compassion towards the animate and inanimate anywhere, anywhen, is the perfect fruition and completion of the mystic way. And the extent to which a person, organization, or artifact radiates impartial compassion is the extent to which he or it transcends the pseudo-mystical and partakes of the essence of authentic mysticism. Moreover, an increase in compassion will always be exactly inversely proportional to the decrease in self-concern, egocentricity, egotism, self-regard, self-consciousness, and selfishness. And the growth in compassion is always partnered by a growth in humility as a realization of God develops.' (The Sermon on the Mount, which provides a wonderful paradigm for this discussion, is, as so often, superlatively concise: so much of mysticism is stated incomparably in the Beatitudes alone.)

'The principle of compassion stems from a deeper vision of the unity of life. The mystic who knows how truly and literally he is one with all men, with all animate and inanimate entities, will be capable of no response other than compassion, literally fellow-feeling. Thus another defining characteristic of the authentic mystical consciousness is a realization of harmony and union and a horror of separative beliefs and actions.' At the same time the compassionate empathy of the mystic prevents him from using force or compulsion to 'convert' or even to 'redeem' the unbeliever. He knows that freedom of thought and action is absolutely sacred; help can only be given to those who want it.

As stated in chapter 1, there is one other indispensable element in the true mysticism: the realization that God is the author of mystical attainment, through his freely given, unearned grace. Thus the fifth and last quintessential article is simply article 28 itself:

'Mysticism is God's work; he is the author of all mysticism. Mystical development is accomplished entirely through his unearned grace.'

To maintain the rigour of the semantic analysis, it is now necessary to show that, according to the factor analytic method, the quintessential articles are not only ideologically central and seminal, but semantically also. This is easily shown. If the reader will now turn back to the essential mystic's credo, Table 1, and check off the thirty main articles, he will see that each one is entailed or implied by, or is a consequence of, one or more of the quintessential articles. Specifically, the analysis shows that:

Quintessential article 1 embodies articles 1–3, 5–6, 13, 15–16 of the essential credo.

No. 2 embodies articles 4, 7–10, 12, 14, 24–6.

No. 3 embodies 11, 17–23.

No. 4 embodies 17–18, 29–30.

No. 5 embodies 28 and 29.

All thirty articles are thus accounted for.

The superquintessence of mysticism

For the sake of that perfection with which mysticism is always concerned, it is interesting to apply the factor analytic method again to the quintessential articles themselves. From that analysis emerges the single article, the ultimate metaphysical and theological statement, womb of all science: 'God, the Supreme Being Who is omnipotent and omnipresent, Ground and Being of all, is Love.'

But for the practical purposes of evaluating mystical candidates, the quintessential five articles provide a manageable yardstick.

There is reason to reject at the outset the possibility that many of the decisions, as to whether or not the authentic mysticism is at work in the case under consideration, will be black-and-white. Human nature being what it is, few movements or persons are either wholly good or wholly bad; there is in most a sort of mixture of the real and pseudo, and it is not a matter of pronouncing yes/no, true/false, guilty/not-guilty verdicts.

Rather it is a matter of deciding, by the just application of the criteria which have been developed, how much of a contribution the entity can make to the mission of mysticism, which is the purpose of the whole discussion. The greater the degree to which the candidate conforms to the five articles, the better he is equipped to contribute to the mission of mysticism, which is of course only concerned with the authentic candidates.

6

The Peak Experience

Abraham Maslow's contribution

In the present era of radical and liberal theology, when attempts
have been made to 'demythologize' and even 'dereligionize' so
many areas of religion, it is not surprising that mysticism has
suffered a similar fate. Abraham Maslow (1908–70), a professor
of psychology in America, and a militant Jewish atheist, set out
to demythologize the mystical element of religion. Maslow has
become world famous as the leader of the psychological
movement which he called the 'third force' (the previous ones
being behaviourism and psychoanalysis), or 'humanistic'
psychology, which is also known as the human potential
movement, and is associated particularly with the West Coast of
the United States. This movement, which has, together with
enlightened religion, been the standard-bearer of mankind
since the Second World War, deserves great praise: its banner is
embossed with the insignia of freedom of mind, body, and
spirit, and its ethos is expressed in the phrase Maslow used to
describe his own vision: the 'wonderful possibilities and
inscrutable depths in mankind'. The atheism of the movement is
no bad thing for religion, because it is the kind of atheism which
sings God's praises while calling him by another name; and no
movement can be bad if it affirms the Kingdom of God within
man, even if it should call it self-actualization.

Abraham Maslow's contribution to psychology and to
mysticism lies in the complex and empirically grounded theory
of human personality, motivation, and nature which he
enunciated in the course of forty years as an academic
psychologist. From his earliest days, even as a student
psychologist, several convictions were his incentive: he detested
religion, and theism in particular, for being woolly and
superstitious, and yet he was determined that man did have a
higher (though secular) nature, and that it had to be given the
prominence it deserved so that the Freudian idea of man could

71

be routed. Over the course of his long career, Maslow became famous for the two terms: 'self-actualization' and 'peak experience'. The author of the first phrase is unknown, but Maslow himself coined the latter term. In doing so he achieved one of his ideals of demythologizing mystical (and plain religious) experience. These two concepts became part of the neatly interwoven whole which was Maslow's theory of human nature – personality and motivation, potential and actual. That theory must be briefly sketched before the concept of the peak experience can be evaluated with accuracy.

The foundation of Maslow's theory of human nature lies in his theory of motivation. His notion of the 'hierarchy of needs' has become famous as the basis of the latter, which is partly formulated in order to refute the Freudian theory of motivation. As is well known, the latter explained human motivation in terms of primitive unconscious motives deriving from unsavoury primeval, atavistic, animal drives. The conscious mind, according to this theory, disguises the real motives, because they would be unacceptable. Thus human behaviour is the product of ignoble, irrational, furtive, and ugly longings from that sink of iniquity, the repository of animal longings, the id. So pessimistic and repulsive a picture had never appeared before or since in relation to human nature, and the human race must have worked off a lot of bad karma by its adoption of the Freudian theory. Certainly there must have been some extrascientific influence at work in making Freud's theory so widely popular: scientifically it was close to nonsense. The evidence was sparse and unbelievably biased, the theory was infinitely plastic and, in the case of art and religion, redolent of contortionism. For Freud, in denying the existence of higher motives, was forced to say that art and religion were all sublimations of animal drives. The stupidity of this view, of course, lies in the idea that the primitive drives of the id could be wiser than the mature conscious mind. Beethoven's Ninth Symphony, for example, or the writings of St John of the Cross, so obviously are inspired by a superhuman wisdom that it is staggering that so cultured a man as Freud could deny it. The human race in the first forty years of this century was evidently afflicted with a temporary lunacy, of which the work of Maslow marks the beginning of the end.

According to Maslow's theory of motivation, animal drives play a part, but when they are satisfied – and they can be – higher needs come into play. Man's basic need is for air, and when that is satisfied he will need food, then sexual emission, then company, then friendship, then esteem, then love, then parenthood or family life, then – in Maslow's terminology – only when all these needs have been met will he fall under the sway of the master motive: self-actualization. Obviously religious people would think of doing God's will in this connection. More secular types will think of career satisfaction.

Maslow's definition of self-actualization was always disappointingly vague, but the general purport of it is self-evident: it is the drive to bring into actuality those potentialities which an individual contains. It is assumed that the state will entail different actions and experiences for everyone. The idea of self-actualization is intimately connected to Maslow's theory of man's higher nature. Having studied all the greatest figures in history, including the religious ones, Maslow became convinced that man had a higher nature, and that self-actualization consisted in actualizing it in each individual, and this is where peak experiences come into the discussion.

The enjoyment of peak experience is one of the marks of a self-actualized person, according to Maslow, and this is the point at which to essay some definition of the term. Conflating various Maslovian definitions into a composite one, the following is the result: The peak experience is what used to be called a mystic experience, in which the experiencer is temporarily overwhelmed in an indescribable happiness, joy, peace, and love, which are accompanied by the certain conviction that the experience is a revelation of reality (or, in Maslow's terminology, a 'cognition of being').

Maslow went on to draw the following conclusions. First, if the experience is veridical – if it is indeed a true cognition of being – the self-actualizing peak experiencers are the advance guard of mankind, as scientists, philosophers, and plain humans. Second, might it not be the case that everyone is potentially a peak experiencer? If so, surely in the peak experience we have identified the gateway to that higher consciousness which is as surely a part of human nature as the infrahuman consciousness named by Freud.

Colin Wilson

Abraham Maslow, in his later years, had a friend and collaborator in Colin Wilson, the philosopher and novelist who has spent twenty years writing on similar subjects. His more recent book, *New Pathways in Psychology: Maslow and the post-Freudian Revolution*, takes Maslow's argument a step further. Wilson, writing from a background of phenomenological and evolutionary existentialism, expands the analysis of peak experiences in both directions – phenomenologically and in terms of evolution. First, he presents an excellent, highly enterprising study of the phenomenological mechanism of the peak experience, in detail for which there is no space here. However, his basic point is that it is possible to train by deliberate exercise the faculty by which the peak experience occurs – its 'muscle', Wilson calls it. He argues that the lacklustre, meaningless mental life which most humans seem to have is the result of slackening the tension of consciousness; but the situation *can* be remedied in the way indicated. Moreover, any perceptual act can create a peak experience if concentration and a search for the hidden meaning is carried on. So much for the phenomenology. On the evolutionary side, Wilson believes that the future evolution of mankind must lie in making the peak experience constantly present in every man.

The peak experience scrutinized

Such are the broad outlines of the peak experience theory which Maslow and Wilson have developed. The question now is the extent to which it satisfies the criteria by which authentic mysticism is identified, and, therefore, whether it has any part to play in the mission of mysticism as here defined. This is an important question, because the idea of the peak experience has considerable currency · internationally, among influential groups; and it appears that peak experiences lie all around us at this time, so to speak. The multiplicity of modern pseudo-religious experiences, the apparent depth of experience associated with modern popular music, and many other species of modern so-called mystical experiences: all these are thought by some to be 'peak experiences', and thereby hangs an issue. Is the peak experience only what used to be called a mystical experience, i.e. by definition qualitatively different from

74

ordinary experiences of such pleasures as good food, a good book, family games, etc., or is 'peak experience' a matter of degree, a smooth continuum from the mildest of pleasures (such as one's train leaving punctually) up to the beatific vision? That is, in the terminology of psychology, is the peak experience continuous or discontinuous with ordinary experience on the one side and the supreme mystical vision on the other? Modern usage of the word has already begun to blur its outlines in the direction of the continuity hypothesis. However, this is not the fruit of reasoned thought but simply the semantic laziness which destroys so many words. 'Peak experience' was used as a metaphor and now many believe the metaphor to be literal, and abuse the phrase in such ways as saying that they are going to their in-laws for a few peak experiences. The best way to answer this difficult question is to proceed to the discussion of the Maslow-Wilson work in the light of mysticism, and return to it thereafter, together with the question whether peak experiences are really ubiquitous in modern culture.

The mystical evaluation of the peak experience

Maslow and Wilson deserve much praise for the way in which they have, in their work on the peak experience, brought to the attention of countless non-religious people the possibility of the higher self of mankind. They have, in an age of doubt, done much to restore man's self-esteem and set him back again on the right trail.

But now the criticisms – and they are many and profound – must be made of this movement. The fact is that both Maslow and Wilson are doomed to failure. Both searched for man's higher self, but both gave themselves an impossible handicap by denying the existence of man's soul and spirit (or, in theosophical terms, the four highest principles of man). Having made this egregious mistake, they were leaving themselves with man's lowest nature to study. Then, finding in it mere echoes of the higher self to which they shut their ears, they were unable to do more than grope ineffectually in seeking to trace these intimations to their source. This is the penalty they paid for denying the soul and spirit of man, denying the existence of God, denying the whole dimension of spirituality (a word which appears in the writing of neither!). This is the penalty they pay for lack of humility and dependence on God's grace: for without those qualities there can be no perception of spirituality. Peak experience research must be guided by the Sermon on the Mount, for only the pure in heart shall see God. Mystical research is nothing without self-surrender to God.

The criticisms may be presented more formally.

According to universal mystical theory, the peak experience, as described by Maslow, is indeed a spiritual experience. This is hardly surprising, since he got the idea from reading about religious experience. Maslow wants to argue that it is man himself, not religion, that is wonderful, as revealed in the experience. Mysticism agrees, but points out that the peak experience is the revelation of the Kingdom of God within man. Colin Wilson, for his part, wonders whether we might all have the potential for constant peak experiences. Many find this an exciting idea. So it is, but it is no more than a pathetic leaf out of the book of mysticism. Mysticism is concerned with having a 'peak experience' all day long. The Bible is full of instructions to that end. The literature of mysticism all over the world is concerned with precisely this aim. It is man's religious destiny, and *a fortiori* his mystical destiny, to have a peak experience incessantly. If we consider just one mystical school, this will be obvious. The raja yoga of Patanjali (*?* *c.* the second century) is a ten-page treatise on *kaivalya* (equals freedom, liberation, oneness with God, the ultimate peak experience). It is not about how to have a *glimpse* of God, but how to see God everywhere at all times and in all things. And it lays down with wonderful conciseness and great exactitude the steps of spiritual self-discipline which is the route to that goal. This includes physical self-culture, moral training in the greatest possible depth, control of mind, right occupation, and ever-increasing meditation and prayer; and Patanjali points out that all these can be disregarded if the aspirant's self-surrender to God is perfect. It is also implied that progress will depend in part upon the individual's past – his karma from this and previous lives.

The penetrating insight of this system of spiritual self-culture is horribly absent from Maslow and Wilson. They do not seem to live in a universe where morality plays a part. They neglect even the simplest religious insights that God, or ultimate reality, is concerned with morality. They neglect even him whom many would say was a fellow-atheist, the Buddha: yet, even he, in his first sermon, described the revelation to him of the moral dimension of being:

> Behold, I show you Truth! Lower than hell,
> Higher than heaven, outside the utmost stars,
>   Farther than Brahma doth dwell,
>
> Before beginning, and without an end,
>   As space eternal and as surety sure,
> Is fixed a Power divine which moves to good,
>   Only its laws endure.

(The Light of Asia, Book 8)

Having omitted the moral dimension of being, they then gleefully experiment with the idea of manipulating peak experiences. But that is nonsense. Once again, the need for humility and the patient waiting for grace are relevant. We can say that if a peak experience is really a religious or mystical experience, it cannot be induced; it can only be enjoyed. This is not to say that it will not seem to be induced. Psychedelic religious experiences come from the hand of God just as surely as do monastic ones. If it was not God's intention for a religious experience to occur, no amount of psilocybin or LSD would induce one. But there is nothing to say that God will not use drugs as his instruments; he allows people to employ music to kindle religious fervour.

Nonetheless, the peak experience movement can make no real progress until it adjusts itself to ultimate reality. And this means the incorporation of a moral and reverential component. We may say that when the peak experience induces not only excitement but also holy fear, then it is indeed a mystical experience. But the issue of whether peak experiences can be had all day and every day is, as shown above, a question to which the answer exists in abundance in the spiritual literature of the world. Religious people and, even more so, mystics, not only believe that mystical 'peak' experience can be perpetual: they *know* that for a fact, they have dedicated their whole life to that goal, and spirituality has given them the methods and attitudes: moral self-cultivation at the heart of self-purification and self-surrender to God. It is almost pathetic to see modern young people comparing notes about their 'really neat' peak experiences and wondering how to perpetuate them, while the entire religious history of mankind points to the simple fact that the greatest religious/mystical/peak experiences are the lot of those who consecrate their lives to God and practise perpetual self-surrender to his will. Yet it is sad for the Church too. The countless youngsters who flee *from* the Church in search of bliss are latter-day Francis Thompsons, desperately flying from the Hound of Heaven who alone loves them. And the Church cannot neglect them. It is a major pastoral duty to learn to speak the language of modern peak experiences and thereby show the young that all their peak experiences are actually pale reflections of the one reality to which the Church is always pointed. We can show them Bach's music to outbid their rock; devotional classics to overwhelm their amoral bestsellers; and we must introduce them to the love of Christ to destroy for ever the need for secular pseudo-substitutes. 'God is Love' is the supreme peak experience, and those who have learnt the reality of the risen Christ have no more need for friendship-substitutes.

Now it is possible to reconsider the question of the continuity of peak, ordinary, and mystical experiences. The answer is that the line is drawn between religious experiences (i.e. all so-called religious experience, mystical experience, and whichever so-called peak experiences belong to these two categories) on the one hand and secular experiences, no matter how intense, on the other. Only the religious experiences are 'cognition of being' or revelatory of ultimate reality. In our present semantic confusion, the epithet 'peak experience' is applied to experiences from both groups. And to decide which is which the quintessential mystical criteria may now be invoked.

Article 1, that 'God is Love', is satisfied in Maslow's secular way, since he holds that in the peak experience there is a revelation of ultimate reality, and that it is good. Article 2 is satisfied, since Maslow does believe in the destiny of all men with the good reality. But the element of fascism which is always in Wilson's writings occurs in Maslow also in connection with the third article: neither believe that *every* man is on the path, and here the two authors fall from grace by repudiating so essential a part of Christianity and universal mysticism. This reminds one that their writings lack real compassion (Article 4), and they are almost wholly lacking in humility and recognition of grace (Article 5).

Much the same applies to Maslow's ideas concerning self-actualization, which, as with Wilson's writings, are marred by pride, lack of humility and compassion, and an impossible handicap of atheism and denial of spirituality.

On the credit side, we may hope that the peak experience and self-actualization are the gateways by which many souls will pass to true spirituality, the welcome of the Church, and the infinite love of Christ. Indeed religion and mysticism have a responsibility towards the peak experience: they have to welcome it, know it intimately, and then transmute it, with the love of Christ, into the reality of which it is at present so pale a semblance.

When the dramatis personae for the mission of mysticism are drawn up, the peak experience will have a small part to play: with its help some will clamber up from the depths of materialism to the lowest rungs on the lofty ladder of mystical development. To the peak experience falls the honour of being for many the kiss which awoke them from their dogmatic slumber to the enchanting land of spiritual reality. The peak experience is the bridge from the mind to the soul; it is a prolegomenon to spirituality.

7
Paramystical Enterprises

A paramystical enterprise is one which more or less closely resembles actual mysticism, in its aims, principles, and methods. It is one of the features of contemporary culture that these endeavours are proliferating in great numbers, in many countries. The task for mysticism is to decide which of these enterprises are part of the authentic mission of mysticism, and which are not. For this purpose the criteria defining the quintessence of mysticism must again be deployed.

Esoteric societies and occultism

In chapter 1 there was a detailed explanation of the true meaning of esotericism and occultism, and it was shown that they are simply the other side of the coin of mysticism. Esotericism is the search for the divine reality behind every appearance; it is secret or esoteric because known by only a few, but it is there for all who seek, as Jesus told his disciples. The ethos of esotericism, its potential universality, lies in the promise, 'For everyone that asketh, receiveth; and he that seeketh, findeth; and to him that knocketh, it shall be opened.' Occultism is a form of esotericism, but its special genius is its embodiment of the quest for mystical perfection.

Esotericism and occultism have existed as long as history. In ancient Egypt the mystery-religion embodied both, and ancient Greece did likewise. Orpheus, the semi-legendary figure at the birth of ancient Greece, was the source of the Pythagorean doctrine of reincarnation, and Plato was similarly indebted.

In certain respects the oriental religions, especially the mysteries, are closer to true mysticism than is Christianity; the Perennial Philosophy, as mysticism is often known, traditionally preaches reincarnation and karma, apparently in opposition to Christianity. But Christianity has often been on the brink of embracing the doctrine of reincarnation – indeed it is in that position now – and that theory is not as incompatible with Christianity as is often thought.

Nevertheless the question arises as to whether particular esoteric schools are trustworthy. This is not, for contemporary students, merely a matter of considering modern manifestations of esotericism and occultism; at the present time many ancient esoteric and occultist traditions are very active. Some we shall have occasion to meet in a later chapter, there to be discussed in detail. For the moment it is sufficient to notice that alchemy, the tarot, the I Ching, astrology, the kabbalah and high magic, and Tantra, all of which are the repository of ancient truths about the esoteric aspects of human nature, are attracting many adherents. There is nothing wrong in these, in themselves; and there is much to gain in personal growth, if they are practised wisely: but they must be practised with the conditions of the quintessential mystical articles. So long as humility is coupled with universal compassion, no harm can come of anything. No doubt this is one reason why Jesus taught the two commandments to love God (humility) and one's neighbour as oneself (compassion), and why St Augustine gave the famous instruction, 'Love, and do what you will.' The modern aspirant who follows those principles will find that within himself are the means by which he will be able to discriminate the genuine from the bogus.

At this point it must be mentioned that a special danger attaching to the paths of esotericism and occultism is that of pride and, ultimately, separativeness. The very fact that knowledge is 'esoteric' causes some of its recipients to fancy themselves a little 'better' than those who are ignorant. This is a near-fatal spiritual error. No man is better than any other, and all may have the esoteric knowledge if they wish it. But the receipt of esoteric lore can intoxicate the aspirant, and this can only, at best, retard him. The possession of esoteric knowledge should be balanced by the awareness of one's infinite ignorance. Without that humbling thought, pride will topple the disciple from his self-proclaimed lofty height.

One especially dangerous area of esotericism is initiation. In many of the great and perhaps even more of the profane esoteric schools of the past, esoteric initiations are conferred upon aspirants. The most famous is the initiation into the Greater

Mysteries in Egypt, when the hierophant led the aspirant out of his body in a deathlike sleep-trance, to show him the ways of death. But countless other initiations are practised to this day. In the tradition of esoteric theosophy, the life of Christ is held to demonstrate the five great initiations of baptism, transfiguration, crucifixion, resurrection, and ascension. Similarly it is stated that in a different scale the fourth initiate is an Arhat, the fifth is a Master, and so on. The question for the moment is the less exalted one of what role the lesser modern initiations have to play in the mission of mysticism to modern mankind.

The quintessential criteria again apply; but on the whole it is probable that, as every man has the Kingdom of God as part of his very being, his essence, as every man is made in the likeness of his Father, God Almighty, so initiation procedures should not be necessary. It must surely be the case that in the ideal religion no one can come between a man and God: every man must be his own priest. Since spiritual development is not a matter of assimilating spiritual wisdom but of exposing it within one's being, initiation must be in reality unnecessary. All the business pertaining to a man's spiritual destiny must take place between him and God. Surely this is implied in the great command, 'Seek ye first the Kingdom of God, and his righteousness, and all these things shall be added unto you.' In a word, God is his own initiator.

Theosophy and anthroposophy

The name 'theosophy', a Greek form of the Sanskrit term Brahma-Vidya, meaning 'divine wisdom', began from about the third century to be used to designate the teaching also known as the Perennial Philosophy. Naturally, this wisdom is by definition authentic mysticism. Theosophy is sometimes defined as the truth common to all religion, and its function of religions is accordingly to lead the aspirant to the One Wisdom.

In 1875 the Theosophical Society was formed in America by H. P. Blavatsky and H. S. Olcott. Its purpose was to make public the ancient wisdom. Its motto was: 'There is no religion higher than Truth', and its stated aims were the formation of a universal brotherhood of man, regardless of colour, class, creed, religion, etc., the investigation of paranormal faculties in man, and the study of comparative religion with a scientific temper. In practice, the society, which has about 20,000 members, including people from most of the world's countries, has certain additional biases. For one thing, although there is nothing in their declared principles to cause them to prefer one religion to another, their actual teachings take yoga and Buddhism as their basis, and tend to reinterpret Christianity in that direction. But they have also propagated a new teaching, the 'Secret Doctrine'. This is, as well as being an actual doctrine, also the name of a gigantic book which H. P. Blavatsky wrote, she states, at the instigation of Adepts (perfected men) who were the real founders of the society, and who are anxious to help mankind. The society also does much good work of healing, teaching, serving, and researching mysticism scientifically, as well as all psychical research.

For another thing, theosophy, along with occultism and esotericism, presupposes a particular theory of human nature. Briefly, this depicts a human being as an ensouled body, having the following 'principles': physical body and its 'etheric double', astral body, prana, mental body, causal body, reincarnating ego, divine spark (atman), lower mind, higher mind, Buddhi (intuition). In this scheme, which theosophists claim to have overwhelming evidential validation by a variety of means, the higher principles reincarnate with a new set of lower vehicles each time.

This is not the place to expound in detail the theosophical schema. It is accompanied by theories of human evolution towards Mastership and Adepthood, always in accordance with the esoteric teachings of the 'Secret Doctrine', and thus has very definite teachings of its own concerning the mission of mysticism. Short of a whole volume on the subject, we must in this book confine ourselves to mentions of the theosophical vision wherever it promises to elucidate the issues touching upon the mission of mysticism to individuals and to the human species.

The question of the role of theosophy, or the Theosophical Society, in the mission of mysticism, can be answered as follows. Undoubtedly the teaching and the society pass the quintessential criteria. This is because theosophy, to a considerable extent, *is* the true modern form of mysticism. As to its actual role, it will be to continue to do what it is doing, but with an ever-increasing emphasis on planning the spiritual reconstruction. No doubt this endeavour will attract the sympathy of such mighty spiritual beings, by whatever name they be called, as are overlooking the affairs of the modern mystics. The society's tradition of scientific occultism will be especially important.

The same cannot necessarily be said of the offshoots of the Theosophical Society, the most well-known of which is probably Rudolf Steiner. For a short time he was head of the German Section of the Theosophical Society, under Mrs Besant, but his differences of opinion with the society became too great, and he was expelled. He formed his own 'Anthroposophical' Society, which flourishes still, and Steiner schools all over the world attest the vitality of his teachings. Steiner was another lofty initiate into arcane wisdom, which he made public. It is a slightly worrying and cautionary fact that nonetheless he disagreed with all the occult facts made public in theosophy. Here we see one of the dangers of the theosophical movement as a whole. Whenever it becomes too obsessed with *knowledge*, it is in danger of falling into the Gnostic heresy. For God is love, and he can only be known by love. St Teresa of Avila taught that it is not necessary to know much, but to love much. St Paul pointed out how all the knowledge in the world would be fruitless if he lacked love, or charity. Thus, though one may greet the theosophical wisdom with delight and eagerly embrace it, it must never be allowed to become an end in itself, or it will stifle the faint breath of love which it is our task to cultivate.

The point is so important that it is necessary to restate it from a different position. The fact is, that in a strict sense, knowledge is spiritually worthless and impotent. The mere receipt of knowledge from books, people, or any other source, is unable to affect the recipient's spiritual stature one iota. It is what is done by the person as a result of the receipt of the knowledge which is spiritually efficacious. The people who heard the original Sermon on the Mount were not at once more spiritually advanced than those who were elsewhere; they had been given an opportunity. There are, basically, only three events which conduce to spiritual growth in any person: morality, as expressed (1) through love of men and nature, (2) through piety and humility, and (3) selfless service of one's fellow-men. Only what a man does from his own volition can have any effect in his spiritual life. Thus esotericism must always caution its *aficionados* that only if their esoteric knowledge engenders moral rectitude can it help them; and the occultist must always bear in mind the unpalatable truth that only when his activities are supervised by high ethical principles can he really achieve self-realization.

There is, in addition, a special danger which awaits those who commit themselves to the path of occultism in any of its many guises. It is unwitting egotism. When the way of occultism is first encountered, the aspirant cannot help but become intoxicated with the vistas of personal development which are promised to him. And he often goes on to a life as an occultist in which self-development is his goal. He will declare, with sincerity, that this is synonymous with spiritual development, but it is not; it is synonymous with self-inflation. For the fact is that isolated self-development is a mystical impossibility. Strictly speaking, the phrase 'personal spiritual development' is a contradiction in terms. *Spiritual* development, because of the absolute unity of life, can only be of the whole. However, the occultist need not abandon his programme of self-culture; on the contrary, it is morally obligatory for everyone to practise self-culture towards spirituality; but it must be done for all mankind. The motto of the occultist must be, 'I am seeking to perfect myself and my powers so that I can become a better servant of my fellow-men', and only those powers which can be thus deployed should be sought.

It should be added that, as pointed out earlier, much occultism does follow these principles; the earnest seeker will easily recognize it.

Another offshoot of theosophy is Alice Bailey, who also made public a vast mass of profound wisdom through the many books which she claims were psychically dictated to her by a great Master of the Wisdom, and through her own 'Arcane School'. There can be little doubt that, like the monumental 'Secret Doctrine', Alice Bailey's gigantic corpus of wisdom could not have been invented by human minds; the teachings are undoubtedly superhuman in origin. Thomas Merton remarks that such teachings are satanic in origin. Perhaps he is right; it is not possible to say at this point. But Alice Bailey is in the empirical tradition of theosophy: she was prepared to make definite statements. In one of her books she preached the imminent 'externalization of the hierarchy': the thesis that the Masters of the Wisdom, led by the Christ, would make themselves publicly known to usher in the New Age of mankind. And Alice Bailey's disciple Benjamin Creme keeps this vigorous tradition alive with his preaching that the Christ is even now incarnate, and will soon reveal himself. Christ himself has warned of the false Christs who will claim to be him; and he told us that we will know it is truly he when 'the lightning cometh out of the east, and shineth even unto the west . . . the sun shall be darkened, and the moon shall not give her light, and the stars shall fall from heaven, and the powers of the heavens shall be shaken . . . they shall see the Son of man coming in the clouds of heaven with power and great glory' (Matt. 24.27, 29–30).

Those who accept scriptural authority will have no difficulty in deciding which are the false Christs and which is the true.

Spiritual communities

Spiritual communities, of which there are now many hundreds throughout the world, are an intense, modern paramystical endeavour. They are obviously a sign of the disaffection of the younger generation with the older generation's mode of living. The former have a particularly virulent detestation of religious hypocrisy and insincerity; their greater spiritual integrity requires them to live, and not just preach, their spiritual beliefs, and this has caused an ever-increasing number of people, mostly young, to 'drop out' of society. Many have gone to traditional monastic communities, but far, far more have formed their own.

In the multitude of 'spiritual communities' every shade of religious and political belief is represented, ranging from near-atheist kibbutzim and Skinnerian 'Walden Twos' to authoritarian religious groups such as the Moonies, and *laissez-faire* spiritual groups. Some of the communities have shown the world the force of spirituality: Findhorn, in Scotland, has achieved miraculous results with horticulture and farming in the spirit of love. There are also healing groups in many places, and many westernized yogic ashrams.

It is impossible in this confined space to give individual

attention to particular communities. In any case, this is not necessary, since our purpose is simply to lay down evaluative principles which may be applied to all and each of the communities. The quintessential mystical criteria, applied here, yield the following guidelines, whose application will determine which of the communities, or which part of each, is likely to play an active part in the mission of mysticism.

Truly spiritual communities cannot be defined so easily in terms of what they will do, since the ways of approaching God are infinite. But they can be defined in terms of what they will not do. They will not regard themselves as superior to outsiders: their aim will always be union, not separateness. Their purpose will be in accordance with the Sermon on the Mount, to let their light shine before men as an example. They will have no hate in their makeup, either for each other or for outside persons. They will be centred on God, by whatever name he is known to them, and they will set aside some time daily to be with him. They will be intensely aware of the need for self-improvement, and will direct much of their time to this end. They will have a true Christian communism of property, and they will have boundless brotherly love for one another. But most of all, the acid tests of humility and dependence on grace will discriminate the truly mystical from the earthbound.

Naturally, in the imperfect earthly world these qualities will be imperfectly displayed. But the discerning onlooker will easily separate the sheep from the goats, thereby learning which of the communities is likely to offer a contribution to the mission of mysticism.

Religious sects

Much the same applies to the almost equally prolific religious sects which are to be found in large quantities all over the world. The student who is looking for a sect to suit his personal temperament and character and personality (and it is in respect of individual differences that there are so many sects) will be able to apply the criteria quite easily. In particular he will look to see if the sect exalts itself over all others (pride, lack of compassion, lack of oneness) and he will look closely at the obligations which the sect imposes upon him. Only actions which express brotherhood are acceptable to mysticism. He will not worry about how they worship but who they worship: what divine attributes do they praise? They should praise love above all, and should observe the spirit not the letter of the law. They should have a lively sense of the need to improve themselves – indeed, character-building leading to religious realization is the only purpose of religion: all else is just so many accidental accretions which are, unfortunately, mistaken for the real thing. Ideally, the sect's tradition of prayer should include meditation or silent waiting on God; for only in the silence will God answer prayers. And highly authoritarian sects are incapable of real spirituality, which thrives only in the garden of tolerance and love.

Other parareligious confraternities

In this survey it remains to mention a number of groups and movements which are undoubtedly of a parareligious nature – that is, they have certain features superficially in common with religion – but which are very clearly not a part of mysticism, and may even be in opposition to it. Most of these are part of 'the occult' (which is nothing to do with occultism, as explained in chapter 1).

It is obvious that anyone who associates with groups or persons, or undertakes practices, in which there is intention of harming another person or persons, or even any part of nature, is not only excluding himself from religion and *a fortiori* from mysticism and its mission; he is putting himself in danger, since he is voluntarily excluding himself from the love of God and leaving himself at the mercy of dark forces which would otherwise be impotent towards him. This is the case with all black magic, whether it is voodoo or sympathetic magic or witchcraft.

Persons associated with this range of activities have traditionally argued that magic is neither black nor white, it is simply the exertion of will over nature. Some modern witches and magicians also claim that if they only work their spells for personal gain without harming others, they can do no wrong. But this is nonsense. The mystic, seeing the One Life in all, knows that the very idea of personal gain is a denial of mysticism. Evelyn Underhill stated this well: 'Mysticism wants to give, magic wants to get.' Precisely. Only by giving can one grow spiritually, so all movements which contradict this are on the wrong path. This includes high magic and ceremonial/ritual magic, witchcraft, wicca, etc. It must also apply to most systems of divination which are more fully discussed in chapter 7. Devices for foretelling one's future for personal gain or safety, whether it be cheiromancy, tea-leaf reading, or crystal-gazing and the like, are equally unhelpful. The wise spiritual man who trusts in God's bounty will live for today and let the morrow look after itself. He knows, with great Christian souls such as de Caussade, that whatever the morrow brings, it will be God's loving gift and the best thing one could wish. And, if he is an occultist, he knows also the seemingly contradictory truth that the only future before him is one which he has made – and will make, and may make – himself; and with that realization the superstitiousness and, ultimately, the binding nature of systems of divination (*as prophets*) is understood.

8

Self-help through Paramystical Means

Of the multitude of paramystical endeavours at large in contemporary culture, a great number are concerned with self-help. At least three traditions, and probably more, have contributed to this feature of modern mysticism and paramysticism. One is the American tradition of the selfmade man, the archetypal all-purpose man who led his families in a wagon train across the American continent, 'to Oregon, or bust'. The pragmatic American spirit has always admired those who helped themselves, and this is still a part of their philosophy. The teachings concerning positive thinking have also originated mainly in America, although the European Émile Coué was probably the first to attempt to use self-hypnosis and related techniques for the purposes of self-betterment: it was he who instructed his pupils to repeat daily, 'Day by day in every way I am getting better and better.' Later, Norman Vincent Peale, an American Christian priest, became famous for literally preaching the doctrine of positive (optimistic) thinking, based on Scripture.

A second tradition is occultism. This, as the science of mystical perfection, is naturally concerned broadly with self-help, though not in a sordid or selfish manner; rather, it is concerned with the unfolding of spirit within, with self-realization.

A third tradition is modern humanistic psychology. This is the bridge between the first two traditions. Preaching the gospel of joy immanent in human nature, it teaches ways of opening up the centres of joy, and it teaches an individual to be more true to himself, in order to become self-actualized. The notion of self-actualization, it may be seen, is a halfway house between the lofty spiritual aim of self-realization and the selfish goal of self-help.

The other origins of the self-help idea can be seen in Christian Science and faith healing, and in the many magical or occult techniques for obtaining information which will further one's purposes.

The question now is to decide which of these schools are consistent with the principles of mysticism.

Systems of divination

In our present industrial, scientific culture a large amount of time is spent on producing, marketing, consuming, and employing instruments of occult divination. The information which it is hoped thus to procure is concerned with the future, or the present, or the past. Usually it cannot be obtained by normal methods of perception, or by science, but there are varying senses in which this may be so. For example, all divination intent upon discerning the form of some part of the future can, if at all, only be obtained by paranormal methods. Science and ordinary discernment are powerless in that dimension. On the other hand, systems of divination may be used to obtain knowledge possessed by someone else – such as a business rival, or a militarily hostile nation. Or it may be used to obtain information which could be known by scientific means, but in fact is unknown: the location of hidden treasure would be an example. Systems of divination have also been used to obtain knowledge of an otherwise hidden past.

As regards the techniques of paranormal divination, there is a large number of diverse methods and associated philosophies. Some hide a noble nature behind a relatively tawdry front – the tarot, for example – while others have a mailed fist of evil inside a velvet glove of innocence – as in the case of the ouija.

As there are so many different types of divination, broadly or narrowly conceived, and because they are so diverse in method and purpose, individual evaluation is impossible. But a brief survey is in order. There is one group of methods which, though purporting to be about the future, are actually techniques for obtaining self-knowledge with the intention of promoting personal spiritual development along the esoteric paths of occultism. Ralph Metzner, in an excellent book called *Maps of Consciousness*, showed how the tarot, I Ching, astrology, and alchemy were and are all maps of the human psyche, to be used on the paths of meditation and prayer trodden by those seeking to perfect themselves. When utilized in this spirit they become a part of genuine mysticism; when used out of idle curiosity, self-regard, or an unconstructive obsession with the future, they are worse than useless to the genuine aspirant.

There is another group of systems of divination which are probably always worse than useless, since they have only the popular façade, and no esoteric tradition to sustain it. These range from the cruder forms of divination such as tea-leaf reading through the darker occult practices exemplified by ouija consultations, to the often sincere crystal-ball gazing and cheiromancy practised on Brighton Pier.

The mystic has only one reaction to all of this: 'Take no thought for the morrow', for it will look after itself. In Ernest Wood's terminology, the mystic is one who has learned that the presence of God sanctifies not only everything in the present, but in the future also. The mystic lives eternal life in the here and now, and is untroubled by the passage of time or the 'threat' of the future. No event can dislodge him from his nirvanic repose, no worry can assail him. In real mysticism, systems of divination have no part to play: all is within, and the task of life is to become ever more and more oneself. And, it must be reiterated, the mystic *qua* occultist knows that he must himself, through the higher self, the god within, design and create every particle of all his future 'down to the last syllable of recorded time'.

Psychism, psychical research, and spiritualism

The matter is not so easy in these cases. Each has a mixture of the authentic and the bogus, and both the investigators and the investigated vary in the purity of their motive. And it is in that respect that the evaluation must lie. It is universally agreed among mystics that, in this universe where the law of morality reigns, it is the motive alone which determines the sanctity of an act. In this chapter our concern is with the use of these activities for self-help. Many borderline cases may be recognized. Psychical research, in itself, is commendable, and has a long and respectable lineage involving both scientists and religious believers. Its aims are one with the third aim of the Theosophical Society, which continues this useful research to this day. It is another matter to resort to mediums. Many bereaved persons do this, and no one can blame them for seeking that comfort, whether or not it is authentic. But the mystic has no use for mediums, because he lives the eternal life even now, he knows that there is no death, and he is one with all creation, so he cannot suffer bereavement in the same way; for him, not only his death but all deaths have 'lost their sting'.

It is far more difficult to speak wisely on the mystic's own unfolding 'occult' powers – called *siddhis* in the Hindu tradition. In the yogic tradition, such as the raja yoga of Patanjali, it is recognized that the practice of the Eight Limbs of Yoga will result in the acquisition of psychic powers, of which two will serve as representative for this discussion. We may consider astral projection, and the recollection of past lives. For those with eyes to see there is no shortage of evidential data showing the existence of these powers. The question is, since they arise in the course of mystical growth, whether they have an important part to play in the mission of mysticism. The answer is that they most definitely do not. The wise commentators on the path all agree that the *siddhis* are nothing better than a snare and distraction which can topple the aspirant from his lofty position if he allows himself to be trapped by them. Patanjali himself warns that the *siddhis* constitute a formidable obstacle to the attainment of the highest *samadhi*. Tulsidas, great mahatma and poet, prays to his beloved in his book *Ramayana* that he may be saved from the temptations of the psychic powers.

It is well worth pausing to consider just why the psychic powers are, so far from being welcomed by the mystic, actually shunned like the plague by him. People often cannot understand why the powers cannot be used wisely and make a major contribution to humanity's interests. The explanation lies in the fact that man is an amphibian. At present he is part spiritual, part material. It is his destiny to learn to be wholly spiritual and to abide permanently in that medium which we call the realm of eternal life, or the Buddhic plane, or the supramental consciousness. The simple fact is that every psychic power, no matter how strong, is 'more of the same' – it holds man back from the purely spiritual realm, and as long as he remains with the *siddhis* he cannot go into the indescribable non-mental 'beyond' of the mind, the realm of contemplation. This is why the mystical life, in every religious tradition, is centred around perpetual meditation upon God with every attempt to minimize the distractions, both internal and external, to the perfect recollection of God, or contemplation. The mystic, concerned as he is with the supramental (and supra-supraphysical/material!), avoids whatever may distract him back to what we call material reality; this is why the great Christian saints were said to be dead to the world and to their own needs. These remarks apply to other psychic powers of the same kind, such as ESP in its many varieties. The only purpose of human incarnation is God-realization, and anything not conducive to that goal is anathema to the mystic.

Psychedelic drugs

These form another category of paramystical means to help oneself, ostensibly for spiritual purposes, and they have enjoyed quite a vogue since Aldous Huxley and several other writers pronounced psychedelia the road to God. This movement has lost a little of its impetus now, with many of its gurus dead, many of its leaders having recanted, and medico-psychological research having given a cooler picture of the claims and their validity.

It must be reiterated that there is nothing wrong in the inducement of spiritual states by the ingestion of physical substances. Millions do it every day during Holy Communion. 'By their fruits ye shall know them', and psychedelic drugs must be evaluated in this light. First, the scientific facts about psychedelic drugs: heroin and cocaine are known to be addictive and ultimately fatal. LSD, mescalin, and marijuana do not seem to have this effect. The effects of the former pair vary enormously according to the individual, but in no case does it seem that by the quintessential mystical criteria the experiences have been desirable. A case might be made for Carlos Castenada, but even with him only a part of his training was drug-controlled, and in any case compassion and humility, to say the least, were lacking from his Yaqui way of knowledge. Marijuana has been legalized in some countries, and it may in due course be as popular and ubiquitous as alcohol and cigarettes. But even though it may cleanse somewhat the doors of perception, so that reality shines forth, it cannot be an easy route to divinity. There are none. And since it tends to cause social withdrawal it contradicts the mystic principle of serving society, which every mystic must obey, in recognition of the great truth of the oneness of all. But most of all, all these drugs are absolutely unnecessary on the one path. It is true, as Patanjali long ago knew, that the psychic powers may be produced by drugs (*Yoga Sutras* 4, 1). And it is equally true that the drugs are as unwelcome as the psychic powers. The three great powers of love, unselfish service, and prayer/meditation contain all the power that the aspirant will ever need, and the pure mystic, watching in awe as the Kingdom of God unfolds within him, can find no purpose for drugs.

Fringe medicine and 'alternative healing'

Mystical approaches to medicine, like psychedelic drugs, are a difficult topic for commentators. Jesus Christ himself showed the reality of spiritual healing, and that it is infinitely more potent than material medicine; and miracles have continued to be worked in his name down to the present day. But the subject is a complicated one. The mystic does not see illness in the same way as the non-mystic. He is aware that ill-health is not an irrational affliction visited meaninglessly upon the sufferer, but rather a 'karmic' opportunity to work through spiritual obstacles which he has created. Pain and suffering, says Geoffrey Hodson, are our best friend, and even Father Butler, author of the famous *Lives of the Saints*, agrees that it is through illness and privation that people return to God, who is their real home. Nevertheless, illness can, if the karma permits, be healed more or less miraculously by anyone who serves as a channel for the divine grace, and this may be a country parson, or a retired housewife, as much as a great Master. Mysticism does not deny the reality, or the authenticity, or even the sanctity of faith healing of all kinds; moreover, the Christian mystic believes that in Jesus of Nazareth there came to earth not just an incarnation of God but God himself, very God of very God, the only true Son of God. Accordingly, he will believe that Christ is superior even to karma, and it is certainly true that the sequence of religious revelations in which the Christ followed the Buddha suggests that while the Buddha told men how to live, and left them to their own fortunes, the Christ came to redeem the suffering there and then: he was able to redeem karma itself. This mystery, amply supported evidentially, evokes great humility in the heart of all mystics. It also suggests that for once the quintessential articles should themselves be set aside in humility, and the matter placed directly in the hands of Christ himself. Then his command is surely that in all matters of illness the mystic will, as all others should likewise do, be self-abandoned to Christ our Lord and Saviour.

The question remains of the role of alternative healing in the mission of mysticism. The answer is that as the mission of mysticism is to perfect *Homo sapiens*, healing must play a part, as men and man are so sick, spiritually even more than physically. The healing of all the sicknesses of man is a precondition for the perfection of the species. But it must be remembered that God sometimes heals by death, and the thesis of this book is that the whole race may have to die the death of crucifixion before it can be healed. In this respect no confident rules can be stated: the only prudent behaviour is perfect self-abandonment to divine providence, in the certain knowledge that illness in the conventional sense is seen as an impossibility to the God-realized mystic, who sees God's grace at work in 'illness' as everywhere else.

Obviously where decisions have to be made about healing by extramedical methods, the quintessential criteria may be applied, and it need hardly be said that no healing should be offered for a price; healing is the gift of God, and cannot have any temporal conditions attached to it.

Humanistic psychology

This is once again the bridge from the secular to the spiritual. The 'human potential' movement of California, inspired by Maslow and many others concerned with human joy and growth, is not religious in the old sense, but is broadly in touch with spirituality insofar as it presupposes noble depths to human nature. This movement has devised (and marketed) literally hundreds of techniques for actualizing human potential: these include the highly various groups of techniques such as encounter groups, humanistic psychotherapy, sensitivity training, self-knowledge, bioenergetics, relaxation training for mind and body, biofeedback, catharsis, concentration, and meditation.

On the whole these may be welcomed enthusiastically. Modern man has become unbelievably 'uptight', to use the excellent phrase of this movement, physically, spiritually, mentally, interpersonally. Enjoyment of life has become rarer and rarer, less and less prominent in the day's events, and constant tension in traffic jams and public transport, together with the acidic pains of frustrated ambition and the sheer pace of life, have reduced to a mockery the supposed joys conferred by 'civilized' life. Man cannot awaken his spirituality without a flourishing interior life of prayer and meditation. But modern man can never relax long and deep enough to make a beginning: even when 'resting' he is troubled by the need to pay for the new three-piece suite, or is perhaps just distracted by the impending broadcast of his favourite television programme. Rousseau was right, though for the wrong reasons, when he declared that man is born free but is everywhere in chains. The chains are of tension and fear.

The human potential movement has begun to restore the dignity of human life, to teach man relaxation and contentment. And it does also show him that he has something resembling a spiritual nature. The yogi welcomes this movement because he sees that all the techniques are valuable, none is harmful, and all have the effect of serving as a pre-yogic training. The Eight Limbs of raja yoga are excellently prepared for by the human potential techniques. This is why they are a bridge from the secular to the spiritual.

As for the choice of methods, each individual must select those which will fit his needs. The application of the quintessential criteria on the one side of his individuality, and the contemplation of the Eight Limbs of raja yoga as the subsequent task, will ensure that a person will choose with perfect wisdom.

Sexuality in relation to mysticism

The final topic for this chapter is also an extremely contentious one. The question of the relationship of sexuality to mysticism has been answered in every conceivable shade of opinion, ranging from that of the complete *Brahmacharya* who sublimates spiritually all sexuality, to that of the devotee of Tantric Buddhism or yoga who employs sexual emission as part of his spirituality. In order to arrive at a balanced view on this controversy it is necessary to go very deep and recall the whole purpose of mysticism. That purpose is to equip man to live in the beyond, the supramental realm of eternal life. If that fact is held firmly in mind, the debate settles quite easily into several layers. The first point is that sexuality, when allowed physical expression, constitutes an affirmation of man's material nature. This may be no bad thing in itself, but from the point of view of the spiritual life it is unquestionably a distraction. It is a fetter which binds the aspirant as he climbs heavenwards. The only way to sever that bond is to embrace chastity, or to become a *Brahmacharya* as it is described in the East. This does not, of course, entail shunning of the opposite sex. In his recent book, *The Sexual Celibate*, which incidentally admits to being at least partially inspired by humanistic psychology, D. Goergan describes with much wisdom the role of sexuality even in the life of the chaste. Fr Herbert Slade, an Anglican priest who leads the Haywards Heath house of the Society of St John the Evangelist, has written with brilliant power and penetration, in his book *Contemplative Intimacy*, of the synthesis of *eros* and *agape* in the Christian tradition, of the perfect integration of sexuality into spirituality.

There will always be those who choose to be married rather than to be single and celibate, and although some pious married souls will reserve sexual congress for occasional procreative acts, others will seek to know whether a life of regular carnal intercourse is somehow compatible with the mystic life.

The answer is that in the earlier stages of the spiritual way it is possible to enfold sexuality as a physical act into the embracing spiritual quest. Plato's divine vision of inter-sex relations points the way: if sexual intercourse is genuinely the carnal expression of the partners' mutual love, then the physical act will be sanctified, for in loving the spouse it is God himself who is being loved. The compatibility of the act with the spiritual life will be in direct proportion to the spirituality of the love expressed by the act. No doubt this is one reason against adultery: any sexual action based on lust rather than love cannot help but take its author further from God. Another mystical reason for abstaining from adultery is the wedding vow, and, furthermore, the fidelity of the spouse symbolizes the spiritual fidelity to God.

Pre-marital sex is a different matter again. Not many adolescents are mystics, and the intense sexual curiosity of that age-group suggests that sexual partnership, under compassionate guidance and with careful contraceptive precautions, might be a helpful policy for all concerned. Of course, whenever any kind of sexual licentiousness is advocated, large numbers of people will try to seize the opportunity, and will pervert the whole endeavour. No doubt in a society in which adolescent sexuality was encouraged, huge numbers of middle-aged people would pay large sums to disguise themselves as adolescents. But the principle remains: adolescents should have some experience of sexual intercourse, so that they can approach it with maturity as an adult, whether it is in a marriage, or as a celibate, or some other role. And from the point of view of the perfection of man, whose body is the temple of the Holy Spirit, it is hard to see why the lifelong denial of a natural and healthy human appetite should be especially conducive to sanctity. In the Christian monastic tradition it is the mortification of the appetites of the flesh which has been the aim here. This is obviously the right strategy for those committed to spirituality, but it is probable that for a man to have perfect self-understanding he must have experienced for himself the nature of the sexual experience; and this should be something which is part of his education, in the care of wise teachers.

But the mystic, who inhabits the farther reaches of the path, will, and must, follow the Christian mystics to the destiny which one day all mankind will embrace: the spiritual marriage, to which end all his vital forces, sexual or otherwise, will be directed and perfectly maintained. The mystic is the man who has renounced all earthly embraces for the perfect union with God in the unitive life of nirvana.

9

Science Fiction and its Derivatives

The significance of science fiction

My recent philosophical survey of science fiction[1] entailed fourteen experts from many different disciplines contributing accounts of the importance of science fiction in their own fields. From this an impressively coherent picture emerged, showing the profound significance of science fiction, as a serious part of human culture, science, intellectual life, philosophy, religion, sociology, psychology, and literature, and demonstrating its centrality in the culture of the younger generation. The survey identified science fiction as the lingua franca of modern man, the embodiment of the hopes and fears, the aspirations, and the mythology which are common to contemporary people from all countries. Science fiction is, among other things, the mythology of the twentieth century.

The conclusions of the fourteen contributors to the study were, for the sake of brevity, set down by me in a series of aphorisms, the quintessential science-fiction aphorisms; they are given here in Table 3. They constitute an approximate guide to what might be called the 'logical geography of science fiction': they are intended to exhibit as a whole the complex, manifold nature of science fiction.

The aphorisms are for the most part self-explanatory. But for the present purposes the most remarkable outcome of the study was the recognition that *science fiction is the evolutionary conscience of mankind*. It is in this that its great significance for mysticism inheres.

---

[1] Richard Kirby, ed., *The Significance of Science Fiction* (with fourteen contributors). Bran's Head Books 1978.

Table 3
The quintessential aphorisms of science fiction

I PSYCHOLOGY APHORISMS

1   Science fiction is part of psychology (theirs is the special relationship).

1.1   Sf explores the nature and limits of consciousness.

1.2   Sf is primarily a study of human nature.

1.2.1   Sf can lead to an alteration of human nature.

1.3   Sf explores and maps inner space.

2   Science fiction unites the brain's two hemispheres and hence it unites science and art.

II SPIRITUAL APHORISMS

3   Science fiction is part of modern man's search for a soul.

3.1   Sf is a quest for the perfection of men and man.

4   Science fiction is a vehicle of spiritual development.

5   Science fiction bestows the science-fiction peak experience, the sense of wonder.

5.1   The sf peak experience may physiologically be localized in the cerebral corpus callosum (the great cerebral commissure).

5.2   The sf peak experience is the messenger of the evolutionary conscience of mankind.

6   Science fiction is the evolutionary conscience of mankind, and the science-fiction peak experience is its messenger.

6.1   Science fiction seeks a new reality with a new consciousness.

6.1.1   Sf intimates immortality and evolutionary fulfilment.

6.1.1.1   Sf is the modern heir of romanticism, of poetry and mysticism.

III MYTHOLOGY APHORISMS

7   Science fiction is of immense contemporary popularity, especially as TV.

8   Science fiction has permeated modern culture in general.

9   Science fiction is modern mythology.

9.1   Sf *re*mythologizes the Bible.

IV RELIGION APHORISMS

10   Science fiction is part of religion.

10.1   Sf coats the pill of religiosity.

11   Religion, contrariwise, is a part of science fiction.

V SCIENCE APHORISMS

12   Science fiction stands at the perimeter of all human knowledge: science, philosophy, mythology, religion, art, mathematics, psychology.

12.1   Science fiction propels man through the eye of the hurricane of partial knowledge.

12.2   Science fiction is humanity's epistemic escape hatch.

12.3   Science fiction stands at the threshold of infinity.

13   Science fiction is part of science; it is science's symbiote.

13.1   Sf inspires astronautics and space science.

13.2   Sf sustains exobiology.

13.3   Sf is the conscience of science.

13.2.1   Sf prepares for contact with aliens.

13.3.1   Sf sets aims in aim-oriented science.

13.4   Sf produces many important inventions and scientific ideas.

13.4.1   Sf calls for applied sf content analysis.

13.5   Sf is science's advance guard, its reconnaissance part.

13.5.1.1   Sf operates at the level of the paradigm and programme more than the level of the project and problem.

13.5.2   Sf is prodromic science, proto-science, anticipatory science, ethereal science, imaginary science, avant-garde science.

13.5.2.1   Sf and science are points on the same continuum. Both have *degrees* of fiction. Sf has more than science.

13.5.2.2   All extant sf may be analysed as conjecture awaiting scientific testing. The conjectures *are* science, in an early stage.

13.6   Science fiction is the inspiration of science in faith as well as in ideas.

13.6.1   Sf may inspire science *teaching*.

VI PHILOSOPHY APHORISMS

13a/14a   (shared origin)
         1. Science fiction is part of mathematics.
         2. Science fiction is part of cosmology.

14   Science fiction is part of philosophy.

14.1   Sf is part of logic.

14.2   Sf is part of ethics.

14.3   Sf is part of futurology.
14.3.1   Sf makes *some* useful predictions.
14.3.2   Sf's telescope (or distorting mirror) shows *possible* futures.
14.4   Sf is part of existentialism.
14.5   Sf is part of metaphysics.
14.5.1   especially new-wave 'dangerous visions'.
14.6   Sf is part of theology.

VII   CREATIVITY APHORISMS

15   Science fiction is the laboratory of the imagination, viz. imaginary empiricism.
15.1   Science fiction is the champion of creativity.
15.1.1   Sf is the champion of problem-solving.
15.1.2   Sf uniquely explores the logical heart of creativity.
16   Science fiction teaches a new use of the imagination.
17   Science fiction is guardian of the generic imagination.
17.1   Sf expunges cognitive rigidity.

VIII   HUMANITIES APHORISMS

18   Science fiction is part of the humanities.
18.1   Sf is a part of ecology and urban design (it has a higher degree of fiction).
18.2   Sf is part of (with higher degrees of fiction) sociology and political science.
19   Science fiction demolishes the arts/sciences distinction; it bridges the gap from science to fiction.

IX   LITERATURE APHORISMS

20   Science fiction revolutionizes literary criticism, and demands a new species thereof.
20.1   Sf generates fanzines.
21   Science fiction is a unique literary genre because it concerns the human species primarily.
22   Science fiction is part of literature.
22.1   Sf generates unique reader commitment.
23   Man is science fiction's real character.
23.1   Sf breaks new ground in characterization.
24   Science fiction studies 'alternative persons' (aliens, monsters, robots, computers, quasi-humans).

LIMITING APHORISM

Science fiction, which is multidimensional and highly multifarious, is primarily concerned to discover; its principal instrument is *change*. Therefore it has no immutable properties or forms except its commitment to unending change, growth, progress, and discovery.

The idea of science fiction as the evolutionary conscience of mankind fits closely with the major theses of the present volume. The mission of mysticism is here defined as the design and creation of the mystical and scientific species which will supersede *Homo sapiens* as *Homo christus*, heir of the New Jerusalem, resurrected man. *Homo christus* is the fruit of the union of science and mysticism, in the age in which man's intelligence has taken him beyond the realm of natural selection to the situation in which he must design his further evolution, with the divine wisdom as his inspiration, science as his method. It is thus because the mission of mysticism is conscious control of the evolution of mankind that science fiction, especially as revealed in this definition, is so important. By describing science fiction as the evolutionary *conscience* of mankind, it draws attention to the fact that man is led from above: science fiction is the modern embodiment of those 'intimations of immortality' which in Wordsworth's day were expressed in romantic poetry. Science fiction is the heir to that romanticism and the principal voice of the teleological beyond, the future state of mankind. Science fiction is an expression of mystical intuition. That intuition has been known by many names: Ernest Wood calls it the Intuition of the Will; H. P. Blavatsky calls it the Voice of the Silence; Mabel Collins calls it Light on the Path. The Bible speaks of it constantly; almost its central theme is God speaking to man and instructing him in how to perfect himself.

The science-fiction aphorism 5 and its sub-sections point out that, as in spiritual intuition as it is more widely recognized, the evolutionary intimations of science fiction are accompanied by, and identified by, the 'science-fiction peak experience', defined previously as the 'sense of wonder' (at man's immortal and sublime potentialities). Science fiction is one of the most widespread constituents of modern culture, and its products are as diverse as they are numerous. Moreover, they vary greatly in quality, and the excessive popularity given to the cruder forms in the mass media has blinded far too many people to the incomparable majesty and beauty of the more noble works. It is, naturally, with the latter that we are concerned in this context. Our attention focuses on science fiction which (a) has a high artistic quality, and (b) deals particularly with matters concerning the possible development of *Homo sapiens*, for only these will confer the science-fiction peak experience which is the trademark of the higher self, or spiritual faculty, which alone can inspire this and the many other varieties of directive spiritual intuition.

A very great quantity of literature and many films do in fact meet these severe conditions. For the sake of continuity it is, as space is so limited, perhaps desirable to concentrate attention on the mystical science-fiction authors mentioned in chapter 2, selecting the 'sacred band of three': the Englishmen H. G. Wells (1866–1946); Olaf Stapledon (1886–1950); and Arthur C. Clarke (contemporary). Of the many works of science fiction written by these three (who, it must be added, are universally recognized as being in the very front rank of science-fiction writers of all time with Wells and Stapledon usually competing for the highest accolade), most dwell upon the subject of the nature of mankind, and what may happen to him or what he will do to himself, his destiny as a species. It is for this reason that aphorism 21 points out that science fiction is unique in that it is, unlike other literature which is about men, concerned with man. Likewise aphorism 1 and its sub-sections describe science fiction as a part of psychology, and speak of the 'special relationship' between the two.

However, just as there are many false Christs but only one who is truly he, so there are para-peak experiences, false stimuli. Science fiction, like all art and literature, can be employed crudely, its genius exploited. It is easy to induce useless pseudo-peak experiences in science fiction as in other art forms. For example, the plot of the American Western story, easily transposed into outer space, can excite in an unproductive way, with emotional outbursts, artificially maintained tension, showdowns at noon, to say nothing of the inevitable symphony orchestra just round the corner. *These* elements, when reproduced in science fiction as they so often are, have little lasting value. The real 'sense of wonder' is unique. It is interesting to note in passing that Plato, in the *Republic*, states that the true motive of the philosopher (which to him was a far more noble idea than to us) is just that, the *sense of wonder*. The science-fiction peak experience partakes of that same Platonic experience. And it is authentic only when it appears in connection with the nature and destiny of man. A few examples make this clear.

Olaf Stapledon, in *Last and First Men*, envisaged the entire future history of the human race, over the next 2000 million years, on several planets, through eighteen species. He shows with icy poignancy what is involved in redesigning the species, and he is unbearably moving in contemplating the suffering of his predecessors. Arthur C. Clarke, for his part, used the film *2001* to explore man's possible origins and future with the development of sentient computers and under the guidance of compassionate extraterrestrial aliens. In *The City and the Stars* he explores the possibility of mankind designing as its successor not another man, but a 'pure mentality', 'freed from the tyranny of matter'. Examples such as this begin to make clear also the symbiotic relationship between science fiction and science (aphorism 13). The sub-sections of this aphorism show the rich interdependence of science and science fiction. They differ in two principal respects: their 'degree of fiction', and the fact that science tests its conjectures. But if testing is the special prerogative of science, conjecture belongs to science fiction, and aphorism 15 points out the unique contribution which science fiction makes to creativity.

As regards mysticism and its mission, these properties of science fiction not only guide and inspire; they also furnish the scientific part of the mission of mysticism with particular hypotheses concerning the design of the new species. Indeed, it is not too much to say that nearly all the thinking on this vital subject has been done, and continues to be done, in the pages of science fiction. For this reason, a recently formed body, the Applied Science Fiction Association, is making a survey of science fiction to compile the relevant ideas. The study from which the aphorisms were taken has also suggested ways in which scientists and science-fiction writers may henceforward co-operate in the design and execution of scientific research, especially in connection with the evolution of our species. In the meantime, the contribution of science fiction to the mission of mysticism will not only be the provision of particular ideas to science; it will also be to continue to act as the evolutionary conscience of the whole race, scientist or non-scientist, and its stories will serve continually to remind mankind about the spiritual potential which, with scientific expression, he must sooner or later make actual. It may also be expected that this modern intuition of the will, the science-fiction peak experience, will become purer and purer in its expression as the time for the metamorphosis draws nearer.

The brainchildren of science fiction: computer mysticism

One of the obsessions of science fiction is with 'alternative persons': aliens, manmade artifacts, mutant men, etc. This is perhaps why one of the leading authorities on science fiction, Brian Aldiss, chose to define science fiction as 'a search for the definition of man'. Many science-fiction stories have explored these possibilities, and it is well-known even among non-enthusiasts that there have been many stories depicting these various entities threatening man, or exterminating him, or superseding him. Sometimes the stories capture the imagination of readers who are moved to take the stories literally. Thus, for example, Christopher Evans, a computer scientist, psychologist, and science-fiction anthologist, has declared his belief that machines will take over evolution within a few decades, and will supersede man, who will quickly become extinct. This must stand as an extreme aberration of atheistic science-fictional science. It is incredible to religious people that so shocking an error could be made, but in a world conceived as soulless there is obviously nothing to stop one from seeing machines take over. After all, René Descartes proved philosophically that man is only a machine – *plus* a soul. And modern atheists have simply subtracted the soul, leaving just the machine. And with those premises, why not design a 'better' machine to take over? Yet, vulgar though these ideas may be, one must respect their fertilizing power: like so much science fiction they encourage constructive thinking about human nature.

Flying saucers

The same applies to an obvious offshoot of science fiction, the flying-saucer cult, also known as ufology (after unidentified flying objects). It is in this matter that the centrality of science fiction to modern culture, its role as lingua franca, its provision of scientific concepts, its action as the modern mythology, its remythologization of Scripture, its role as intermediary between science and religion, its embodiment of the hopes and fears and aspirations of our time, are seen most clearly. A brief factual survey of the field will illustrate these points.

The first fact is that, according to recent surveys, the majority of people in the western world now declare a belief in the existence of flying saucers. The second issue is the question of the evidence for the contacts.

Never has evidence for allegedly factual occurrences been as slippery as in the case of UFOs. Many thousands of people have apparently 'sighted' one (an indigenous jargon has now developed) in the sky, similar numbers have reported seeing them land, lesser numbers but still a substantial number of people claim to have been speaking with aliens, and some – no mean number – claim to have been on board the UFOs, and there to have undergone various experiences, ranging from free joyrides to being seduced by an alien.

This all seems, if a little far-fetched, not beyond the bounds of reason – after all, the number of 'sightings' is so large, and the integrity of many witnesses so unimpeachable, that surely there must at least be a hard core of fact? But even this moderate conclusion is not beyond doubt. There is something very strange about the evidence: despite the many thousands, perhaps even millions, who report sightings, not one indisputable fact has withstood scientific investigation. There is nothing to prove the personal contacts, no physical relic, not even a universally accepted photograph. But for all this, many of the world's governments have declared their official belief in the existence of UFOs, although no one has decided what the official human response should be.

One important feature of the data is that reports almost all speak of the aliens as being not hostile.

Moving a little deeper into the subject, one finds that many

UFO sects and factions have already arisen, in greater or lesser states of organization. There are many scientific groups, eager to get to the factual bottom of the UFO mystery. There are many groups at the opposite extreme, the extreme of gullibility, and for them UFO magazines have already begun to reach the mass market, publications in which alleged UFO experiences share the space with 'factual' articles on the subject. There are science-fiction UFO groups, who are concerned to explore the relationship between the science-fiction traditions concerning extraterrestrial aliens and the UFO data. There are professional authors who are reaping a handsome harvest writing books about UFOs, with more or less degrees of seriousness. The most popular of these, with over thirty million worldwide sales, are Erich von Däniken's: it is evident that the present-day recipe for bestsellerdom is a combination of science fiction and mysticism – the gospel according to science fiction, religion remythologized, with not Christ but aliens coming down from heaven to save us.

And finally, most interestingly, there is the developing field of esoteric ufology, whose British leader is the theosophist Rex Dutta. His approach to the subject is far more serious, more intelligent, and more penetrating than most. To appreciate it properly it is necessary to recall C. G. Jung's contribution to the topic. In one of his last books (1958), the great Swiss psychiatrist turned to the subject of flying saucers. He had studied the particular nature of the data and he came to the interesting conclusion that the phenomena were both real and imaginary, both subjective and objective. He believed that the collective unconscious of man was creating the saucer-images and projecting them, there to be seen by the conscious man and to play a needed part in creating a modern mythology, religion having, for many, been killed off by science. This would explain the slipperiness of the data.

Rex Dutta takes the discussion a stage further and relates the whole problem to theosophical literature, to the esoteric metaphysics of *The Secret Doctrine* and to occult meditation. And while agreeing that the UFOs may not be physical-material in nature, he disagrees with Jung's conclusion; instead, he argues that the objects are extra*dimensional*. This, granted the premise of the alternative planes of reality which theosophy subsumes, also goes a long way to explaining anomalies in the data, e.g. the instantaneous disappearance of UFOs travelling at a colossal speed. It is an explanation which is most relevant to the mission of mysticism, since for the first time it effects a reconciliation of the data of ufology and science fiction on the one hand, and spirituality, religion, mysticism, and esotericism/occultism on the other. And it makes an important contribution to the new metaphysics which must eventually bind together these diverse schools of thought regarding reality. Rex Dutta's approach, which he calls Viewpoint Aquarius, is at present only the sketch of an adequate theory to embrace all the phenomena, and his pugnacious, polemical, hectoring tone, with contempt of the uninitiated, lack of compassion, and pronounced intellectual arrogance runs contrary to many of the articles of the quintessence of mysticism. But when an articulate theory *is* developed and related to the mystical-religious and esoteric-occultist factions in more detail, a very important task in the mission of mysticism will be complete.

In the meantime, some interim conclusions must be drawn concerning the role of ufology in the mission of mysticism.

It is obvious that extraterrestrial aliens, or extradimensional beings, especially as they seem kindly towards man, may have a major part to play in inspiring the design of *Homo christus*. And it may well be that God's agents in this era will be some latter-day 'scientific' version of angels. Perhaps lofty spiritual beings will preach from the open doors of their spacecraft. To the mystic, it is of little importance whether superior beings wear green or blue, have three eyes or drive a rocket instead of a chariot. He is interested only in the *moral stature* of any sentient entity. An intriguing question is the relation of the inner life to UFO recognition. Among the psychic powers listed as the fruit of raja yoga are included the abilities to see great spiritual beings. If Rex Dutta is right, it may be through the cultivation of the inner life that future humans will be able to see these strange beings unequivocally. It is also possible that the 'sightings' of UFOs correspond somehow to the intuition of the will, as spiritual intimations. But perhaps the most intriguing prospect for ufology is that it may serve in the mission of mysticism by uniting mankind and by shattering his parochial complacency concerning himself as lord of creation. Moreover, it may be through UFOs, real or imaginary, that mankind comes as a species to feel a true mystical oneness with all creation; and finally, ufology may be the stimulus for man to adapt to the cosmology of modern science.

These are the possibilities regarding the role of ufology in the mission of mysticism. It is an important role, but at present it is only hypothetical. However, whatever is the final truth about what we now call flying saucers, it is certain that the design of the new species will have to take the ufology metaphysic into account. Mankind has, with ever-increasing momentum since the Copernican revolution, become a citizen not only of the whole earth but even of the whole universe, and his mystical thinking has now to consider the mission of mankind to the universe with which it is so intimately one. In this realization we see again at work the joint action of science and mysticism which is the central theme of this book: science shows us the pitiless, boundless, severe universe and reduces us to an infinitesimal speck; but mysticism reminds us that God is in all, and we, his children, are an integral part of this universe of love and union, we are bound in brotherhood to all beings everywhere, everywhen. Ufology, if it did nothing but sustain this great vision, would have a profoundly important role in the mission of mysticism. From it we must learn to think in terms of the role in the universe of mankind as a whole – not just our role *on* earth – and of course ufology encourages the uniting of all human races and countries, if only in fear of a common enemy, later from motives of real brotherhood. Ufology combines with science fiction in being the stimuli for man's expansion into the numberless stars, if such colonization is his destiny; and who knows what extraterrestrial entities it may be our duty to evangelize? For, as Pierre Teilhard de Chardin has reiterated, we are the devotees not of some merely terrestrial leader, however great: we are the flock lovingly guarded and succoured by the cosmic Christ, Lord of all Creation, Guardian of the galaxies like grains of sand.

Science-fiction religions

It remains in this chapter to mention another major offshoot of the science-fiction consciousness, the new pseudo-religions which have sprung from it. The most well-known of these is scientology, which was created by an American science-fiction novelist, L. Ron Hubbard. The religion began as Hubbard's idea, 'Dianetics: the science of mental health', and reliable witnesses have stated that he said, at about this time, that the best way to get rich quick was not to write science fiction, but to found a new religion. And he was, apparently, right. Scientology has been shown by Christopher Evans to fit any reasonable definition of religion: it was he who called it the first science-fiction religion. As far as its doctrine is concerned, it is a crude marriage of B-movie science fiction with an amalgam of eastern religions, garnished with psychotherapy. There is not necessarily any harm in this, but the 'religion' has proved itself vengeful and dogmatic, as well as prone to badgering people who might be interested. As far as the mystical criteria are concerned, they need hardly be involved, but it can be reported that the only ones which are satisfied even in part are those concerning man's capacity to make some sort of progress. And this goes to show a very important truth: that a school may be religious in the semantic sense without being mystical at all, or in other words, since mysticism is the quintessence of religion, it is easy to formulate a religion which evades the taxing demands of mysticism altogether. Indeed, it seems that Jesus had that opinion of the Jewish religion nearly 2000 years ago!

The mission of mysticism in respect of science-fiction religions is simply to insist that its criteria be strictly applied to all candidates for the souls of men and women.

Scientology is the first fully-fledged science-fiction religion; but there are junior versions. One such is the Aetherius Society, which believes in UFOs, cosmic wars, fighting through prayer-power stored in boxes, and Jesus living on Venus. This has a considerable number of devotees, and is in some ways preferable to scientology. At least it makes people happy. As to its mystical cogency, its main failing is its esotericism in the bad sense, the belief by the members that they are the elect. This vitiates all the good points, such as the desire to serve Jesus. Élitism kills mysticism instantly, for the latter cannot survive except in an atmosphere of universal compassion. Bad esotericism always routs humility, which cannot coexist with belief that one is the sole repository of the most important knowledge. There seems, moreover, to be in these religions a puzzling combination of Christocentricity and atheism. True mysticism is based on complete self-surrender to the God of all things made and unmade, and if that is absent a slender belief in a ufologized Jesus cannot suffice. And it must be added that the idea of Jesus living on Venus and sending us messages is contrary to Scripture, except insofar as it recalls the warning against false Christs.

In conclusion it should be said that the mission of mysticism to science-fiction religions should be not wholly one of destruction. We have seen that science fiction is the language of the new mythology, and we see that modern man, so far from being unreligious, is desperately seeking ways to express spiritual needs scientifically. Science fiction and its derivatives are the main contemporary expression of this, and science fiction is primarily a spiritual phenomenon, whose function it is to be the very clothing of *Homo christus*, at least in his design stage. This being so, it behoves the spiritual commentator on science-fiction religions to speak compassionately and helpfully. It does not matter to us if we conceive our religion in terms of angels or aliens, chariots or UFOs; the conceptual clothing is irrelevant. Religion, and even more so, mysticism, is a matter of morality, and the mission of mysticism to science fiction and its offshoots is primarily to work with the remythologizing (of Scripture and other spiritual documents and principles) now so furiously under way in our culture, ensuring that its mystical integrity is preserved; above all that the moral dimension, which alone is true religion, is at the heart of the new expressions of the eternal religious verities. For science fiction's part in the mission of mysticism is to rehabilitate religion and spirituality in the psyche of modern man.

10
Serious Modern Mysticism

The subject of this chapter, 'serious modern mysticism', is the elements of contemporary culture which, as part of serious contributions to the cultural scene, considered in its broadest sense, make a deliberate contribution to mystical thought. But it also discusses those elements which have made such a contribution unwittingly.

The traditional religions in modern times

The traditional religions are naturally prominent in the dissemination of mystical thought, now, as in earlier times. The general nature of these contributions was described in chapter 2. In Christianity, there is a great deal of mystical thinking which goes on almost unnoticed in the most conservative parts of the Church. Thomas Merton, a Roman Catholic monk and a prolific author on mystical and spiritual subjects, was eminent in this respect. Indeed it must be remembered that the very existence of monasteries, nunneries, and the many related institutions is itself an attestation of mysticism's continuing vitality, since they presuppose the truth or validity of at least Christian mysticism, and often they endorse respectfully the mysticism of other religions. It is interesting to note that this kind of mysticism, however, is non-progressive in the scientific sense: it is content with the body of mystical literature which it has always employed, and it has no part in mystical research of the kind conducted by theosophists.

Another kind of Christian spirituality, if not exactly mysticism, is the charismatic movement which has seen a revival in recent years. But a more general Christian hunger for mystical experience has expressed itself in the proliferation of Christian groups for spirituality. Christianity is rapidly adding to its repertoire for the laity such enterprises as silent retreats, ecumenical meditation groups, and practices combining Buddhist and yogic techniques with Christian prayer and meditation. In doing this it is undoubtedly going to make up some of the deficit, the congregations it has lost through a lack of direct religious experience for the parishioners. The remainder of the deficit will be further reduced when Christianity adjusts itself to the science-fiction culture. But despite these relatively superficial desiderata, Christianity is bound to have a vital part to play in the mission of mysticism as here conceived. The universe will remain a moral universe, and no amount of cultural change will alter that fact. Christianity is a recognition that there is a law of good which has to be obeyed, and it may confidently be predicted that whatever the vicissitudes in respect of the outer garb of the religion, Christianity will remain, if only as a solid nugget of truth, inside the flimsy and ephemeral costumes of culture. But this is the irreducible minimum of Christianity's contribution; in fact its role is vastly greater, no less than to form the backbone of cosmic culture.

As the last chapter of this book will make pellucid, the mission of mystics is, *par excellence*, a Christian mission – in its most literal and traditional sense.

Let us recapitulate the thesis of this volume. It is that we have reached a point in humanity's career, in the schemes of terrestrial evolution, where three major facts now coincide for the first time in human history. The first is that man is apparently in imminent danger of extinction for internal and/or external reasons. The second is that science and technology have almost developed to the point where mankind can be redesigned in the most fundamental way. The third fact is that the risen Christ points the way for mankind; he is the leader and also the prototype of the new men, *Homo christus*, who will inhabit the New Jerusalem. And we ourselves will in some sense also be present there. Obviously Christianity is at the very heart of such a mission. Or is it just Christ himself who is? What we call Christianity may be superseded by a Christianity more directly relevant to the mission here described, and throughout this book suggestions have been made as to the changes Christianity might make in itself in order to meet the future. Briefly, it is suggested that not only *de*mythologizing religion is necessary, but that the Church should play a part in *re*mythologizing Christianity to make it credible to modern man. But perhaps the biggest change which Christianity needs to make is towards the teaching that all men must be like Christ, must become Christs in due season, and that the faith must be built on a personal relationship which everyone is to have with the risen Christ. Our task is not just to praise him and petition him but to alter ourselves so as to allow him more and more access in the depths of our being, until we can truly say that we are one with him, that he is risen indeed, that our nature is his nature and that the Kingdom of God as Christ lives as our most essential part.

By comparison, the role of other religions is small. The eastern religions are doing important work currently in the West: they are introducing spirituality, mysticism, and religious experience to vast multitudes who ten years ago had hardly heard of the word 'meditation'. They are teaching people organization in their inner lives, and they are teaching them that the world within the mind is greater by far than that which they call reality normally. The shortcoming of these enterprises is that they tend to be atheistic: western meditators are often escaping from a personal encounter with God into a supposedly safe harbour of atheistic religion in meditation. But really the only purpose of religion of any kind is to lead individual men to a confrontation with Christ in whom they must recognize their destiny, which is to become transformed by his grace into his likeness. And there is opportunity for meditation to play its part so long as the backdrop is always the Christ. One may in this context recall the Hindu mystical saying, *Tat tvam asi!* ('That thou art!') which the guru at a certain point says to his disciple in reference to the divine nature. To look at the risen Christ and say, 'That thou art!' is the beginning and end of religion and mysticism.

Modern art

Art is the voice of God; aesthetics is the translation of the language of the Holy Spirit. For this reason art has always had, and will always have, a major part to play in mysticism. And there is no doubt that this is especially true of music. Music is the language of the soul, as many composers and writers have affirmed. William James, in his great survey of religious experience, wrote that '. . . not conceptual speech, but music rather, is the element through which we are best spoken to by mystical truth. Many mystical scriptures are indeed little more than musical compositions.' Elsewhere James remarked that 'music gives us ontological messages which non-musical criticism is unable to contradict . . . there is a verge of the mind which these things haunt; and whispers therefrom mingle with the operations of our understanding, even as the waters of the infinite ocean send their waves to break among the pebbles that lie upon the shores' (*The Varieties of Religious Experience*, 1902 edn, pp. 420–1).

In similar vein, Evelyn Underhill's monumental exposition of mysticism observes that:

> The mystery of music is seldom realized by those who so easily accept its gifts. Yet of all the arts music alone shares with great mystical literature the power of waking in us a response to the life-movement of the universe: brings us – we know not how – news of its exultant passions and its incomparable peace. Beethoven heard the very voice of reality, and little of it escaped when he translated it for our ears (*Mysticism*, pp. 76–7).

The mystics themselves often used the same metaphor. Ruysbroeck spoke of contemplation and love as 'two heavenly pipes', which, blown upon by the Holy Spirit, play 'ditties of no tone'. And J. W. N. Sullivan, in his famous short treatise on Beethoven's spiritual development, ranks that composer with the greatest mystics, showing how Beethoven, like them, passed through the Dark Night – in his case, deafness – and triumphantly passed on to the most exalted heights of contemplation, showing the world in his 'third period' compositions, especially the late Quartets, states of spiritual consciousness hitherto undreamed of, but nonetheless definitive portraits of the soul of ultimate reality.

In surveying modern art in search of resources for the mission of mysticism, we begin with music. But first it must be noted that, in this connection, 'modern art' includes not only art created in the modern age, but also art appreciated in the modern age. And thus the entire corpus of what we call classical music is relevant. All of this is today the subject of study, performance, and appreciation as much as at any time, and we may quickly say that everything that we call serious or classical music (which includes 'romantic' music also) is a part of the mission of mysticism. Indeed, it is a part of mysticism itself. Its exact *role* in the mission of mysticism is to provide (a) spiritual sustenance (for with its soothing ministrations we can go on temporary retreats into the garden of the soul), and (b) spiritual direction (for it points the way to new states of mystical consciousness, which the mystic can follow up in meditation and prayer, and later in thought and word). In fact the great task of redesigning mankind as *Homo christus* can only be done in the presence of great art. One may picture the following scene as an image for this task. It is as if the 'whole earth' was to unite in meditative prayer for the design of the new man. Each person would have before his eyes the works of art which move him most deeply, and in his ears the most profound and beautiful music known to him. In this way each man's unique glimpse of reality, of truth, would be at hand to contribute to the supreme venture of fashioning the new mankind. Perhaps for many Christians the vision would be clearest during a choral church service in a great cathedral. Others might choose to spend the time in the British Museum, accompanied by such music as Mahler's Resurrection Symphony.

But if all the great music has a guaranteed place, what of the truly modern music? This century has seen the creation of 'pop' music, jazz, 'rock', 'modern folk', 'blues', and several other types. And the total number of devotees of these genres far exceeds that of classical music's *aficionados*. The situation in this respect has a certain resemblance to that of science fiction. The question is whether the new music is of a comparable stature and value to mysticism. It is not an easy question to answer, but it is a very important one. We must briefly examine each of the new genera.

Jazz music is indispensable to the progress of mankind. Its creation this century is one of the most uplifting events of a troubled period. Jazz may not communicate exalted states of consciousness in the same way that Beethoven's work does, but its purpose is different. Jazz is the voice of freedom, of man's existential liberty. It bears an image of man which must be part of the new species, an image of a creature born of infinity which, regardless of rule-formation and classification, can never be

118

pinned down. Jazz affirms, with a delightful insouciance vis-à-vis musical rules, the godlike character of Proteus which inheres in human nature. It is a vision which must be retained, with the body of traditional and modern jazz. Jazz *singing*; Al Jolson, Judy Garland, etc., is a special, unique expression of this vision.

Rock music is the voice of the heart of the younger generation. And for that reason it must be taken very seriously, for it is they who will for the most part bear the task of reconstituting mankind. Already the corpus of rock music is so great that many different types and strata may be discerned. But one commentator, David Wingrove, holds that essentially rock music is in our culture the music counterpart of science fiction. In surveying the field he notes that the images and themes of science fiction are now prevalent in rock, and the spirit or world-view of science fiction is beginning to pervade rock. Rock is like science fiction in several ways. One is that in it the audience sees more relevance to their situation than they can find in older art-forms. Rock speaks directly to them. Another is that both rock and science fiction are experimental. Science fiction has become the accepted medium to which most vital literary innovations may be assimilated, but it is not only style or form that is altered in science fiction; it is philosophy, psychology, science, the very substance of the received world-view which is being combated. Science fiction, it has been said, is the laboratory of the imagination. In this respect it is matched by rock, in which no rule is sacrosanct; even more than in jazz, anything is possible in rock. But if rock music is even more anarchic than science fiction, still it is richly purposeful. For rock music, just like science fiction, is a search for a definition of man, and if science fiction explores the effect of science and technology on man and our image of him, rock music explores the nature of post-industrial man, man in whom the optimism of much science fiction is present, but also the despair of anomie, alienation, civilization at the end of its tether. Anything which has so much to say about mankind is an absolutely indispensable addition to the mission of mysticism, and rock music is therefore part of that mission. It is irrelevant whether the musical 'quality' is 'inferior'. The many kinds of music cannot be judged by the same rules. In a sickroom it may be appropriate to speak in a whisper; as a cheer-leader it is necessary to shout. The different types of music speak to different situations, and all are valid in principle, even if particular examples of a type may be shallow and inauthentic.

Thus folk music, ancient/traditional or modern, is also indispensable, as it too contains magnificent essays on man and his vicissitudes, often made hauntingly, bewitchingly beautiful by the melody. To hear Richard Tauber, the great tenor, or Peter Dawson, the great baritone, or the modern Bob Dylan, or Pete Seeger, is to experience as a great revelation the validity of every kind of folk music.

Much the same remarks apply to the other forms of modern music. We must pass over blues, rhythm-'n-blues, reggae, soul, and others with a respectful nod, recognizing the contribution which each is making to our self-understanding, so that we can speak of 'pop' music. This is a genre which evokes mixed feelings, even among those who are eager to enjoy any kind of music. On the credit side there is a good deal to mention. We may consider just exactly what it is. The very idea of 'pop' music, like that of 'pop' art, is enough to excite the sympathetic musical onlooker, for, like jazz, there is an element of liberation. And the idea of enriching the lives of millions of people who have had no chance to learn to love so-called serious music is a moving one. The question is whether this aim was achieved. To an extent, pop has become the choice of the people, especially the underprivileged. But there is something disturbingly 1984-ish about the present role of pop in society. The 'news' in pop centres around the weekly 'charts' – statistics allegedly showing in rank order the week's top twenty bestselling records. These charts are very influential in record-buying, because the radio stations 'plug' endlessly the bestsellers. The weekly 'chart' is basically the only systematic evaluation, and it is based on quantity, when the charts may be considered representative. And such is this commercial situation that the records tend to be simpler and simpler because the artists dare not depart from the typical bestseller. In practice, therefore, the pop scene is characterized by very many records all sounding more or less the same, the words being banal repetition of archetypal love-story clichés, the music uninspired. This illustrates how a valid art-form can be sabotaged from within, and fail in its mission.

Of course there has despite all this been much that is good in pop. The Beatles are widely recognized as musical geniuses, and many other gifted musicians smuggle quality music into 'the charts'. For the mission of mysticism, the question is not one of evaluation *per se*, but simply whether pop adds to our self-understanding, to our vision of the universe, to our maps of consciousness. And the answer is that *some* does. It is fairly obvious which pop is valuable *sub specie aeternitatis*, and that must be gratefully welcomed by mysticism.

The last major type of music is a rich and heterogeneous one, which may be called 'religious music'. This rather vague appellation is the only one which is broad enough to encompass the entire panoply of liturgical music, hymns and carols, and all other musical elements of church services and offices, and the entire range of religious music which has expressed itself in the language of classical music: Masses, cantatas, Te Deums, etc., on one side, and symphonies and other purely instrumental music on the other. The fact is that religious music has penetrated every type of music-form – even rock music has its 'Godspell' and pop its 'Jesus Christ Superstar', and folk music overlaps with religious music at every point, carols and hymns especially.

Of the integrity of this great body of music there can be no doubt; and its quality is equally sure. The question is just what part it has to play in the mystical-scientific reconstitution of mankind. It might seem obvious that the more religious the music, the more relevant it would be. But this is not necessarily so. A great deal of music of a religious nature is concerned purely with worshipping God – this is, after all, the purpose of liturgy. Worship, and devotion and gratitude, are certainly sublime, even divine, but they do not tend to differ among themselves in the music which is relevant to the task at hand. Rather, the most useful type of music is that which describes the attributes of our great forerunner, Jesus Christ, especially when there is reference to mankind and his own properties, needs, and hopes. From these we have much to learn towards the redesigning of humanity.

In general it appears that almost all music has a vital part to play in the mission of mysticism. That mission can begin even now. Music is as vital to the soul as air is to the lungs, and those in search of mystical development need not delay for a moment; they can even now begin to design the musical atmosphere in which the developing soul within will draw breath. Each person has thus to construct his musical ambience, using those things to which his soul most deeply responds; and this atmosphere, if he breathes it as often as he can, will ensure spiritual growth.

Non-musical art-forms

All that is said of music in general can be applied to art in general. The plastic arts, the visual arts, architecture, and the many other art-forms, all have a unique part to play in man's new career. They are the breath of the Holy Spirit, who is the true designer of *Homo christus*, and to listen attentively to his intimations is the best response to art.

Where vocal music speaks often about man and his relationships with the world, much art shows man beauty in the world or in man which he had not hitherto noticed. The artist copies reality, but it is a reality which, until he copies it in wood or oil or stone, he alone knew. Artists are the sixth sense of mankind. They see not only unsung beauty, but unremarked horror. Many artists have captured on canvas visions of horror which are also part of reality. To see all these is the duty of the new mankind, and thus art and artists will be prominent.

So far we have spoken of art and music appreciation. But the enaction is equally important. *Homo christus* will be a consummate artist and an accomplished musician and composer.

In literature the mystic values every genre. Drama, poetry, prose and *belles-lettres*, short stories, novels, biographies, and many others are an automatic part of mysticism in its widest sense, and certain contributors to the great mystical task. In this vast range of thought that we call literature we see ourselves from a million different perspectives, and our role in the universe. We see nature in countless ways, many previously unguessed at. We read in fiction of what we might do, or might have done; we read in poetry, as we see in paintings and hear in music, the hymn of the universe. Every serious work of literature is welcomed by the mystic; every library in the world is part of the data bank needed by those striving to perfect human nature, for it is in literature that the secrets of human nature are mostly to be found, at least the material ones. Of course, those secrets, like all art and everything on this lower plane, are only second-hand; they originate in the mind of God, where they are read by the awakened eyes of artists, writers, musicians, and scientists. But the day will come, in the future man, when all those psychical expressions will be redundant, when every man, through practice of contemplation and *samadhi*, and contemplative prayer, will have built for himself a new 'I' with the materials of contemplative experience, and he will be able to live in the beyond of the kind, the supramental consciousness which is the mind of God in its lower aspect. Ernest Wood writes sublimely on this prospect:

> The mind is swifter and freer than the body, and beyond the mind is the spirit, which is swifter and freer still. Love is more possible in the quietude of the heart than in any outer expression, but in the spirit beyond the mind it is divinely certain. Reason and judgement ever correct the halting evidence of the senses, and the vision of the spirit will discern the truth without organs and without mind (*Concentration*, pp. 151-2).

When that day dawns there will be no need for art, except perhaps as signposts: the man who lives in that beyond will perhaps use a work of art as a reminder or a pointer; but he will not dwell on it, he will go straight to the divine segment of reality which it represents, and will dwell there in the supramental consciousness, one with the original object of the art. Another yogi, I. K. Taimni, points out that many philosophies, including Plato and the Vedanta school, postulate forms, principles, eidola or idea(l)s in that beyond of the mind. He states that 'the positive qualities like courage, compassion, etc., are not vague, nebulous things as they appear to the lower mind but real, living, dynamic principles of unlimited power which cannot manifest fully in the lower worlds for lack of adequate instruments.' And he adds that through contemplation the yogi can become one with each and every quality: and this applies not only to character qualities but to archetypes and to the divine reality which is copied in art and music and literature. That is the realm in which *Homo christus* will reside.

Mystical aesthetics

In the light of this analysis, it may be suggested that a new department of art evaluation should be created: *mystical aesthetics*. Its purpose, which is important for the mission of mysticism, is to extract from all art-forms the vision of reality which must be taken into account in the creation of our successors. Mystical aesthetics promotes the discernment of two types of information through artistic experience: as the language of the soul, it teaches us about the nature of the Kingdom of God, and, since that Kingdom is a part of our most integral being, it is teaching us about ourselves, our Christ-nature, our resources, our potential for development, our possibilities. The heights and depths of experience which we undergo in the apprehension of great literature, music, or art are in fact revelations of self-knowledge, intimations of the properties and attributes of our own souls.

Mystical aesthetics includes person perception: it inspires one to see each and every human being as a work of divine art, a veritable and literal incarnation of God; yet all are different from one another, each is the unique expression of a sublime individuality. And a wealth of such material is already in existence, spiritual wealth which would bankrupt the material kingdoms of infinity. Art, music, literature, *in toto*, lie before us, waiting to be analysed as if for the first time; in them all we see intimations of what we must become, and we can only share the awe of Keats when, 'On first looking into Chapman's Homer', he felt

> like some watcher of the skies
> When a new planet swims into his ken;
> Or like stout Cortez when with eagle eyes
> He star'd at the Pacific – and all his men
> Look'd at each other with a wild surmise –
> Silent, upon a peak in Darien.

Mass media

The last group of influences to be considered is the mass media. These have more power over modern man than any despotic dictator of old ever had, as previously mentioned in connection with television. Two questions remain: what is the present mystical content of the mass media, and what is its possible role in the mission of mysticism? The first question was answered previously, and may be restated by saying that the mass media are on the whole neutral, and they only mirror the mystical (or any other content) of culture. Thus, in answer to that question nothing more need be said, as we have spent six chapters discussing the mysticism of contemporary culture. The second question is a stimulating one. Naturally, any cultural product with as much power as mass media have been observed to have must have a role in the improvement of the species. We must consider what that role would be in a culture which was unanimously working for that noble goal.

The principal functions of television (and cinema) are mass communication, the presentation of fiction, and the delivery of feedback, especially in a closed-circuit system. Each of these has some relevance. The mass communication, in a society which was enlightened or mystically awake, would symbolize the unity of man. The presentation of fiction would be marvellously useful in giving flesh to conjectures as to how mankind may be perfected (this should be the function of all television), and the feedback would give mankind self-knowledge in general, and especially in respect of his attempts to restructure himself.

The functions of the printed mass media are similar. Newspapers, and their first cousins the periodicals, could likewise be part of the common externals of all men. 'News' would always be concerning the perfection of man, and sectarian interests would fall away as the sense of universal compassion grew. Men would still be mainly concerned with their own family and work, but as a real part of the entire human endeavour, and in lovingly recounting their own contribution and experience they would be doing the best they possibly could for the human race.

Lastly, the radio has properties which make it something like a halfway house between the television and the newspapers, and its function would be correspondingly situated.

In conclusion, one may say that the mass media have a terrific power for good or ill, and their potential contribution to the great mystical work lies ahead of mankind. Their greatest single opportunity is to perfect the whole-earth consciousness, to teach all men the universal brotherhood. Many media commentators feel that television has done more to create this global sense than any previous influence; one can only hope and pray that the complete terrestrial circuit of human minds united in a single identity is completed before nuclear war, accidental or deliberate, destroys for ever even the possibility of such unity. It will be a desperately close race.

PART THREE

*Criticisms of
Mysticism*

11

An Introduction to Contemporary Criticisms of Mysticism

Although there is currently a great deal of enthusiasm for mysticism, or at least for its imitators, there is also much criticism. Some of it is wise and some foolish, some new and some old. But whichever of these it may be, every criticism deserves an answer, for mysticism is preparing to take on a greater responsibility than any discipline has done hitherto, and its cogency must be checked meticulously. On the other hand, criticisms which can be shown to be wrong must be rigorously refuted, for erroneous criticisms of mysticism are not only wrong but are actually detrimental to the interests of mankind, since they may partially close the avenue down which man should be going.

Is mysticism 'unscientific' and subjective?

Certain remarks can be made about criticisms of mysticism in general. The main point is that critics accuse mysticism of being unscientific and subjective. But the mystic points out that he is scientific; he sets up stimulus conditions and waits for the response. But in mysticism, where the scientist is the mystic himself, the stimulus conditions are basically those character qualities hymned by Jesus in the Sermon on the Mount: poverty and humility in particular, also universal love. Without attempting even a little in these directions, the 'scientist' will know nothing except second-hand reports of mysticism, for his choice will have shut the channel of his potential enlightenment. Strictly speaking, enduring mystical experience can only come to those who have consecrated their lives to God, and who live accordingly. Critics speaking solely from a 'scientific' viewpoint are bound to frame inapplicable complaints, and they miss the point that mysticism is the supreme science, more scientific than material science. The same argument applies with equal force to philosophers, among whose ranks there have always been critics of mysticism. One of them, an eminent contemporary, John Passmore, calls mysticism 'the auld enemy' of philosophy. But philosophers who seek to understand mysticism have to become mystics first. One may say that as a matter of definition a philosopher who *is* a philosopher by choice, and has been for some time, will never understand mysticism, since it is a fact of spiritual evolution in the individual that one passes through philosophy on the way to mysticism. Nobody who has once seen the real mysticism, even for a moment, can remain a philosopher. The philosopher is supposed to be rather objective, sorting out the wisdom from the mere knowledge. But the mystic has learned that mysticism *is* wisdom! It was Plato who originated our prevailing conception of a philosopher, but he never lost sight of the spiritual truth which he knew to be the only wisdom. Philosophy since then has lost its way, and tried to play off one mental realm against another. But wisdom has nothing to do with the mental realm at all. Its concern is the beyond of the mind, the divine planes. Philosophers who seek mysticism in the intellect are doomed to misunderstand it, for it can be attained only by love, not by words. Philosophers who refuse to undertake the spiritual discipline called for in the awakening of spiritual faculties, but criticize mysticism for being too subjective, are like laymen who disbelieve in scientific results, but, though in possession of laboratory and equipment, refuse to use them. In fact philosophers are, vis-à-vis mysticism, in the same position as the infamous colleague of Galileo Galilei, who, when the latter invited him to see the moons of Jupiter through his astronomical telescope, which was newly invented, refused to look through the telescope at all, at the same time denying the existence of the moons. Thus it can be seen that the philosophical criticisms of mysticism, far from being vindicated, become a source of embarrassment to philosophers, as their criticisms rebound on to them, picking up momentum from their unavailing sortie with mysticism, and showing them to be guilty of that which they denounced in mysticism. Indeed philosophy without the central fire of mysticism installed in its heart is not only a futile enterprise, it is lacking in rigour and objectivity, and is veritably *unscientific*.

Religion and theology

Of criticisms originating in religion it need only be said that as mysticism is the very essence of religion, there can be no quarrel between the two when both are genuine. The persecution of mystics and the anathematizing of certain mystical doctrines in various countries around the world is not only contrary to mysticism but to religion itself. There is no room in religion for any kind of persecution whatsoever. Tolerance is the spirit of religion, and when Jesus taught us to turn the other cheek he was surely telling us that any kind of hostile action, no matter what the provocation, must snap the slender cord by which we are in touch with our higher selves.

Theological criticisms are a different matter. Insofar as mysticism can be discussed at all, it naturally overlaps with theology, and there is bound to be much debate between them. But, as Aldous Huxley pointed out in the preface to his *Perennial Philosophy*, it is incumbent upon theologians as much as scientists and philosophers to nourish their theology with the vitality of mystical experience. Theology with no religious experience to sustain it will make the same mistakes as science and philosophy in criticizing what they do not understand. Theology is sometimes described as the science of God, even as the queen of the sciences; but God does not appear to order in test-tubes or microscopes. We cannot 'study' him except insofar as he works in us. What we call theology can never be more than an infinitesimal fraction of the theology we can experience without being able to communicate it, for God is the beyond of the mind, and the beyonds beyond that beyond, and he cannot be reduced to the formulae of the puny intellect. For this reason Shri Shankara Charya, the supreme philosopher-mystic of the East, bequeathed us the greatest example of theology inspired as it always must be, by mysticism. The various modern theologies, radical, liberal, etc., often fail to see this point. To those who know that Christ lives and personally relates to those who seek him, it is absolute nonsense to speak about Christianity without religion, or religion without God, or even religion with the 'myths' removed. Surely, in presenting such ideas as these, theologians such as Bonhoeffer, Tillich, and Bultmann are confessing to Christianity without religious experience. Their results may be poignant, profound, erudite. But if the mystical element of religion is left out it can be nothing more than empty formulae, *Hamlet* without the prince.

Sociology

There are also sociological criticisms of mysticism. One of the best-known is Karl Marx's dictum, that religion is 'the cry of the oppressed creature, the heart of a heartless world, the drug [or opium] of the masses'. The criticism is a *non sequitur*, which nevertheless is logical, since the use to which an argument or belief is put is not relevant to the accuracy of the argument or the cogency of the belief. And secondly, Marx's point manifestly does not apply to mysticism, which is hardly the cry of the oppressed – Plato was aristocratic, St Augustine was well-to-do in his early life, etc. Moreover, mystics at advanced stages of the way are perpetually content, unlike Marx's working classes, and they enunciate a highly cogent and articulate metaphysic totally at odds with that of Marx or of his oppressed peoples.

Mysticism seems, with its noetic certainty, to provide an irresistible target for sociologists, who are accustomed to treating belief systems as epiphenomena of social structures and practices. The quintessential sociological criticism of mysticism, as of religion, is that it serves some sociological purpose discerned only by sociologists. Even one wise enough to know better, Sir Karl Popper, presents this argument in *The Open Society and its Enemies*. Let us examine the argument. Laid out syllogistically, it is:

Premise   (1)   The behavioural aspects of mysticism play some part in a social structure.

Conclusion   (2)   *Therefore* the metaphysical propositions of mysticism should be disregarded.

The argument (a failed enthymeme?) is simply non-existent. We can twist the tails of the sociologists a little bit, and reply to illustrate the point vividly:

(1)   The sociology of religion plays some part in the social structure (indisputable: for if it did not, according to the sociologists' own universal rule, it could not *be* in society at all).

132

(2)   Therefore the *arguments* of sociologists of religion are false.

(3)   Therefore their criticisms of mysticism are invalid.

Popper recovers himself in the second volume of *The Open Society* enough to contribute a chapter called 'The sociology of knowledge', in which he amplifies *in extenso* the fallacy of sociological theorizing. And his remarks make the point memorably:

> Socio-analysts invite the application of their own methods to themselves with almost irresistible hospitality. . . . The sociology of knowledge hopes to reform (by making people) aware of the social forces and ideologies which unconsciously beset them. But the main trouble about prejudices is that there is no such direct way of getting rid of them. For how shall we ever know that we have made any progress in our attempt to rid ourselves from prejudice? Is it not a common experience that those who are most convinced of having got rid of their prejudices are the ones who are most prejudiced? The idea that a sociological . . . study of prejudices may help to rid ourselves of them is quite mistaken; for many who pursue these studies are full of prejudice; and not only does self-analysis not help us to overcome the unconscious determination of our views, it often leads to even more subtle self-deception.[1]

There is, however, a more general philosophical issue underlying this matter: it is the logic of sets. It was proved in mathematical logic at the turn of the last century that no system can refer to itself with total accuracy; so when sociologists blithely attempt to undermine the foundations of other disciplines, they are digging their own graves.

A final criticism which will be considered in this chapter is also illogical, but one can at least feel some human sympathy towards it. It is that same criticism which comes up from time to time in many places (we will meet it again with a psychologist): this particular manifestation of it arose from a critic reviewing a life of Jung. The critic read that Jung had spent much time with middle-aged analysands in the Second World War dealing with

---

[1] From *The Open Society and its Enemies*, vol. 2, pp. 216ff. Routledge and Kegan Paul 1945.

their problems of self-development and mystical (numinous) experiences. This enraged the critic, whose critique was as follows:

(1) The world was at war, people dying and suffering.
(2) Jung, a Swiss, was happily ignoring the war and attending to his patients' experiences of the numinous.
(3) They were well-off and middle-aged, not at war.
(4) Being a neutral country in a world war is a good place to have complacent experiences of the numinous.
(5) *Therefore* mystical experience is reprehensible.

There are many loopholes in this 'argument'. The critic neglects to include in his premises the facts that (a) real mystics are infinitely compassionate towards suffering humanity, and put themselves to work for mankind; (b) mystical experiences, being the flowering of human thought, automatically enrich the culture of any society, and elevate its humanity, thus contributing to the prevention or mitigation of war and similar practices; (c) only through mysticism can mankind rise to the moral stature whereby war can be averted, for war must be nullified by mysticism, not war; (d) only through mysticism can mankind rise to the philosophical stature necessary to see with mystic eyes the true nature of the universe, the divine comedy wherein love is emperor.

Faith and experience

There is a more subtle point of philosophy here. It is a question of the interaction of reason and actual experience in the creation of philosophical theories. The question raised above all by mysticism is whether one can understand its philosophy without having had something of the experience. The only answer is that understanding proceeds in parallel with experience: partial experience engenders partial understanding, great experience great understanding, negligible experience negligible understanding. Most mystics themselves agree that perfect understanding is not possible for incarnate souls save the great avatars, for: 'Now I see through a glass, darkly, but then I shall see face to face.'

Some scholars urge that mystical philosophy is irrational if it requires experience not open to all, if it renounces the sovereignty of intellect and claims that unaccompanied reason cannot encompass the real. But this argument is false, because it is improper to decide arbitrarily that the universe is so constituted that insight into its working is possible by reason alone. This is itself an act of *faith*; where the mystic has faith in God's love, the atheistic or agnostic scientist or philosopher has faith that the universe is reasonable. He cannot *prove* that it is so. In fact it just so happens that in order really to understand philosophy and cosmology, to see God, to enter the kingdom of heaven, one must lead a life of spirituality. And not philosophy, but poetry and music, are the best ways of expressing and encountering the world of spirit, if one must try to capture it with symbols. Therefore, to give further weight to the argument that spirituality and mysticism is understood in proportion to mystical experience, here is a little mystical poetry to stimulate perhaps a faint flicker of mystical experience. This poetry does not replace philosophical reasoning; it supplements it. And the correct way of construing it is to regard it as the equivalent for mysticism of empirical data for science and philosophy. The 'data' of mystical philosophy are mystical experiences originating in the perception of the poetry of the universe and the music of the spheres.

The following extract[1] from Sir Edwin Arnold's poetical life of the Buddha, *The Light of Asia*, describes one aspect of the path of mysticism, nirvana, and depicts truth in a way beyond discursive philosophy.

> If any teach Nirvana is to cease,
> Say unto such they die.
> If any teach Nirvana is to live,
> Say unto such they err; not knowing this,
> Nor what light shines beyond their broken lamps,
> Nor lifeless, timeless bliss.

And to those who see mysticism as a barren desert of self-denial, another stanza from the same source is salutary:

> Enter the Path! There spring the healing streams
> Quenching all thirst! there bloom th' immortal flowers

[1] From the end of Book 8 of *The Light of Asia* by Sir Edwin Arnold. First published in the late nineteenth century; many editions still in print.

Carpeting all the way with joy! there throng
Swiftest and sweetest hours!

But undoubtedly the greatest number of modern criticisms of
mysticism are those which may be called psychological; they
merit a chapter to themselves.

12

Psychological Criticisms

Many, perhaps the majority, of the most influential criticisms of mysticism have originated in traditions of psychological inquiry, broadly or narrowly conceived. Taken together, philosophical and psychological criticisms of mysticism have often formed a powerful opposing faction – powerful in influence if not in argument. A meticulous defence of mysticism must therefore pay close attention to psychological criticisms and their refutation.

Neither psychology nor mysticism is monolithic. To speak of 'psychological' criticisms as if they were an organized unity, or of 'mysticism' as if it is a homogeneous entity, is to perpetuate a myth which may be prejudicial to the accuracy of our inquiry. Nevertheless it is necessary to subscribe occasionally to this myth, for two reasons. One is that shortage of space precludes the possibility of differentiating between all the different types of mysticism; the other is that the actual criticisms of mysticism *have*, on the whole, treated it as a single set of beliefs and practices. It is therefore necessary, in order to give a satisfactory reply to each criticism, to adopt temporarily the convention that mysticism is unitary.

The psychological inquiries in which criticisms of mysticism have originated are also diverse and heterogeneous. For example, criticisms have been levelled by Freud (depth psychology/psychoanalysis); Watson (behaviourism); Eysenck (experimental psychology); Sargant (medical psychology); Stephen Rose (physiological psychology). However, the critics have no more organized their criticisms than have the mystics organized their visions. The many criticisms have much overlap. It is therefore pointless to discuss the criticisms arranged by critic, since the substance of a criticism does not depend upon the identity of its progenitor. The practice of this chapter, therefore, is to treat the criticisms in the order in which they best present themselves for discussion, but also crediting a critic with the criticism if he was the first to utter it.

In an attempt at reasonable thoroughness, *seventeen* criticisms of mysticism have been gathered for presentation here. These criticisms were culled from a very wide range of literature; and psychological criticisms were found not only in psychology but also in philosophical, political, sociological, and other literatures. It can be assumed that the seventeen criticisms do cover the majority of the criticisms of a psychological nature. For ease of reference, the criticisms are listed in Table 4.

Table 4
Psychological criticisms of mysticism

1 Mysticism is purely subjective, and, *eo ipso*, erroneous in its principal assertions.

2 Mental states are dependent upon physical states (according to the philosophy of materialism); therefore, the human experience must end with the death of the body and brain, and therefore mystical ideas about life after death, and spirituality, etc., must be in error.

3 Mystical states or experiences can apparently be induced by drugs. This calls their validity into question.

4 Mystical states or experiences can apparently be induced by brain damage; this seems to call into question their validity.

5 Belief in mystical revelation does not produce consistent effects on behaviour. This implies that mystical 'insights' are untrustworthy.

6 Mystics may withdraw into contemplation, in which case they may find ecstasy or nirvana, but this does not seem very helpful to the rest of us.

7 When mystics try to propagate their ideas, they all disagree. And since some must therefore be wrong, why should any be right?

8 The only evidence for mystical assertions is the individual mystic's own experience, and this is unsatisfactory because unscientific.

9 Mysticism seems to render the individual immune from reason and evidence; it is therefore utterly irrational.

10 Mysticism produces dogged and narrow-minded evangelism.

11　Mysticism is a poor guide to conduct, since it is mainly concerned with contemplation.

12　Mystics claim to be in touch with a new 'reality'. But psychologists agree that reality cannot be directly apprehended; it can only be constructed.

13　Mystical experience is a childish aberration. For in it the mystic effectively 'regresses' to infantilism of thought. Mysticism is akin to an early stage of development, before the child can speak, and when its separate identity is still latent. Therefore the 'achievements' are no such thing; they are simply regression. They are the opposite of maturity.

14　Mysticism resembles madness so much that mysticism and madness can both be regarded as extreme aberrations from normalcy; mysticism, like madness, is the brain *in extremis*. Needless to say, this view requires that the claims of mystics be regarded as dangerous delusions.

15　So-called mystical experiences are simply the bursting into consciousness of unconscious needs and desires originating in the Id. Therefore all the 'insights' of mysticism are illusory.

16　Mystical states are classifiable along with dreams, reverie, and hypnosis, and are therefore as untrustworthy in their implications as any of the ideas which come to consciousness in the other states listed in this criticism.

17　There is definite evidence that mystics are medically sub-normal and sometimes pathological in mind and body. They have fits, trances, hysteria, and all kinds of bodily affliction. It follows that their mental trustworthiness as witnesses of any scientific worth is small.

However, mysticism is no more unitary than psychology is, and recognition must be given to this fact at the outset of this chapter. To begin with, it must be asked what 'mysticism' denotes for these critics. Its denotation includes the following very different referents:

1　Mystical *experience*: reports of (a) 'oceanic' feeling; (b) 'cosmic consciousness' (Bucke's term); (c) intuition; (d) vision; (e) grace; (f) revelation; (g) spiritual perception; (h) *samadhi*: eight different types.

2   Mystical *behaviour*: (a) exceptionally prolonged prayer and meditation, passing into trance states; (b) unusual physical phenomena, such as stigmata; (c) *siddhis* – psychic powers, such as levitation; (d) superlative contentment evident to onlookers; (e) enunciating metaphysical theories in words spoken, and in prose; (f) exemplary behaviour, ranging from simple altruism and humility through to the highest reaches of saintliness.

An examination of the above denotations of the genuinely mystical – to say nothing of the misuses of the term to mean 'vague' – shows how big an error it is to speak of mysticism without specifying one's target more precisely. It is apparent that many criticisms of mysticism have badly misfired for the following reason: they take claims for one kind of mysticism – say, its resultant metaphysic of love – and use another kind (such as stigmata or trance) to prove the absurdity of such grand ideas. This tactic, of course, falls to the ground when a synoptic view of mysticism, as set out above, is studied.

But this confusing of the part for the whole, which is so typical of psychological criticisms of mysticism, is much more deep-rooted than even the above discrimination of twelve aspects of mysticism may suggest. For it reduces to six the mystical experiences, or states of consciousness. But there are actually dozens of states of consciousness which could broadly be classed as mystical; and these are all treated as one by psychological criticisms.

This is a serious state of affairs. It appears that the psychologists and philosophers who accuse mysticism of vagueness, inexactitude, and subjectivity are making the same mistakes, only much worse.

States of consciousness

To see just how bad this situation is, it is necessary to present a detailed study of the multifarious mystical states of consciousness. But to understand it properly, such a study would have to be presented in the context of other states of consciousness, including those regarded as normal. It is, indeed, becoming more and more widely appreciated[1] that the

---

[1] See Charles Tart's two anthologies, *States of Consciousness* and *Altered States of Consciousness*. New York, Wiley 1969.

comparative study of states of consciousness is one of the major modern roads to psychological *and* religious understanding. Accordingly, Table 5 has been devised to meet the stated need. In two parts, it firstly enumerates 150 states of consciousness, including data from psychology, medicine, occultism, religion, psychiatry, and mysticism. In part 2 it groups these states into twelve divisions. The Table is self-explanatory, but it is noteworthy that no less than *twenty-four* mystical states of consciousness – each of them a potential mystical 'experience' – are listed. And the category of 'occult states of consciousness', which is regarded by many authorities as a part of mysticism (they call it practical mysticism), includes a further *thirty-eight*. And this is not including 'landmarks on the spiritual path', many of which are classical parts of mystical experience.

In fact the Table shows at least *sixty-four* mystical experiences. The failure of psychology to come to terms with this diversity is a very serious indictment of its criticisms.

But now it is time to meet these criticisms face-to-face.

Table 5
States of consciousness[1]

Part 1   Ungrouped

1	Normal waking consciousness
2	Samprajnata Samadhi
3	Asamprajnata Samadhi
4	Samadhi
5	Samadhi
6	Dharma-Megha-Samadhi
7	Cosmic consciousness (Bucke)
8	1st Initiation
9	2nd Initiation
10	3rd Initiation
11	4th Initiation (Arhat)
12	Satori

[1] This Table is not intended to be absolutely complete, but to show the range and diversity of spiritual states of consciousness, and those which are related to them. No doubt the reader will be able to add to the list.

13	Masterhood
14	Mahatmahood
15	Devahood
16	Kaivalya
17	Nirvana
18	God-realization (H. P. Shastri)
19	Buddhahood
20	Christ-consciousness
21	Ordinary happiness
22	Peak experience
23	Mystical experience
24	Science-fiction peak experience
25	Cinema peak experience
26	Love
27	Romantic love
28	The Cloud of Unknowing
29	The Dark Night of the Soul
30	Infinite or absolute bliss
31	Anxiety-state/reactive
32	Anxiety-trait/neurosis
33	Mild depression
34	Psychotic depression
35	Schizophrenia–agitated
36	Schizophrenia–catatonic
37	Psychopathy
38	Uncontrolled mania
39	Hypomania
40	Kama Loka (post-death)
41	Deva Chan (post-death)
42	Deep sleep (stages 1–4 NREM)
43	Primary dream sleep
44	Secondary dream sleep
45	Astral projection
46	Concentration (Dharana)
47	Meditation (Dhyana)
48	Contemplation (Samadhi)
49	Prayer-worship
50	Prayer-intercession
51	Prayer-petition
52	Prayer-thanksgiving
53	Hypnogogic imagery
54	Hypnopompic imagery
55	Memory imagery
56	Eidetic imagery

57	Iconic imagery
58	Imagination imagery
59	Death
60	Purgatory
61	'Right Rapture'
62	'Right Loneliness'
63	'Right Thought'
64	Heaven
65	Hell
66	Hypnotic trance
67	Post-hypnotic subordination
68	Sexual orgasm
69	Shock
70	Amnesia
71	The divided self
72	Instantaneous conversion
73	Slow conversion
74	The sick soul
75	The religion of healthy-mindedness
76	Alcoholic intoxication
77	Marijuana
78	Peyote
79	Mescalin
80	LSD
81	Nitrous oxide, etc.
82	'Eternal life'
83	Musical peak experience
84	Athletic peak experience
85	Unconscious mentation
86	Preconscious mentation
87	Incubation
88	Illumination
89	Exogenous intuition
90	Endogenous intuition
91–3	3 advanced types of Cognition: inspirational, imaginative, intuitional (Rudolf Steiner)
94	Stream of consciousness
95	Logical thinking
96	Conscious dreaming (Rudolf Steiner)
97	Reading the Akashic record
98	After meeting the Lesser Guardian of the Threshold
99	After meeting the Greater Guardian of the Threshold (Rudolf Steiner)
100	Antahkara (Alice Bailey)

* The above 'G' scores represent Gurdjieff vibration levels.

Part 2 States of consciousness organized into groups[1]

Note: some states of consciousness appear in more than one group. This is intended.

I PRAYER

49–52: Worship, intercession, petition, thanksgiving.

II MEDITATION

46–8: Dharana (Concentration), Dhyana (Meditation), Samadhi (Meditation) (after Patanjali); 61–3: Right Rapture, Right Loneliness, Right Thought (Buddhist nomenclature).

III DRUG-INDUCED

76–81: Alcohol, marijuana, peyote, mescalin, LSD, nitrous oxide, etc.

IV IMAGERY

53–8: Hypnogogic, hypnopompic, memory, eidetic, iconic, imagination.

V PATHOLOGY

31–9: State anxiety, trait anxiety, mild depression, severe depression, agitated schizophrenia, catatonic schizophrenia, psychopathy, uncontrolled mania, hypomania. And 70: Amnesia.

VI OCCULT STATES

8–11: First through 4th Initiation; 13–15: Master, Mahatma, and Deva-consciousness; 19–20: Buddhahood and Christ-consciousness; 40–1: After-death states: Kama Loka and Deva Chan; 45: Astral projection; 91–3: 3 types of occult cognition (from Rudolf Steiner): inspirational, imaginative, intuitional; 96–9 (more states of consciousness described by Rudolf Steiner): conscious dreaming, reading the Akashic record, meeting the Lesser Guardian of the Threshold and after, meeting the Greater Guardian of the Threshold and after; 100: Antahkara (A. Bailey); 104–9: The 7 Astral planes; 127–35: Lilly's stages of consciousness (see part 1); The Tarot.

[1] Likewise, the groupings are for heuristic purposes; they are not intended to be a definitive organization of the states of consciousness. No human could succeed in such a task.

VII   MYSTICAL STATES

2–7: 5 types of Samadhi, and Cosmic consciousness; 16–20, 22: Kaivalya (Yoga), Nirvana (Buddhism), God-realization, Buddhahood, Christ-consciousness, Peak Experience (23) 30: Absolute Bliss; 23: General Mystical Experience; 64: Heaven; 82: 'Eternal Life'; 115–19: Yoga (the state), the 3rd eye open, Vairagya, Para-vairagya, Purusha-Khyati (all yogic states); 123–6: Ernest Wood's vision: The Intuition of the Will, the Nirvana of the Earth, the Nirvana of the Soul, the Nirvana of the Self.

VIII   THE INTERFACE BETWEEN NORMAL AND OCCULT STATES OF CONSCIOUSNESS

64–7: Heaven and hell, hypnosis and post-hypnotic subor-dination; 45: Astral projection; 89: Exogenous intuition; 120: Recollectedness (Ouspensky).

IX   'NORMAL' STATES

1: Waking consciousness ('middle C' – C. Wilson); 148: Infatuation; 26: Love; 27: Romantic love; 21: Ordinary happiness; 42–4: Sleep and dreams; 68: Sexual orgasm; 69: Shock; 75: The religious outlook of healthy-mindedness; 87–8: Incubation and illumination in creative thinking; 94–5: Stream of consciousness, logical thinking; 149: Birth; 59: Death.

X   LEGENDARY STATES

101: Being a ghost;   113–14: Group mind, racial mind (Stapledon).

XI THE OUTER LIMITS OF NORMAL HUMAN CONSCIOUSNESS

64–5: Heaven and hell; 149: Birth; 59: Death; 60: Purgatory; 70: Amnesia; 76–81: Under the influence of drugs; 86–7: Unconscious mentation and preconscious mentation; 102–3: Mob and crowd consciousness; 110–12 Charismatic inspiration; 120–2: Recollectedness, delirium, DTs; 150: Hallucination.

XII   LANDMARKS ON THE SPIRITUAL PATH

2–20: (The samadhis, the initiations, the highest states of yogic and Buddhist consciousness, and theosophical classification); 28–9: The Cloud of Unknowing and Dark Night; also divided self (71);

XIII PEAK EXPERIENCES

This epithet is applicable to any of the states of consciousness which have a pleasing affective tone, though Maslovian psychology includes as 'peak experiences' many additional secular experiences.

The psychological criticisms themselves

1 The briefest, and most well-known, psychological criticism of mysticism is the charge that it is 'purely subjective', and, *eo ipso*, erroneous in its assertions. This is the psychological counterpart of the philosophical criticism, or accusation, of 'subjectivity' and is wrong for essentially the same reasons, those that were enunciated in the previous chapter, dealing with philosophical criticisms.

2 'Mental states are dependent upon physical states,' the materialist philosophy asserts, 'therefore, the human experience must end with the death of the body and brain, and therefore mystical ideas about life after death, and spirituality, etc., must be in error.'

Reply: The materialist philosophy and metaphysic is not a proven fact; it is a mere assertion. The developing tendency of mind-body theorists is to regard the brain not as the generator of mind but as the *instrument* of mind. When the brain decays or dies, its instrumentality is diminished and lost respectively, but the mind is merely deprived temporarily of its instrument. Evidence from a host of sources corroborates this view, and mysticism emphatically endorses it. The argument is set out formally in William James's *Human Immortality*. But once again, the only evidence that would satisfy a materialist is to experience himself as separate from his body. Mystical training permits this. Ernest Wood says:

> People say: 'I doubt whether the higher things exist.' Then they remain in that state. But you must help yourself to knowledge. He who lives the life shall know the doctrine. Therefore cease to worry about the matter, but provide the conditions which make direct knowledge possible. Until that is done, the feeling of uncertainty is itself an obstacle to progress (*The Intuition of the Will*, p. 102).

Again we see that mysticism is *scientific* in its specification of exact stimulus conditions; but the critics veer away from this because it implies the need for spiritual purgation. The fault certainly does not lie with mysticism.

3   'Mystical states or experiences can apparently be induced by drugs.'

Reply: So what? So can most attitudes of mind, and beliefs, including materialism. Are they therefore invalid? Of course not; the argument is puerile. The full reply is set down in Aldous Huxley's *Doors of Perception* and in chapter 1 of William James's *The Varieties of Religious Experience*. In any case, this is a criticism which, *par excellence*, confounds all the different types of mystical experience. There is also no evidence that drug-induced mystical consciousness is permanent, as saintliness and yogic kaivalya and Buddhist nirvana certainly are; and when drugs have produced mystical experience, it is usually something that was due to appear anyway in reply to previous researches: as Martin Israel points out, the drug is just the precipitating factor in a peak experience which was due to happen anyway.

4   'Mystical states or experiences can apparently be induced by brain damage.'

Reply: So can most other states and beliefs (same point as above: this objection has no *logical* force; and in any case it is addressed to the tiniest aspect of the great tree of mysticism).

5   'Belief in mystical revelation does not produce consistent effects on behaviour.'

Reply: Not so! The existence of monasteries and nunneries refutes this assertion. Also, the authentic mystical scholars, such as Evelyn Underhill and Aldous Huxley, have pointed out the remarkable unanimity of the testimony of mystics. William James likewise remarks the oneness of behaviour among mystic-saints. Indeed, true saintliness is the invariable and inevitable outcome of true mysticism; for those who truly believe and live in accordance with the mystic's credo are thereby taking upon themselves the attributes of saintliness. Saintliness is, therefore, the consistent behaviour produced by mystical revelation. For the critic to ignore this is an error explicable only by the probable confusion by the critic of pseudo-mystics for real mystics.

6 'Mystics may withdraw into contemplation, in which case they may find ecstasy or nirvana, but this does not seem very helpful to the rest of us.'

Reply: This is a shallow mish-mash of different kinds of problem, absurdly argued. A five-point reply is called for. First, for any individual to find nirvana is his own consummation; and *ipso facto* this is a triumph for mankind – for the fulfilment of the one is the enrichment of all. Second, it is an occult law that mystics always return, from the very gates of heaven (nirvana) in order to help suffering humanity. Gautama, Lord Buddha, did this; and it will be recalled, as the simplest refutation of this vacuous criticism, that he then spent fifty years teaching his doctrine to the suffering. And Jesus, having spent forty days in retreat and discovered his divine duty, did not 'withdraw'; he preached and healed (is this supposed by the critic to be 'unhelpful to the rest of us'?) and, however one may regard the theological implications of his crucifixion and possible resurrection, he died a hideous death for the sake of the suffering. Third, the very existence of a nirvani or mystic is sufficient to raise the consciousness of all in touch with him; contemplation is therefore not only the best but also the *most practical* of actions for mankind. Fourth, mystics are the explorers, the trail-blazers, the vanguard of mankind. They seek, as did the Buddha, the mystical solution to the world's woes, and they return with their solution for suffering humanity. Lord Buddha brought back from his mystical peregrinations the doctrine of the Noble Eightfold Path, which has supremely justified his 'retreat' into contemplation by the untold suffering it has dissipated. And fifth, as the veriest novice knows, it is possible and even obligatory in certain spiritual circles to practise contemplation in an active life. St Paul exhorts us, 'pray without ceasing' (1 Thess. 5.17), and the Bhagavad Gita tells how karma yoga exemplified this self*less* mysticism which is far more widespread in serious religious circles then the self*ish* pseudo-mysticism with which the critic is evidently confusing it.

7 'When mystics try to propagate their ideas, they all disagree. And since some must therefore be wrong, why should any be right?'

Reply: It is good to see the critic showing signs of the awareness of more than one kind of mysticism, but his criticism is badly conceived, since, as repeatedly pointed out earlier in this book, there is a striking unanimity among mystics. Indeed, they subscribe with little departure to what was called the mystic's credo. And the teachings which follow from this are also mutually consistent: that if man develops his spiritual faculties through self-discipline, compassion, morality, and prayer, he will be doing that which was intended for him, and he will come to fulfilment, thereby enhancing the life of all in contact with him, and raising their level of consciousness too. Again, the critic may have been thinking of such pseudo-mystics as Charles Manson, who organized the murder of Sharon Tate, and other self-styled demagogues and pseudo-authorities whose lack of compassion at once proves them impostors as far as mystical enlightenment is concerned. The primary criterion, of judging a man's worth according to his universal compassion, is a good rule for determining which persons are real mystics and which are bogus. And the former will be found to be unanimous in the pith of their teaching.

8 'The only evidence for mystical assertions is the individual mystic's own experience, and this is unsatisfactory because unscientific.'

Reply: The same as above. The critic can verify for himself if he fulfils within himself the same spiritual conditions.

9 'Mysticism seems to render the individual immune from reason and evidence.'

Reply: As above. It seems thus because the critic only has the material picture. And until he grows in spiritual stature he will remain thus.

10 'Mysticism produces dogged and narrow-minded evangelism.'

Reply: Impossible. The enlightened mystic is possessed of universal compassion and is literally incapable of forcing anyone to do anything. Only pseudo-mystics or narrow-minded religious dogmatists engage in hard-sell evangelism.

11 'Mysticism is a poor guide to conduct, since it is mainly concerned with contemplation.'

Reply: Nonsense, as is apparent from previous answers. Mysticism gives great incentives to help others physically and spiritually, and this is what most mystics do. Mysticism is an excellent guide to conduct, since it sharpens all the faculties involved in making ethical decisions, and polarizes the individual's life around the need to be of service.

12 'Mystics claim to be directly in touch with a new "reality". But cognitive psychologists such as Freud, the Gestaltists, the Harvard School of Bruner, Piaget, Bartlett, etc., are unanimous in their declaration that reality cannot be known directly; it can only be constructed.'

Reply: Mystics postulate an intuitive, spiritual faculty, called *Buddhi* in the Hindu-Buddhist-theosophical tradition, with which reality may be directly apprehended. It is only the lower mind (*manas*) which cannot perceive reality. Man is a spiritual being, and it is through his spiritual faculty that he has mystical transactions with reality. In any case, the mystic learns that what is known as 'reality' in the West is merely appearance masking the true reality.

13[1] 'Mystical experience is a childish aberration. For in it there is something akin to a deep regression of thought back into infantile ways. Mysticism corresponds in some sense to an early stage of development, before words become available (hence the "ineffability" of mysticism), and when the individual feels himself to be at one with the rest of creation, not yet a distinct individual. This explanation was indeed proposed by Freud. If it is correct, the achievements of mystics can hardly be said to constitute progress. In important respects they represent the opposite of maturity.'

Reply: The full value of the earlier analysis of mysticism into different parts, and the enumeration of many mystical states, is here apparent. For the criticism manifestly applies only to the 'oceanic' mystical experience, which is almost purely emotional. The cognitive aspects of mystical experience are here ignored. There is an amusing analogy to point up the lunacy of the criticism. It is as if one were watching a television programme with the sound turned off, and was to judge the import merely from the non-vocal communication. This criticism might apply to Maslovian 'peak experiences', but these are also denuded of their noetic (intellectual) content. But in any case there emerges from real mysticism a deep and profound metaphysical teaching, which would be impossible for the merely 'oceanic' experiences. It is important to recall that the Buddha's teachings came to him in a mystical experience. The critic, who elsewhere speaks warmly of Buddhism, forgets that its doctrine originated in the despised mystical experience.

14 'Mysticism is an aberration, the brain gone haywire, and is therefore akin to, or is a form of, madness.' This criticism was made in a recent book, *The Conscious Brain*, by the self-proclaimed communist materialist biologist Stephen Rose.

Reply: To anyone who has studied any mystical literature this criticism looks to be madder by far than that which it condemns. Only by the most egregious arbitrary playing with words, of the standard of Humpty-dumpty, could mysticism be thought to be

[1] These thirteen psychological criticisms were taken from the debates between the authors in John Radford and Richard Kirby, *The Person in Psychology*. Methuen 1975.

madness. Or, if it is, so is all else, and all are therefore sane. The simple fact is that if one formally examines the mystic's credo against conceptions of mental health and illness, one sees that mysticism is found to be the most superior item on the scale of *positive* mental health. The whole of the next section of this book is devoted to showing the positive achievements of mysticism.

It is clear that this 'criticism' is based on a shockingly shallow grasp of mysticism, and apparently on the most scanty acquaintance with real mysticism and spirituality. It is evident, of course, that the critic has in mind the 'oceanic' experience – perhaps contemplating one's navel. At any rate, sheer ignorance makes of this criticism one of the most vicious. The sting in its tail is disarmed forever by a simple study of the tables in this chapter, especially Table 6.

15   'So-called mystical experiences are simply the bursting into consciousness of desires and needs lying submerged and latent in the unconscious (another Freudian idea). This naturally invalidates the experiences.' (Evelyn Underhill abstracts this criticism from many similar ones.)

Reply: This idea has had much currency, but suffers from logical problems and empirical problems.

The noetic (intellectual) content of mysticism defies this explanation of the origin of mystical experience. And the criticism, apart from being merely an assertion, and an *ad hoc* one at that, is also a *non sequitur*; for the invalidity of mysticism cannot be proved by studying its *origin*. On the contrary, spirituality must express itself to the physical vehicle through some medium, and William James concluded his empirical survey, *The Varieties of Religious Experience*, with the speculation that spiritual experience is indeed effected through the medium of the unconscious. The criticism is as illogical as a man disbelieving a letter because it came by pony express rather than pigeon post, or vice versa. Moreover, it is easily forgotten by those who think Freud a scientist that the very notion of the unconscious was vague, tendentious, and so loosely articulated as to allow almost any explanation to hide under its generous shade. The 'unconscious' is merely a convenient term for the aggregate of those powers, parts, and qualities of the whole self which at any given moment are not conscious. And it is no embarrassment for mysticism that its roots are in that same capacious repository, the unconscious, that houses animal instincts and personal memories, as well as occult connections with the whole universe (as occultists assure us). As Aldous Huxley said, if Freud proved that mankind's mind has a basement, or lower, animal self, then mysticism proves that it has an attic, or higher self, wherein originate the impulses of the spirit. And perhaps it is time that someone pointed out that the assertive emperor has no clothes; the edifice of the Freudian critique of spirituality is the most slender house of cards; the effort in attacking others is sufficient to blow down itself. Moreover, mystics have really outgunned the depth psychologists (as the school of psychoanalytic thought is known) on their own territory, with their own weapons. As Evelyn Underhill points out, the mystics have been more scientific and more thorough in studying the nature of mind than have the psychologists, whether of psychoanalytic or Wurzburg affiliations. Indeed one of the earliest and greatest mystics, Shri Bhagawan Patanjali, writing around the time of Christ, interweaves his exposition of mysticism with a magnificent, still unmatched, account of the nature of the human mind. So one might sum the matter by saying that psychoanalysts and experimental psychologists have merely theorized about mind, while mystics have, from a desperate personal need, found out about its properties by the hard way of personal purgation.

Speaking more generally, the same pattern may be seen to emerge in respect of psychological criticisms of mysticism as was the case with philosophical criticisms. It is the biter bit. Psychology, like philosophy, not only fails badly in its poorly conceived, ill-informed, pusillanimous objections to mysticism; it is itself badly damaged by the exchanges. Let us suppose that psychology regards itself, in old-fashioned terms, as the science of mental life, or, more recently, as the science of behaviour or experience studied as behaviour. It has a responsibility to discover important truths which will help mankind to fulfilment. But almost all the important subjects have been left to mystics to research: the nature of consciousness, for instance, was explored by yogis thousands of years ago. It is the very fount of all psychological problems, yet is still hardly explored within formal psychology. Similarly psychology has shunned after-death states, while the Egyptians and Tibetans codified them in their respective Books of the Dead thousands of years ago. Psychology became an official science, at least in its own eyes, in the late nineteenth century, when a group of Germans flattered themselves that they were doing something new when they attempted to introspect scientifically the contents and processes of their own minds. They soon gave up, baffled by the appearance in their minds of ineffable *Bewusstseinlagen* ('unanalysable states of consciousness'). Psychology then retreated into the embrace of the founder of behaviourism, John B. Watson, in America; this gentleman solved the matter by declaring that psychology is about behaviour, and it has duly not heard about consciousness since. Yet the scientific study of introspection had been solved by every mystic since Patanjali!

This abysmal record has not prevented psychology from levelling further ingenuous criticisms at mysticism, and this chapter closes with a consideration of two more such. The further one examines these criticisms impartially, being well read in mystical literature, the more one realizes the irony of the situation; for mysticism is the living embodiment of what psychology has always striven to be: a science of mind, exact and practical, with an associated technology, and with a grasp of the deepest, broadest, and highest components of human nature, including a conception of the nature of human fulfilment. Mysticism has all these; psychology lacks them. The reader must judge for himself after reading Patanjali, Buddhist scriptures, Ernest Wood, H. P. Blavatsky, Rudolf Steiner, St Paul, and the like.

16 Our penultimate criticism in this chapter is this: 'Mystical states of mind are classifiable with dreams, reverie, and the results of hypnosis, for in all these cases and mysticism too the normal waking consciousness is deliberately or involuntarily lulled, the images and ideas connected with normal life are excluded, and images and faculties from "beyond the threshold" are able to take place.'

Reply: Actually, of course, this is no criticism but a simple practice of the illogical technique known as guilt by association. It is implied that dreams are known to be fantastic, hypnotic delusions to be imposed, so why not mystical states too? Apart from the lack of logical licence to this 'criticism', the short answer is that neither dreams, reverie, nor hypnosis are enduring states, while the mystic states of, to name but three, satori, nirvana, and kaivalya, are all definitely said to be permanent and indeed irreversible by the theorists and Masters of Zen, mahayana Buddhism, and raja yoga respectively. And neither dreams, reverie, nor hypnosis yield hypotheses which are consistently verified by experience, whereas the growth to mystical consciousness proceeds with the measured and reliable tread of a scientific investigation (see *The Science of Yoga*, by I. K. Taimni; Wheaton, Illinois: Quest Books). And, finally, neither dream nor reverie nor post-hypnotic suggestions are so powerful as to revolutionize an entire life; yet such happens regularly to mystics. A well-known case is that of Dr R. M. Bucke, who near the close of the last century suddenly experienced an intense mystical consciousness, which he described as follows:

... a sense of exultation, of immense joyousness accompanied or immediately followed by an intellectual illumination impossible to describe. Among other things, I did not merely come to believe, but I saw that the Universe is not composed of dead matter, but is, on the contrary, a living Presence; I became conscious in myself of eternal life. It was not a conviction that I would have eternal life, but a consciousness that I possessed eternal life then; I saw that all men are immortal; that the cosmic order is such that without any peradventure all things work together for the good of each and all; that the foundation principle of the world, of all the worlds, is what we call love, and that the happiness of each and all is in the long run absolutely certain. The vision lasted a few seconds and was gone; but the memory of it and the sense of the reality of what it taught has remained during the quarter of a century which has since elapsed. I knew that what the vision showed was true. That view, that conviction, I may say that consciousness, has never, even during periods of the deepest depression, been lost (*Cosmic Consciousness: a study in the evolution of the human mind*, Philadelphia 1901).

This classic account of mystical experience and the effect it has on the life of the recipient – just the one vision, of a few seconds' duration, enduring an adult lifetime in its effect – illustrates perfectly the difference between mystical experience and dreams, reverie, and hypnotic delusions. And one could add hundreds of volumes of hagiography, recounting the lives of saints and showing how the most wonderful, most admirable of all human lives – Jesus, Buddha, Socrates, were inspired *and sustained* by mystical experience.

17 The last psychological criticism to be considered here (though not of course the last in existence) is another example of the 'smear' technique (as the imputation of guilt by association is crudely known nowadays). The substance of the criticism is this: 'Mystics are notoriously subject to numerous illnesses and physical malaises, natural and unnatural. Probably these pathologies are sufficient explanation of their visions, without the need for supernatural explanations.'

Reply: To show a willingness to appreciate the critic's argument, let us recall that critics have seized upon such evidence of pathology in mystics as self-hypnosis, apparent monoideism, delusions of grandeur, physical disturbances which accompany the ecstatic trance, and the like. They have sought by this evidence to attribute all the abnormal perceptions of contemplative genius to hysteria or other disease. They called St Paul an epileptic, St Teresa the 'patron saint of hysterics', and have found room for most of their spiritual kindred in the various departments of the pathology museum. Critics also point to frequent bad physical health in mystics, and the reaction of mystical processes on the body.

The reply will once again be divided into two parts: logical and empirical. They will be taken in that order.

Logically speaking, this criticism (actually a group of criticisms) is illegitimate. Indeed it once again, as so often with 'criticisms' of mysticism, actually embodies several classical logical fallacies. First, let us consider whether a person's ill-health threatens the integrity of his ideas.

Logically it cannot; and indeed the *antecedents* of an argument or theorem are totally irrelevant to its validity. But let us flesh out the logic by reminding critics of the following creators whose creative output is respected despite their known bodily – and even mental – pathology. We may mention Immanuel Kant, whose physical feebleness should lead us to discard his *Critiques*, the most influential of modern philosophy; or Beethoven, whose deafness should, according to this logic, cause us to dismiss his post-deafness compositions, which include the Mass in D, the Ninth Symphony, and the last Quartets! Or we might remember the madness of Robert Schumann and Virginia Woolf. A more spectacular example is Milton; his blindness requires us to commit to the flames his *Paradise Lost*! Thus one can see the stupidity of this criticism.

The criticism must not be left with that, however; it must be used as an example, and thoroughly demolished, for it has other faults. It is an argument from the few to the many. If the syllogistic structure is spelled out, we see that it is:

Some mystics have bodily afflictions.
Therefore all mystics have bodily afflictions.

This inference is obviously illegitimate and wrong, and is no better if the critic tries to save it by arguing that:

Some mystics have bodily afflictions.
Therefore they are the only ones relevant to this dispute.

Of course this begs the question and is invalid. However, the main thrust of the argument comes in this:

Some mystical enlightenment is accompanied by physical pathology

(concealed premise: therefore the mental aspect, i.e. the mysticism, is also pathological).

Therefore all mystical revelation is delusory.

This too is false. The inference of the concealed premise, that somatic pathology always co-occurs with mental pathology, is simply wishful thinking. There is no medical licence for such a thesis; indeed the evidence is clearly to the contrary.[1] So, logically speaking, this criticism falls heavily to the ground. But for the sake of thoroughness we should expose another logical

[1] See Richard Kirby and John Radford, *Individual Differences*. Methuen 1976.

fallacy embedded in this criticism: the fallacy of causation inferred from correlation. The critic observes, let us say, a somatic disorder in the life of a mystic. The reasoning is then:

GIVEN	1	There is somato-pathology.
	2	There is mystical consciousness.
INFERRED	3	1 caused 2.
	4	*Therefore* 2 is pathological in origin.
MAIN CONCLUSION	5	*Therefore* 2 (the mystical insight) is fallacious.

Again, this is riddled with errors in reasoning. The principal error is that of arguing from correlation to cause. As is well known among logicians, an observed case of correlation between two variables, X and Y, has at least *five* possible explanations, namely:

1 X causes Y.
2 Y causes X.
3 Y and X affect one another.
4 The correlation is due to chance or random factors.
5 Both X and Y are affected by ('regress on to') a third factor, Z.

In this case the critic *assumes* without evidence that the explanation of the correlation is X causes Y (somato-pathology causes mystical experience), whereas the most likely contingency is actually Y causes X, since the bodily pathology commonly occurs *after* the mystical practices have begun. Or it may be a case of number 5 above, wherein factor Z causes the co-variation of X and Y. In this instance the Z factor is spiritual development, which encourages bodily austerity (leading to pathology) and also engenders spiritual enlightenment.

So much for the logical fallacies of this criticism. To turn to the empirical aspect, the first point to be made, after the long excursion into logic, is that the actual amount of evidence for physical pathology in mystics is diminutively small compared with the healthiness and longevity of most mystics. For every St Paul and St Teresa mentioned by the critic, mystics may cite a dozen such as Plato, Eckhart, Suso, St Augustine, Ruysbroeck, Gautama the Buddha, Thomas à Kempis, Annie Besant, Sri

Aurobindo, C. W. Leadbeater, Sri Ramana Maharshi, Teilhard de Chardin, Aldous Huxley and Ralph Waldo Emerson.

A second empirical point is that even if some mystics may have had some bodily weaknesses or ailments, mystics actually excel in many respects concerning physical and mental health. On the whole they have the most widely developed of all human minds; and they know contentment, joy, and compassion as no others do. They are of high intelligence even when (as in the case of Boehme) they are uneducated. In self-discipline they are again heroic and exemplary, and their acceptance of laborious, sometimes lifelong travail, is legendary. We should not be surprised by these virtues: they are among the fruits of the Spirit hymned by St Paul some 1900 years ago as the inevitable consequence of spirituality (mysticism).

Also a moderate application of mystical practice, after the instruction of yoga, leads always to perfect physical health; and indeed, as mystics hold that all illness is a manifestation of spiritual disharmony,[1] they would say that they are the only ones who have even a chance of total, deep-seated health; for they are the only people who try to live their lives in accordance with the spiritual laws which govern the universe.

Evelyn Underhill, in further extenuation of mystical illness, suggests that it is helpful to look upon the strange psychophysical state of some mystics as just a rebellion of the body against the exigencies of a way of life to which the nervous and vascular systems are not yet adjusted. This is as may be; but it is well to bear in mind that the somatic aberrations associated with mysticism are mainly western; in the East, although there are such religious cranks as fakirs, the true mystics – yogis, Buddhists, and Sufis primarily – always treat their bodies with great respect, for they know, as did the Jews, that the body is the temple of the spirit, and they regard the body as a vehicle for the expression and perfection of mystical consciousness. Therefore they practise moderation – the Middle Way or Golden Mean of Aristotle – even in meditations, and never allow themselves to be so lost to the body that it suffers in the way of certain ascetic mystics. The true mysticism, in other words, is after all completely exempt from the seventeenth criticism.

[1] See, for example, Geoffrey Hodson's *Health and the Spiritual Life*. Theosophical Publishing House 1926.

Conclusion

This section of the book has covered a great deal of territory in the course of expounding and rebutting a score of major criticisms of mysticism. Apart from objections of scientists, philosophers, sociologists, and theologians, these criticisms have come not only from academic psychologists (who are quite a recent breed) but also from doctors and psychiatrists, and experts from other disciplines such as politics and biology, and even poets and novelists. The *origin* of the criticisms is of course irrelevant to their validity, just as the origin or vehicle of a mystical insight is irrelevant to its truth. It is, however, worth asking whether there is some general pattern characterizing the criticisms, with which this account might conclude.

The answer is that the main pattern lies in the common deficiency of the criticisms. On the whole they are vitiated either by a fairly crude logical mistake, or by being ill-informed concerning mysticism. From these facts it is possible to suggest the conditions which critics should satisfy before they attempt a criticism, if it is their intention to make a useful criticism which has at least the elementary virtues of serious scholarship. First, the critic should study the standard texts concerning mysticism, such as Evelyn Underhill's stupendous essay, *Mysticism* (1910). This at least gives familiarity with the standard objections and equally standard replies, and would save a modern critic from wasting time. Second, a critic should learn the diversity of mysticism, and should familiarize himself with the mystical literature of Egypt and the Middle East, India, China, Japan, Europe, and America, in all periods, and not confine himself to his own time and place. Third, it is necessary to read some of the mystics in their own words, for their writings are of a sublimity which is not captured by summaries. In this respect the teachings of Jesus, Gautama, and Socrates are obligatory reading, and those of Ernest Wood, Dante, Olaf Stapledon, William Blake, H. P. Shastri and Thomas à Kempis, to name but a few, have a glory which has to be read in itself.

But all these conditions are themselves second-hand; only first-hand knowledge of mysticism can give complete satisfaction in the rebuttal of criticisms. The fourth requirement, then, is that the critic should seek personal direct knowledge of mysticism. The circumstances under which this knowledge will be forthcoming has been laid down with great scientific accuracy by many great teachers; indeed the instructions are so well known that they have become clichés. They can be summarized very simply and briefly in view of their familiarity, and also their inherent simplicity. At its very simplest, the spiritual life begins with a sense of the difference between good and its absence; and the first growth of ethical thinking. Anything which diminishes egotism, anything that reduces crime or antisocial behaviour in a person, anything which leads a person to reflect on appearance and reality, on life and death and love – any and all of these will sow the seeds of mystical intuition. 'He who leads the life', said Ernest Wood, 'shall know the doctrine.' H. P. Shastri's extraordinary booklet, *A Path to God-realization*, a mere twenty-eight pages, provides a brilliantly succinct account of the route to mystical knowledge; or, for the more esoterically minded, Rudolf Steiner's classic *Knowledge of the Higher Worlds and its Attainment* is well stocked with practical instructions in the attainment of mystical cognition.

To sum up: criticisms of mysticism which come from 'exoteric' sources, from the uninitiated, are completely misconceived and destined merely to return to plague their inventor. The cogency of mysticism is not merely a matter of logic and evidential data (although even in these respects critics have been sorely lacking); it is something so integrally a part of the very structure of the universe that it can only be understood by someone who is prepared to exert himself to satisfy the ethical requirements of the universe. For mysticism shows that love, not logic, is supreme governor of the universe. The critic who expostulates that this is 'irrational' is simply chanting an empty formula: let him remember that 'The letter killeth, but the Spirit giveth life' (2 Cor. 3.6); he will then find that the spirit of mysticism itself 'kills' small-minded criticisms, leaving resplendent the truth which it embodies.

PART FOUR

The Mission of Mysticism

13

The Mission of Mysticism to the Individual

The mission of mysticism to the individual is to present him with an opportunity of riches beyond his wildest dreams: spiritual riches which lie hidden in the depths of every human soul, divine powers of love, thought, and will on the scale of Christ himself; for he told his disciples that they could not only achieve his stature, but actually do greater things. The mission of mysticism to the individual is, very simply, to take every individual to the state of Christhood. When that has been achieved with every human being the mission of mysticism to the human race will also have been fulfilled, for we will have become what our spiritual destiny intends for us: a race of Christs, veritably the species *Homo christus* which lies immanent in *Homo sapiens*.

At the level of the individual the mission of mysticism is, paradoxically, to disestablish individuality or at least individualism. Mysticism is nothing so much as an affirmation of the radical unity of men, the rooting of all in the One Life. Anything which recognizes and promotes that unity or the perception of it is part of the real mission of mysticism to the individual; anything which promotes individual growth cannot, by definition, be spiritual development, still less mystical growth: for mystical growth is only possible for the whole of mankind.

Such is the mystical vision from the religious end of the spectrum of mysticism. But although it denies the possibility of individual development in the spiritual life, it recognizes the possibility of spiritual development for the individual so long as his motive is one of altruism. Spiritual practices undertaken for all one's brethren are sanctified, and mystical growth will take place. And so long as the individual continually reconsecrates his growing spiritual power to God in the service of his fellow-men, that growth must continue.

The task facing the aspirant is therefore to develop a twin

vision, with which he can instantly change his perspective from a self-regarding one (which is essential in some cases of personal development) to a unitive one: from the thought, 'This will improve me' to 'This will help my fellows.'

In the next chapter we will examine in more detail the actual spiritual practices used in different mystical traditions. For the moment it is helpful to point out that the true religious vision, at its simplest and purest, avers that spiritual development comes above all through self-forgetfulness in service of humanity. 'He who loses his life shall save it.' In Christianity, love, humility, and service provide every spiritual power needed, and progress is certain for one who lives by those principles.

Occultism

However, as we have seen earlier, in opposition to religion, at the other end of mysticism's spectrum, lies occultism, whose special genius is precisely the guidance of souls on the spiritual path. In an ideal world occultism would be unnecessary, for all would tread the simple religious path. But this is not an ideal world, least of all from the mystical point of view. People are spiritually weak, alienated from their higher selves, beset by sin, and for the most part unable to undertake the Christian mystical path. One reason for this is that the path of Christian mysticism starts too far forward to entice most men, who (necessarily being at a less exalted level) quite simply do not see what there is in it for them, for they have yet to learn the truth that all are one, and that my brother's riches are mine also. It is to such people, whose spiritual life is awakening but who still desire a reward for their spiritual practices, that occultism speaks. Occultism's purpose in the spiritual life is, among other things, to entice people on to the spiritual path by the offer or promise of personal, individual growth – not necessarily in power, but often just in peace and happiness and fulfilment. And once people have been thus led to spirituality, they may choose either the authentic occultism or religion to be their guide in the higher stages of the path.

For the remainder of this chapter and some of the next, we shall study the occultist approach to mystical development, always bearing in mind that the practices will bear fruit in proportion to the unselfishness with which they are undertaken. The main reason for presenting the view of occultism is that it

166

has a far richer literature concerning what men become through spiritual growth, and its guides to the spiritual path are uniquely comprehensive. Thus, by attending to the vision of occultism we will strengthen and enrich our conception of the mystical destiny of our whole species.

In addition, it would be naive to pretend that the occultist vision of spiritual development is not far more attractive to most people than is the religious approach. Thus an important reason for giving generous space to the occultist path is that through it more people are drawn to mysticism, and they will enter the hall of spirituality by the doorway of individualism. A smaller number of innately religious souls will reach the same destination more directly: they will not have to divest themselves of the garb of egocentricity.

It is important to bear in mind at this point that, in the last analysis, God is the author of all mysticism. The true mystical awakening is by him, and when it is his call, notions of personal gain in power are seen expunged from the mind of the aspirant. Then the purification of the self begins, and mysticism becomes a uniquely insistent goad to self-improvement. The Christ-principle, the Kingdom of God in each man, will intermittently goad and direct an individual towards the way of mysticism, where alone he will find fulfilment, peace, and joy. In modern terms, mysticism is the organizer and director of every one's quest for self-actualization (called God-realization in Vedantic terminology, self-culture in occultism, self-realization in esotericism and theosophy). A more old-fashioned name for the process (which precedes the spiritual path) is character-building or character-development, and a more secular term is self-development (called self-help by the Victorian author Samuel Smiles). Traditionally religious folk think of it, if at all, as plain religion, while the more mystically inclined among religious people speak of spiritual growth, spiritual development. Teilhard de Chardin spoke of 'divinization', while Maslovian humanistic psychologists instruct their clients to approach self-actualization by finding out who they really are, their 'true selves'. Earlier philosophers, such as Rabelais, urged their followers to 'Do what thou wilt', which enlightened later writers have interpreted to mean, not unbridled licentiousness, but finding one's vocation.

Self-improvement is the language of the path at its outset; it continues to be necessary all the way, and to the very end. Just what that end may be has been suggested by many authors in occultism. Here is an example:

> If you have said: 'I will', then choose what you will have, and the nearer your choice is to the spiritual heart of things the sooner you will succeed. Give rein to your fancy and picture to yourself the liberty, and the might, and the love, and the knowledge that will be yours. Your chariot shall be the lightning flash, and your raiment the splendour of the sun, and your voice shall be the thunder of the spheres. The divinest knowledge shall be your food, and the ethereal blue your home. Yours shall be the strength of mountains, the power of the tempest, the force of the ocean, the beauty of the sunrise, the triumph of the noonday sun, the liberty of the wind, the gentleness of the flowers, the peace of the evening twilight, the purity of eternal snow.
>
> Do you say that this is extravagant? It is not so. It is true that you may not achieve this success in one brief lifetime. But believe in your own immortality, then realize that the future is full of splendour without limit, of achievement beyond and beyond and beyond again the most avaricious dreams of imagination, yet that the achievement is a matter for your choosing now. Death is but a trifling episode in our agelong life. Through its portal we will go as one who rises from a bed of sickness to go out into the sunshine. If we set our hearts upon the superhuman things, then we shall achieve. If we fix our ambitions in human life, these, no doubt, we shall attain. Rather, believe in your own immortality; give wings to your imagination; say: 'This is within my reach, I WILL ACHIEVE' – and success will come sooner than you expect. Do you dread time? If so, you have not willed but only wished, for if you had willed you would know that the result is certain, and what is sure is as good as though it were already here. Fix your thought upon your aim; it will come, and its time is as good as now, and, in the light of that certainty, what may happen to us between now and then can matter not at all, and of no moment can be the road we take to that stupendous goal (Ernest Wood, *Concentration*, pp. 153–4).

Such is the mystical occultist's vision of human life and

development; such is the message of mysticism to each human being.

The vistas of this vision dwarf any merely secular scheme of self-development; the author shows us precisely what are the implications for ordinary people, not necessarily in sympathy with mysticism, of the insights of mysticism. And therein lies one of the justifications of the 'retreat into contemplation' of mystical thinkers.

Ernest Wood shows the practical implications for ordinary people of the discovery of the truths of the mystic's credo. The realization of the reality of life after death, of immortality and, eventually, eternal heaven and of the operation of personal karma, together with the knowledge that every ensouled being does move up the path (most probably through a long sequence of incarnations, in this and other worlds), and must reach the goal eventually – these revelations must cause a huge transformation in the lives of those who come to understand the truths of mysticism. Let us quickly specify the main implications of the mystic's credo for personal conduct.

1 *Optimism* is implied. For 'all shall be well'; God is Love; pain and destruction are illusory; there is no death; every man is destined for supreme happiness in the fulfilment of doing what he is best suited to do.

2 An *inner life* of prayer and meditation, concentration and reflection, is necessary. But it is not a trial but the greatest of joys, the flowering of human thought.

3 *Morality* – truth, service, and generally the religious commandments – must be followed, not out of piety, but because such observation is the fastest road to happiness. Morality is the fastest vehicle on the spiritual path, and it is a vehicle possessed by all.

4 *Personal planning* must expand its range to transcend the perspective of a single lifetime. And it can aim at a superhuman career.

5 *The finitude of personal suffering and faults* is realized.

6 The aspirant has to raise his sights to the target of godhood itself for his aims; when he realizes his divine nature, all becomes possible.

The aspirant on the path comes to understand that he has created all his vehicles and all his 'fate', though not necessarily by actions in this life. With this recognition comes a change in his idea of what constitutes his 'self', and a new appreciation of the supreme wisdom of the habitual advice of the ancient oracle at Delphi: 'Know thyself.' The aspirant begins to find his sense of 'self' going back in time, and understands that the extent of his good and bad luck, his character and personality, family and work, good or ill health – all these are self-created and must be remedied by action by the self. This is certainly a very 'occult' truth, but it can be verified by anyone who is prepared to study the classic literature, and study himself. Such a study leads to the knowledge of the finitude of all problems; and the mystical cognition that death is not the end of the self enables the student to understand that there is, no matter how desperate things seem, time enough and to spare for 'all manner of things' to be well. We should not forget the familiar affirmation of St Paul, pillar of mystical orthodoxy:

> Listen! I will unfold a mystery: we shall not all die, but we shall be changed in a flash, in the twinkling of an eye, at the last trumpet-call. For the trumpet will sound, and the dead will rise immortal, and we shall be changed. This perishable being must be clothed with the imperishable, and what is mortal must be clothed with immortality. And when our mortality has been clothed with immortality, then the saying of Scripture will come true: 'Death is swallowed up; victory is won!' 'O Death, where is your victory? O Death, where is your sting?' (1 Cor. 15.51–5).

This quotation is perhaps over-familiar to western readers; and it is not unfair to say that disbelief in its message has become equally familiar. But *practical mysticism* equips one to understand this vital declaration.

The fact is that a belief in personal mortality is utterly at odds with mysticism. The two cannot coexist; one must be banished. Indeed, in mystical development the first requirement is not a conviction of sin, but a willingness to *hypothesize* that one's identity lies in the possession of an immortal self. The willing practice of the simple exercises of the spiritual life, be they Dr Steiner's, Ernest Wood's, the Bible's, yoga's, Buddhism's, or any other, will then provide the evidence to show that the hypothesis is true and personally applicable. In particular, meditation is the means of providing spiritual data. Meditation is to the spiritual aspirant what a laboratory is to the scientist.

We have spoken of the happiness engendered by mysticism; we have studied how mysticism is the goal of human personal and spiritual development, how indeed mysticism transmutes personal development into spiritual development in its higher reaches. And, of course, mysticism provides the most profound solutions to personal problems and the satisfaction of personal aspirations. However, we have hitherto stopped short of details as to the life on the mystical path. All the details so far addressed to the actual practices have been concerned with the foothills of the path, that part known as the preliminary way, the way of purgation or purification. Now it is time to talk of the main path itself.

The spiritual path

The principal concept which will be employed in speaking of *practical* mystical development is 'the spiritual path'. It is an attractive teaching device, because it yields imagery which is highly instructive concerning spiritual development. Mysticism, it has been argued, is a progression from a condition of zero compassion to infinite (divine) compassion (to use the Buddhist word) or love (the Christian or Sufi word). From the point of view of yoga, mysticism is the process by which the individual becomes 'yoked' (hence the word 'yoga') with the divine. All of these are so many metaphors, of course, and each new metaphor has a chance of bringing out some new aspect of spiritual evolution. Thus one might equally describe the goal of mysticism as 'perfectly doing God's will'; or, to those who are slightly discouraged by theistic imagery, it would be better to say that the goal is 'realizing one's full spiritual nature'. And so on. Now these are the end states, the goal of mysticism. But what of the route? It is this to which the concept of 'the spiritual path' is the answer.

Most humans alive today, it need hardly be said, are not in a state of yoga or spiritual fulfilment. They are near the beginning of the human section of the path, and it is with their condition there that we must dwell a moment. Most humans suffer greatly, even if they do not admit it to themselves. They are in a state of 'original sin', because they are living contrary to their spiritual natures. And they are unhappy because of it. The Buddha's Four Noble Truths included the Noble Truth of (the ubiquity of) Sorrow:

> Be not mocked!
> Life which ye prize is long-drawn agony:
> Only its pains abide; its pleasures are
> As birds which light and fly.
>
> Ache of the birth, ache of the helpless days,
> Ache of hot youth and ache of manhood's prime;
> Ache of the chill grey years and choking death,
> These fill your piteous time.
>
> Sweet is fond love, but funeral-flames must kiss
> The breasts which pillow and the lips which cling;
> Gallant is warlike might, but vultures pick
> The joints of chief and king.
>
> Beauteous is Earth, but all its forest-broods
> Plot mutual slaughter, hungering to live;
> Of sapphire are the skies, but when men cry famished,
> No drops they give.
>
> Ask of the sick, the mourners, ask of him
> Who tottereth on his staff, lone and forlorn,
> 'Liketh thee life?' – these say the babe is wise,
> That weepeth, being born.
>
> (*The Light of Asia*, Book 8)

The question, then, of this chapter, is how can the individual progress from the state of sorrow to the destination of mystic union? And the answer is: 'By steadfastly treading one or more of the spiritual paths.'

It is a fact less familiar than it should be, that there is a multiplicity of spiritual paths. Table 6 enumerates fifty-five of them, and it is only a moderately comprehensive list, by no means exhaustive. Actually the explanation of the large number of paths is that, quite simply, there is an infinite number of them, and all that is done in Table 6 is to select those which will be most relevant to readers of this book.

It is something of a mystery how there should be so many

paths, perhaps more mysterious that there should be an infinite number, and most of all it may seem shocking that such activities as rock music and even insanity should be included. Let us seek in one explanation the reason for these puzzles.

Table 6
Spiritual paths[1]

CHRISTIANITY

1 Monastic seclusion (nuns and deaconesses; monks)
2 Mysticism
3 The priesthood
4 The imitation of Christ
5 Christianity in everyday life
6 Judaism: the kabbalah

BUDDHISM

7 Zen
8 The Noble Eightfold Path

HINDUISM AND YOGA

9 Adhyatma yoga (H. P. Shastri)
10 Raja yoga (Patanjali)
11 Jnana yoga
12 Karma yoga
13 Karmasanyasayoga (Bhahgavad Gita ch. 5)
14 Atmasnyamayoga (Bhahgavad Gita, ch. 6)
15 Bhakti yoga (Bhahgavad Gita, ch. 12)

ISLAM

16 The Muslim Way of the Koran
17 The Way of Sufism

CHINA AND JAPAN

18 Taoism
19 Confucianism
20 Shinto

[1] Table 6 is not intended to be perfectly encyclopaedic, but to illustrate the range of paths. The reader is likely to be able to add to the list.

OTHER

A spiritual path is, of course, a path to God (or heaven, or enlightenment, or independence, or wisdom, or eternal life, etc., etc.) Its aim is simply to take the best route within its own powers to that supreme goal. Human beings, for their part, differ enormously in temperament, personality, intelligence, faith, upbringing, occupation, etc., and it is not possible for them all to tread the same path *and make progress at the same speed*. These individual differences are recognized in the geography of the spiritual realm, and many different paths are available for all the different types of persons. That is, in fact, an understatement. For spirit is infinitely capacious, infinitely hospitable, and it can furnish as many spiritual paths as there are human beings. And this implies, quite rightly, that *there is in fact a unique spiritual path for every individual person*. This is partly what is meant by saying that the number of routes is infinite.

There seemed, however, to be a second puzzle about spiritual paths: what is their nature if there can be so many, infinitely many, all leading to the same goal? The answer is sublime. It is that although there is an infinite number of paths, in reality there is only one: the one in which the aspirant consecrates all that he does as an offering to the Lord. Moreover, on the one path the disciple is able to pay tribute to God everywhere, for God is in all. This is of course a perception impossible to most people, but the development of the insight into it as one proceeds along the path is well described by Ernest Wood:

A simple worshipper at first regards God, manifested in a particular form, as the proprietor of all things, and desires to perform all the acts of his life in order to please. Next he begins to see that the finer qualities, which he first discovered in the divine form, are to be seen in some measure in other forms also, and he then begins to realize that there is something of divine nature in all – that God pervades where he possesses. Thus expanding his devotion the worshipper begins to perceive God in all forms and to feel for them an ardent affection, inasmuch as they manifest him.

Slowly another dawn breaks upon the devotee, and now, instead of feeling that there is something of God in all forms, he will realize that all exists in God, that each represents and reproduces him, though not in his fullness, yet just so much of it as there is, is God, and if anything seems to be evil or ugly that is because he feels there a little absence of something else of what he knows to be divine. In these lesser things it is as though the devotee, though looking only at the feet of his God, yet loves the whole of him. He is learning the absolute presence of the divine (*Concentration*, pp. 146–7).

That is the description of the path of paths: the direct consecration of all to the Lord. Of course, Ernest Wood's perception is that of a man very far along the path; yet to novices also is the short path open: for any action is a spiritual path. The Bhagavad Gita portrays the Supreme Being telling his disciple:

> Whoso loveth Me cometh to Me.
> Whoso shall offer Me in faith and love
> A leaf, a flower, a fruit, water poured forth,
> That offering will I accept, lovingly made
> With pious will. Whate'er thou doest, Prince!
> Eating or sacrificing, giving gifts,
> Praying or fasting,
> Let it all be done
> For Me, as Mine. So shalt thou free thyself
> From *Karmabandh*, the chain which holdeth men
> To good and evil issue, so shalt come
> Safe unto Me – when thou art quit of flesh –
> By faith and abdication joined to Me!
> (Bhagavad Gita, trans. Edwin Arnold)

But it is rare to find, in the western world, people who can sustain such a vision even for a moment, let alone all their domestic and business life. For we the vast majority, therefore, the mystical way to spiritual development is not by that path of paths the short path, but by commitment to one or more spiritual paths. But before turning directly to examine the options before us, it is necessary to dissolve one more puzzle about spiritual paths, as represented in Table 6. It is simply this: how is it that such apparently irreligious activities as rock music, to say nothing of such nakedly painful experiences as insanity, can constitute spiritual paths?

The short answer to the question of rock music and its ilk is a reiteration of the point that *anything* (other than definitely harmful practices) can be dedicated to the Lord – and that is sufficient to render it a path for the practitioner. Anything which brings man to increased spirituality is a path. And this explains also the role of mental illness (alias insanity) in this respect. Mental illness is, in fact, the expression of an underlying spiritual crisis, as all illness is; and it is no more than an intensified purgative path, in which the 'doors of perception' are cleansed, so that man's spiritual sight is restored. Mental illness is no more than a secularized version of the 'Dark Night of the Soul' which many mystics undergo as part of their purgation before mystical illumination.

The general topography of spiritual paths

The manner in which every mystical novice must seek progress is by treading one or more spiritual paths. It is therefore now in order to inquire of their general and specific natures, so that the pilgrim may have some kind of map to hand on his journey. No 'official' map exists, but the records and counsels of many mystics in past eras make it a relatively easy task to assemble an outline of the general topography of the paths.

We should start with the obvious again: the beginning and the end. At the beginning is sorrow; at the end is total peace, joy, and fulfilment. What lies in between?

The great mystics unite to tell us something very comforting: the journey is not endless. Every step we take covers real distance, and diminishes the remaining distance. We do not have a milometer in the spiritual life, but we can be assured that spiritual actions are furnishing the fuel which is immediately consumed by the engine of our spiritual vehicle, thereby bringing us perceptibly nearer to home (for such is our destination).

We know the journey will be bumpy; there will be valleys of unhappiness as well as hills of joy. But we are assured that the journey is like an ascent to the highest mountain; as we wind ever higher and higher the air becomes continually fresher and cleaner, more sweet-smelling, more bracing, more enriching, simply purer. We may interpret this to mean that as we proceed along our path, *our* lives will more and more be filled with this fragrance, which merges imperceptibly into that peace which passeth all understanding – or as the Buddhists put it, 'carpeting all the way with flowers'. To put the matter in the crassest of material terms (though it is not wrong to speak thus if it will help the aspirant), more hours per day are happy as one treads the path.

We know from the Masters that there may be unexpected reverses on the path. Illumination may be followed by despair, or vice versa. Trusted guides may fail or disappoint one, prayers go unanswered, inner tranquillity depart. This is to be expected and endured. The eastern authorities declare this to be the intrusion of bad karma from past lives, given the chance to be burnt up in the developing flame of spirituality. It is this positive aspect of suffering which makes it bearable, or can make it bearable. The ancient saying that suffering is good for the soul is absolutely correct. Suffering, in the writings of Dr Martin Israel, is the way in which we build up the spiritual body which is to be our home at the physical death. Suffering must be endured in the certain knowledge that it is serving the best interests of the spiritual man. Mystical authorities have expressed this vividly. We may recall from chapter 12 that Geoffrey Hodson, in his book *Health and the Spiritual Life*, attested that

> Pain may be taken as a sure indication of that lack of harmony which causes resistance. There is some obstruction against which the Divine Life is pressing and by which its vitalising flow is impeded.
>
> Pain is, therefore, our best friend and our teacher, especially at the early stages of our progress.

Another authority, Edward Bach, writing an explanation of the 'real cause and cure of disease', shares this view:

> Disease, though apparently so cruel, is in itself beneficent and for our good and, if rightly interpreted, it will guide us to our essential faults. If properly treated it will be the cause of the

removal of those faults and leave us better and greater than before. Suffering is a corrective to point out a lesson which by other means we have failed to grasp, and never can it be eradicated until that lesson is learnt.[1]

This, then, gives great heart to those on the path who meet terrifying obstacles. For they learn that suffering and illness are, incredible though it seems, indeed simply additional powers for the journey along the path.

In due course aspirants inherit the entire world, for they learn, as did the Stoic Epictetus, that whatever they have, do, meet, or undergo is in fact the best thing for the development of their soul. This realization is the first major initiation on the path; and thereafter the aspirant knows indeed the occult truth that this is 'the best of all possible worlds' for him. Later he realizes that it is the best of all possible worlds for others too. And finally he attains to a level of spiritual perception so profound that there is not one small event in his life, not the picking up of a pin or the tying of a shoelace, which is not lighted with spiritual significance; every small thing, every small action has become divine, far-reaching, universe-shaking. All things have become new, and filled with light.

Such are some of the landmarks – not the goal, which is ineffable – on the path. It is time to turn to the choice of one's own path or paths.

---

[1] See Edward Bach, *Heal Thyself: an explanation of the real causes of disease.* Daniel 1931.

14
Mystical Growth on the Spiritual Path

Choosing one's spiritual path

It must be said at once that there is actually no obligation for an individual to commit himself to one path only; a combination of many is quite permissible and common. The reason for sticking to one, however, is that the simplicity of the requirements is such as to promote faster progress. Persons who combine many paths may end up so confused that they will be moving unnecessarily slowly.

In order to make a wise choice of a path one must have two important data: the paths which are available, and what they each entail; and one's own individuality with all its idiosyncrasies of personality and habits. In the latter case, 'Know thyself' is once again the operative instruction. Now it must be explained in more detail. Table 7 shows some of the projects which are involved in attaining to self-knowledge of the kind required in this endeavour.

Table 7
An introduction to practices directed towards self-knowledge for spiritual purposes[1]

1   Keeping a record of all remarks made about oneself by others

2   Soliciting opinions from others concerning oneself

3   Keeping a file on oneself, impersonally, recording dispassionately all one's attributes, non-evaluatively

4   Making an impartial list of one's habits of thought, behaviour, work, play, recreation, family life, interpersonal relationships, religion, emotions

[1] The same applies as to Table 6. It is impossible to be complete here; however, the projects are designed to lead the reader to a position where he will know precisely what to do next towards further self-realization.

5   Listing all the personality traits which have been imputed to oneself by self or others

6   Describing the structure of one's personality – its constituents, their manner of relationship, and the architectonic properties of the whole

7   Describing the structure of one's character – as in previous item

8   Describing one's life aims, great and small, and after-death aspirations; also one's ambitions, broadly interpreted so as to include all unfulfilled desires

9   Answering in 500 statements the question 'Who am I?'

10   Recording the exact role-specification which one accepts for all the roles one plays – father, husband, son, uncle, employer, employee, Christian, centre-forward, gardener, wine connoisseur, etc.

11   Stating fundamental attributes – who one is, what one does, all physical characteristics, all mental characteristics, all past achievements and failures, qualifications and possessions

12   Stating impartially one's strong points and faults, including good and bad habits respectively

13   Analysing every friendship one has ever had, discerning one's patterns of relationship

14   Studying every occasion when one has made an enemy, seeking patterns of behaviour – the cause of the rift, the sustaining of it

15   Recording all one's illnesses – their start, course and finish; one's use of them

16   Recording all the accidents one has been involved in – causes, and effects on oneself

17   Recording all that one has read; and one's reading habits

18   Recording all that one has viewed on television or a larger screen; and one's viewing habits

19   The nature of one's spiritual life – habits of prayer, meditation, church attendance, good works, study of spiritual literature

20   One's sports and pastimes – the extent of involvement in each, one's skill or prowess or knowledge or expertise, extent of emotional involvement, money expended upon them, what one receives from them

21   One's affiliations to groups and associations – their nature, one's part in them

22   One's current circle of immediate friends, and the nature of the friendship

23 One's family life – relationship with spouse and offspring, parents, etc.: the quantity and quality of each relationship, and properties of the whole

24 One's work: job specification, relationships, success, job satisfaction

25 Practices of a biological nature – eating, sexuality, etc.

26 One's socio-politico-economic attributes – class, sex, political affiliation, area of residence, etc.

27 One's education at every level – teachers, subject, success, exam. results, attitude to each subject, teachers' evaluation of self and work

28 All one's clothes, including circumstances under which each is worn, reason for purchase, effect on self-image

29 All the places, home or abroad, which one has visited, and why; what one learned in each case

30 Self-image – of body, personality, mind, soul, and social self

31 All one's 'problems' – *everything* which one feels obstructs spiritual development towards one's spiritual heritage – the realization of the Kingdom of God

32 One's aptitude for study and scholarship: exam. skills, memory, concentration

No doubt there are some who will greet this Table with horror, regarding it as obsessionally meticulous, morbidly self-indulgent, and above all impossibly arduous and lengthy (they would be even more horrified to learn that it is no more than one per cent of the total task, a task which can never be completed). In fact the task as laid down *is* lengthy: it could take from two to five years for a person who devoted some of his spare time to it, though only a couple of months for one devoting all his time to it. But we should not think of it as excessively long. The man leading the spiritual life knows that he has all the time in the world, and, after all, it is the richest of rewards which awaits the student who completes the task.

It is necessary to say some words of explanation about the practices advocated in Table 8. They are not arbitrarily devised by the present writer, but have been chosen and expressed so as to present in western and secular terms some of the many religious, mystical, occultist, psychological, and educational techniques for self-improvement. But whereas merely secular self-improvement schemes cannot see beyond the death of the individual, this Table has a longer-term purpose in mind. That is why such thoroughness is necessary. And it must be clearly understood that the wisdom of mysticism decrees that a man must design his own future. No one else can or may do it for him. He must take every step himself – this is one of the greatest of occult truths, hiding behind a veil of apparent simplicity. And no man can get far without self-knowledge, which is why these practices have been introduced at this point. The especial features of the programme of self-discovery are thoroughness and impartiality. Thoroughness is essential because one is building one's own castle with one's bare hands; and no brick must be missing or improperly aligned. And impartiality loosens the choking grip of materialism and the false self. By self-study as if one is another, one finds that one *is* another – an immortal soul, richer and more joyful than the small self which one is analysing. In this sense self-study can be a spiritual path itself. But it is a path chosen by very few, and we must suppose that, for most, self-study will be but one part of a spiritual programme of which treading a spiritual path is the principal part. We thus return to the question of the choice of a path, though this time we do so, we may assume, enriched by the perspective of self-study. The mystical pilgrim will find that with increasing self-knowledge comes increasing discrimination among paths, and vice versa.

An examination of the spiritual paths specified in Table 6 shows that the paths fall into clear categories. A basic distinction can be made between three superordinate categories: religious (nos. 1–23), occultist (nos. 24–45) and secular or semi-religious (nos. 46–55). It is, of course, open to any individual to tread a path from all three categories, or to cobble together his own path with ingredients from all three. Indeed, in reality this is what all must do, for human diversity is such that each must, in a sense, create his own path. Nevertheless, it is instructive to compare the attributes of the three groups. The paths in the first group have the advantage of being routinized, reliable and predictable, prestigious, and usually welcomed by the parent society. Thus, it could hardly escape the attention of those who chose a Christian path that there is, on average, a church every 300 yards in this country! Those seeking safety and opportunities for sharing growth with a large group are obviously well served by traditional religions.

On the other hand, the contemporary generation has shown a greater passion for the second group, the occultist. We have seen that this is mainly due to the apparent rewards of occultism, plus the charm of esotericism – that is, the sense of doing something secret. The 'secret' aspects of these paths are being published in huge numbers now, but this does not seem to affect their 'esoteric charm'.

The third group, the secular paths, is the shortest. It is probably the one requiring most explanatory comment, since its members seem to be without reference to mysticism. This is a fallacy, of course; all of them have mystical qualities in great evidence, and in them all it is possible to reveal and express spirituality, the coinage of mysticism. When they are employed as spiritual paths it is simply a question of bringing these qualities to the forefront. They have been described here as secular on the assumption that they can be used by atheists and still serve as paths. It may seem odd to cater for atheists in discussing spiritual paths and mysticism, but such a view would be the result of narrowness of conception of God. These secular paths are all ones in which there is opportunity for the aspirant to self-development to practise love, compassion, *arete* (the Greek concept of general excellence or virtue), to create and revere beauty, truth, and unselfishness. And it must be realized that these are all spiritual qualities which result in the ever-increasing refinement of the consciousness and spirituality of the aspirant, until he becomes a practical mystic. And then it does not matter by what name one calls the Supreme Being. For wherever love is abroad, there also walks God. Hari Prasad Shastri, superlative and divinely articulate mystic, explained thus the relation between God and the soul:

Love is the golden thread which binds the soul to God.

Love means the realization of beauty and selfless devotion caused by that element which produces bliss. When beauty in nature, art, or literature makes an aesthetic appeal, know this beauty to be the divine expression of the bliss of God.

A moment's reflection on this passage will show how such as poetry and rock music can become spiritual paths. But the same author has more to say on this topic, and it illuminates brilliantly the manner in which the 'relationship' paths (marriage, parenthood, family life, nos. 46–8) can be spiritual routes to mystical achievement:

Love, when impersonal, is a manifestation in man of the ray of God. The relation between love and beauty corresponds to that between the ray of God and divine bliss.

Love is polluted and rendered powerless when directed towards temporal and selfish ends. Love must be dynamic and transcendent, progressing from the individual to general ethical principles and from these to truth. The culmination of all love is the realization of one's own Self as the divine Self (Atman).[1]

To sum up, the secular paths fall into two broad groups: ones in which beauty is the platform to the mystical heights (poetry, music, etc.) and those in which personal love is the foundation. A smaller group could also be built of those paths devoted to the ray of God which we call truth: this would include philosophy and science. Finally, nos. 51 and 52 (self-actualization, and training in consciousness) are really religious, belonging to no. 10, since they are in fact part of the methodology of raja yoga. It is nonetheless stimulating to list them as secular, and to encourage students to discover for themselves how rapidly secular programmes of self-inquiry and self-improvement merge with religious systems.

Methods and principles used on the spiritual path

The pilgrim is always seeking to be in motion. He knows roughly where he is, in personal and spiritual development; he knows where he wants to go, but does not always know how to go there, or how to move at all, or even how to face in the right direction. But there is, on this path, something, or rather many things, which correspond to fuel, the provision of which will

[1] From H. P. Shastri, *A Path to God-realization*, pp. 9–10. Shanti Sadan 1974.

cause him to locomote in the desired direction. These are the methods used for progress on the path. They are listed in Table 8.

Table 8
Methods and Principles used on the Spiritual Path

The contents of this Table are not impious formulae for instant holiness; they are simply practices which Scripture or spiritual literature exhorts the pilgrim to begin or increase. Their effect, progress on the path, is becoming nearer to God.

Part 1   Christian

THE THEOLOGICAL VIRTUES

Faith
Hope
Charity

THE CARDINAL VIRTUES

Justice
Temperance
Fortitude
Prudence

DANGERS TO AVOID

THE ENEMIES OF THE SOUL

The Flesh
Concupiscence of the flesh
Concupiscence of the eyes
The pride of life

The World
Worldliness
Christianity for personal gain

The Devil
Temptation to sin
Temptation to evil

THE CAPITAL SINS

Pride
Envy
Anger
Covetousness
Gluttony
Lust
Sloth

REPENTANCE

Compunction
Confession
Satisfaction

MORTIFICATION

Avoidance of favourite sins
Poverty (renunciation of possessiveness)
Mortification of thought
Mortification of desire
Mortification of judgement
Mortification of self-will, egotism

THE SACRAMENTS

Baptism
Confirmation
Penance
Holy Communion
Matrimony
Holy Order
Unction

PRAYER

Intercessional
Thanksgiving
Petition
Liturgical
Confession-penitence

MEDITATION

Concentration
Meditation (Raja Yoga)
Meditation (Zen Buddhist)
Meditation (Christian)

CONTEMPLATION

Contemplative prayer
Samadhi

RECOLLECTION

CHRISTIAN VIRTUES

Poverty
Chastity
Obedience
Truthfulness
Morality of behaviour

CHRISTIAN SERVICE

Serving others
Almsgiving, charity
Sharing unattractive work

THE TWO COMMANDMENTS OF JESUS

Love of God
Love of neighbour as oneself

THE TEN COMMANDMENTS OF GOD TO ISRAEL

Recognition of the one God
Non-idolatry
Not taking God's name in vain
Observing the sacredness of the Sabbath
Honouring one's father and mother
Refraining from murder
Refraining from adultery
Non-stealing
Non-lying
Non-covetousness

THE MASTER PRINCIPLES

Love
Humility
Service

Part 2   Eastern Religions

YOGA (RAJA)

SELF-RESTRAINT

(*Ahimsa*, harmlessness)
Non-injury (in thought, word and deed)
Truthfulness
Non-theft
Spiritual conduct
Non-greed

OBSERVANCES

Cleanliness
Contentment
Austerity (*Tapas*)
Self-study
Attentiveness to God

ASANAS

(Postures)

PRANAYAMA

(Control of breath and vital force)

PRATYHARA

(Control of senses)

CONCENTRATION

MEDITATION

CONTEMPLATION (*SAMADHI*)

BUDDHISM (Eightfold Path)

RIGHT DOCTRINE

('Walk in fear of *Dharma*, shunning all offence;
In heed of *Karma*, which doth make man's fate;
In lordship over sense')

RIGHT PURPOSE

('Have good-will
To all that lives, letting unkindness die
And greed and wrath; so that your lives be made
    Like soft airs passing by.')

RIGHT DISCOURSE

('Govern the lips
As they were palace-doors, the King within;
Tranquil and fair and courteous
Be all words which from that presence win.')

RIGHT BEHAVIOUR

('Let each act assail a fault or help a merit grow;
Like threads of silver seen through crystal beads
Let love through good deeds show.')

RIGHT PURITY

RIGHT THOUGHT

RIGHT LONELINESS

RIGHT RAPTURE

Part 3   Occultist

PHYSICAL PRACTICES

Vegetarianism (or veganism)
Chastity
Fasting
Moderation: the Golden Mean

MENTAL PRACTICES

Perseverance
Dispassion/non-attachment
Practice of mind-control (untiringly)
Relinquishing the fruits of one's actions
Meditation

ATTITUDES

Loving everything and everyone
Contentment
Patience
Humility
Courage in adversity
Constant determination to achieve spiritual growth unceasingly
Strength of purpose for spiritual growth

PROJECTS

Reading

Thinking discursively

Discussion

Systematic education

Establishing a relationship with a guru or spiritual director

Systematic self-study

Nightly recollection of day's conduct, with moral evaluation

Daily study of personal aims

Decision at the beginning of each day for everything to be done during it

Regular and systematic generation of new spiritual goals and aspirations

Studying the holy in music, art, literature, history, saints, coevals

Dispassionate recognition of personal faults

CHARACTER-BUILDING

Meditation on virtues, leading to contemplation

Meditation on great, exemplary men (saints, mystics, philosophers, etc.)

Regular examination of own character

Regular redesigning of one's character structure and content in the light of personal experience relevant to spiritual growth

Belonging to a spiritual group in which mutual character-building occurs.

Common to every tradition

SUFFERING

Suffering is hardly a practice or an action, but it occurs to everyone, and it plays in the spiritual life a very important part which cannot be overstated.

Pain is the purest fuel on the spiritual path. When used wisely, it purifies and strengthens the sufferer's soul. Suffering takes many forms, and not all are of great spiritual potency. It is, technically speaking, the suffering which constitutes sharing Christ's crucifixion which is the most powerful spiritually – for by undergoing it we are taking his Way to the Life and the Father. Physical pain is the least potent in this respect; it is mental suffering which is most valuable, especially in its extreme forms such as mental illness, in dying, and particularly in empathic suffering, for this is taking part in our Lord's vicarious atonement. Thus, as so often with Jesus, familiar ideas are stood on their head, and suffering, which we dread, is seen to be our best friend. And in the very nadir of its quintessence – anguish and despair – we are moving most swiftly towards our Lord and our God.

Nobody has yet drawn up a mathematical score-sheet, but the practices listed in this Table are all time-honoured ways of progressing along the path. The purpose of them all is the same: to make the pilgrim's whole being at one with God. Sometimes the practices are passive, as in silent prayer; sometimes they are active, as in study, and in helping other people. It is no doubt a great pity that God did not equip us with maps on our heads, so that we could get our exact spiritual location at any moment. As it is, one will often know roughly where one is, and one will recognize landmarks that mystics have spoken about. But there will also be times when one does not know where one is, when one feels lost (in both senses of the word) and near to despair. Certainty is lost, one doubts whether there is a path at all, and life seems a futile delusion. This is where so many people give up, but they would not if they knew the great spiritual law that it is in those moments that one is actually moving fastest along the path. *Suffering has no purpose whatsoever except to speed the pilgrim on his way; it ranks with love and charity as the most powerful of spiritual fuels on the path.* When we feel splendid, that 'God's in his heaven and all's right with the world', we are not necessarily making spiritual *progress*. At best we are standing still. When a man says, 'I feel well, and I've earned it, the theory of karma is just right!' he is regressing. When he says, 'I'm ill and I don't care if the theory of karma is true, whatever I did I don't want justice. I want help. God help me!' he is making progress in humility and through suffering, although he may not think so. Truly Jesus said that the man who loses his life shall save it.

It will no doubt seem to some that it is entirely contrary to the spirit of religion, let alone mysticism, to attempt to sort it into little parcels of principles and techniques, each with its own 'speed-rating' on the path. It appears to many devout religious persons that it is sacrilegious to reduce God to a concatenation of marketing methods, to limit the illimitable Holy Spirit. But the argument of the present book is that, just as modern man needs to be proficient with both halves of his brain, with logic and language as well as intuition and love, so the mystic needs to partake both of religion and occultism. The former corresponds to the right hemisphere of mysticism's brain; the latter to the left hemisphere. Occultism, earlier defined as practical and intellectual mysticism, is concerned with spiritual progress, development, evolution; and its practical urgency supplements the timeless, God-fearing attitude of religion. Both are essential. The prescription of practices and principles should not be criticized by Christians; for Jesus himself set an illustrious example, and, of his many teachings, the Sermon on the Mount is a clear example of occultism in the sense defined here: it is an exhortation to men to perfect themselves (occultism), to become mystics, to win eternal life. With that divine example in mind, it is permissible to examine more closely the suggestions embodied in Table 8.

The principles and practices presented in Table 8 are drawn from Scripture (in the case of part 1, the Christian section); from Patanjali's raja yoga *Sutras* and Sir Edwin Arnold's Life of the Buddha, *The Light of Asia* (part 2, eastern religions); and, for part 3, Occultist, from Ernest Wood's many texts presenting the practices of self-culture in the service of spiritual development. Obviously it would have been possible to expand all these lists, especially the middle one, but this book is not an encyclopaedia. The purpose of the Table is simply to introduce the idea of approaching spiritual development in this deliberate, almost calculating fashion, and to present an elementary compilation which anyone moved to pursue the matter might develop to his or her personal needs.

The items in each list are, of course, not of equal importance. The relationship between them is subtle and complicated. In the case of raja yoga, for example, the practices are hierarchical and cumulative, in the sense that the aspirant is expected to master the moral requirements before he can proceed to the spiritual ones; similarly in Christianity the basic Commandments of the Old and New Testaments must be as second nature to the disciple before he can proceed to Christian mystical practices. The explanation of this is not so much spiritual as psychological. It is a fact of human nature that an immoral person cannot engage in spiritual practices – the two are mutually exclusive, although God may awaken at a stroke an erring person and thus free him through grace to begin the true spiritual life.

Generally, the practices of the religions and of occultism follow a common pattern. Their aim is to clear away the rubble of the egotistical self and personality, and the obstructions posed by imperfect minds and bodies, so that the light of the Higher Self, God, the Soul, the Christ-principle may shine through and illuminate, to an ever-increasing extent, the consciousness of the person. For this reason strict morality is required as an essential precondition, in order that the basic behaviour may be in harmony with the soul-qualities. But then the mind and body must be cleansed, purged, improved, perfected, for the Christ-consciousness must, in incarnate souls, manifest through them. Perfection of mind and body means perfect health for both, and perfect self-control over all their appetites, and it is the attainment of these states that is so difficult for rapacious, self-indulgent modern man and his mind – necessitating the multitudinous practices of occultism, aimed solely at creating a pure channel for the spiritual consciousness. It is worth reiterating the point that the body and mind have served their purpose when *perfect* God-realization (i.e. the last nirvana) is achieved or conferred; but it is equally important to remember that this is an unrealistic aim for most humans *in this life*. Naturally we keep one eye on the ultimate goal; with the other we continually appraise our present state of moral, bodily and mental imperfection, and the feebleness of our religious practices. For most of us, to remedy that situation will be more than the work of this lifetime: certainly they are the subjects which the spiritual school of life requires us to study as best we may before we move on to the greater university of many mansions which welcomes the discarnate.

Conclusion

Our survey, of the occultist approach to the mission of mysticism to the individual, is now complete. As promised, it must be rounded out with the religious perspective. The two taken together will perhaps provide a balanced picture of mysticism in relation to the individual.

The driving force of occultism is the desire for freedom. Not the freedom of infinite power, but the freedom from bondage to circumstances. This freedom is what is really attained in nirvana or (in raja yoga) kaivalya. Onlookers often mistake that desire for cupidity, and say that it is power which occultism seeks. It is not, in the genuine occultist; it is a striving for liberation from contingency. The Buddhist conception of nirvana, as expounded in *The Light of Asia*, makes it clear just what the freedom is:

> All life is lives for him, all deaths are dead;
> *Karma* will no more make new houses.

And the point is made even more clearly in the Buddha's cry of Enlightenment (equals Buddhahood):

> Many a house of life
> Hath held me – seeking ever him who wrought
> These prisons of the senses, sorrow-fraught;
> Sore was my ceaseless strife!

> But now,
> Thou builder of this tabernacle – Thou!
> I know thee! Never shalt thou build again
> These walls of pain,
> Nor raise the rooftops of deceits, nor lay
> Fresh rafters on the clay;
> Broken thy house is, and the Ridge-pole split!
>   Delusion fashioned it!
> Safe pass I thence – deliverance to obtain.

It can be seen that this is very far from the fruit of cupidity – especially when one realizes that the truly 'Noble' Eightfold Path is the way to it. Anyhow, such is the goal of the occultist.

The driving force of religion is the desire to serve – to serve God and other people. Where unswerving perseverance and intense one-pointed purpose is the trademark of occultism, in religion it is humility partnered by unselfish love. On the religious path to mystical realization the only forces are suffering (purgation), service, love, humility, and brotherhood.

The religious attitude is, at its most extreme, the utter abrogation of self or ego, the very erasure of identity as an individual. Desires for the self drop away altogether, and the aspirant leaves himself utterly self-abandoned to God. The aims of occultism would seem to him to be self-inflation.

The religious ideal and aim, insofar as there are any other than to serve God, rests upon ever more perfect imitation of Christ by deprivation and suffering coupled with universal compassion. From the viewpoint of religion the individual response to mysticism is to practise ever greater charity and mortification, and the aim is the simple (though infinitely exalted) one of ever more close union with God. Where the occultist plans for the after-death life, the religious mystic rests in the present in the desire to achieve the spiritual marriage.

It can, therefore, be reiterated that religion provides the simplest mystical path, but it is one which is so stark as to attract few adherents outside the monasteries. Occultism will no doubt remain, for the time being, the more exciting in appearance, and will thus draw more aspirants into the path; but in all probability it will be to religion that even the advanced occultists will eventually turn, as they perceive the gold beneath the glitter, and, knowing themselves to be built in God's image, yearn for the perfect simplicity of union with him. That state may be achieved through yoga, through Buddhism, or through Christianity, for the liberation aimed at by the former two is the same as the spiritual marriage of the latter, the step which is achieved by all religions prior to the attainment of Christhood, the perfect fulfilment of the mission of mysticism to every human being.

A return to the source

After this prolonged excursion into the details of self-study, and the choice of paths, it is requisite to review what has been achieved. In this consideration of personal development it is very fitting to do so, for we thus evoke a distinguished occult-mystical image, the Ourobouros, the circle formed and transcended by the snake which bites its own tail. If we tuck the tail of this discussion into its mouth, what do we find?

We began with the astonishing mystical-occultist vision of the omnipotence or divine destiny of all creatures. We end with the provision of tickets for each and every one for the great journey. What can Ourobouros tell us, what are his parting words as all the trains bearing the pilgrims move away and upwards from their buffers? Surely his wisdom is to remind us that *all our journeying is in his image*; we too must individually take his form. Jacob Boehme, the great Protestant mystic, was once asked, where does the human soul go at death? He answered, 'There is no need for it to go anywhere.' Our tail, in other words, is already in our mouth. Surely, we learn from Ourobouros, T. S. Eliot was right to aver that 'the end of all our exploring will be to arrive where we started and know the place for the first time'. Or, as Professor Shastri stated, the realization of one's own self as the divine self – which is only another way of saying that God is within each man – or even that this is what is meant by saying that man is made in God's image.

At any rate, we must humbly recognize that the great paths are all shrouded in mystery. We know their destination as far as we can comprehend it now; we know its starting point, for we are that beginning; but the exact nature of the bridges and fords, streams and rivers, natural hazards and unsung glories – all these are hidden from us. With humility and eager expectation the pilgrim must tread his chosen way and savour the sublime uniqueness of his journey.

This chapter precedes the last pair, which present the culmination of the whole book and its argument, the discussion of the mission of mysticism to the human race. And it is no accident that causes the chapters on the mysticism of the race to be immediately preceded by those describing the mission of mysticism to the individual. For the two are inseparable. The mission of mysticism to the human race can only find its expression in the enlightenment of those individuals who comprise the race. And mystical illumination *eo ipso* confirms the realization of the unity of life, the *de facto* universal brotherhood of man. We have seen that *separatist* mystical realization is impossible by definition.

Thus, these chapters have described not merely an op-portunity for individual men and women; they are stating a *duty*, a duty to follow the Way, the Truth, and the Life, to obtain Christ-realization of the Kingdom of God within, for the sake of every member of the one brotherhood of man, thus simultaneously fulfilling the mission of mysticism to the individual and to the species.

15
The Mission of Mysticism to the Human Race

Mysticism has expressed itself in many human contexts, but it really has only one purpose: the perfection of the human race. Mysticism is the conductor of the symphony orchestra of human perfections in art, science, religion, philosophy, and every other human cultural enterprise. There can be no dilution of this vision; it is *nothing less than perfection* to which mysticism calls mankind.

In order to achieve this perfection it is necessary to perfect every facet of humanity and its products. Art, religion, and science, in particular, are destined to be perfected.

To recapitulate the argument of this book, it may be valuable to repeat that human perfection is not difficult to understand or to envisage: it is the eventual destiny of every human being, and many saints have shown the way, led by the most perfect of all, Jesus Christ. Because man is made in God's image, his *real self* is already perfect; perfection is simply becoming what one already is, by consecrating one's life to God and practising self-abandonment to divine providence. And to the Christian this is a duty, as Jesus commanded men to become as perfect as God himself. And, just as Jesus showed us the way to perfection, so mysticism is our constant reminder that perfection is possible.

The above remarks are essentially timeless; they apply to almost any era of human history. But it has been argued in this book that the present juncture of history is unique even by the standards of mysticism's remarkable history. For not only religion but several other important influences have fashioned a dramatic era for mankind. Firstly, the human race is now, for the first time, frighteningly close to extinction from internal or external causes: nuclear war, famine, pollution, ecological imbalance, or extermination by putative non-human entities. Secondly, the 'Aquarian Age' is now upon us, and the paramystical consciousness is encircling the globe, while more and more people profess a conviction that the Second Coming, or some great religious revelation, is at hand. Thirdly, the advent of science has for the first time made man superior to nature, and thus put an end to 'natural selection'. Man is the first creature with the power to take control of his own evolution. And it is science which makes this possible. Thus, for the first time, science and religion find themselves facing identical tasks. Science, which has always been the servant of man, becomes at one with religion in the quest for the perfection of man. It appears, therefore, that the unique mission of mysticism to modern man is to unite science and religion at the highest point of each; and there can be no mistaking what this will entail: their joint purpose is the design and creation of a new human race, *Homo sapiens* perfected, a race of Christs, *Homo christus*.

Science-mysticism

As yet, science has not engendered the mysticism based on itself which so obviously lies immanent in it. The nearest to that vision have been Julian Huxley and Teilhard de Chardin, but neither pursued their arguments to their natural conclusions. Probably it is the ignorance of science fiction which has caused this oversight in philosophy, and this in turn is the result of self-defeating intellectual snobbishness and narrow-mindedness posing as refined discrimination. Actually, more insight into the real possibilities of science has appeared in the pages of science fiction than in 'serious' non-fiction. And it is now timely to sketch these possibilities.

In the popular consciousness, God in the religious sense may not have many followers who believe in his omnipotence, but science does have such a following. To the secular mind God's attributes are taken over by science. All around them every day, people see evidence of the magical, miraculous powers of science, but not (they suppose) of God. To many, science *is* God. (It is worth considering what would be the 'theology' of science, taken as a religion, and, for that matter, of science fiction. Surely western theology could only benefit from such a study.) Moreover, science appears on the whole to be beneficent, just as God is said to be. Admittedly the lost souls of Hiroshima might dispute this evaluation, but on the whole we regard science as our friend. And like God, science appears to be omnipotent.

This is no exaggeration. In the last hundred years science has come close to vanquishing death in several ways, such as artificial organs, cryogenic suspension of life, direct attack on biological mechanisms of senescence. And many others are in sight: genetic reprogramming, the storage of identity in computer data-banks, brain refurbishing, the near-complete mechanization of the physical parts of man, and much that is beyond this, such as the complete suppression of the physical, mortal elements of man, the transcendence of the dependence of mind upon matter. The science-fiction novel mentioned earlier, *The City and the Stars*, depicts a united humanity which collaborates in the creation of their heir: the 'pure mentality', an entity of near-infinite intelligence with no material embodiment, which is but 'patterns of thought embossed on space itself, thriving on electromagnetic and "yet higher" forms of energy'.

Such conceptions reveal that there is a special type of mysticism which must be called *science-mysticism* or *mysticism of science*. As with all other types of mysticism, it is concerned with the immortal possibilities and infinite depths of human nature (indeed every type of mysticism is a theory of human nature). But it deals in the physical and mental, whereas the religious variety deals mainly in the spiritual. There is, of course, no reason why science must ignore the spiritual realm. On the contrary, its destiny is to assimilate it and be assimilated by it. However, a glance at the quintessential criteria of mysticism shows that whereas religious mysticism is fundamentally an ethical or moral system, science is, in itself, amoral (though humans make it serve ethical ends). And in this unconsciousness of the ethical realm lies the danger of science. Science, without mysticism to pacify it and bless it, *to make it a sacrament*, is as dangerous as a homicidal maniac who has been given the key to an arsenal. The mission of mysticism is, therefore, to effect this overdue synthesis of science-mysticism and religious mysticism, consecrating both to God, perfecting science in the religious sense, and putting both to the service of man in the improvement of human nature.

The end of Homo sapiens

Like all works of mysticism, the present book is a theory of human nature. But this is rarely explicit in religious writings, while here it is absolutely central. In an earlier book, *Individual Differences*, I pointed out that in order to understand every dimension of human nature it is necessary not only to understand what man is and has been, but also to show what he may become, to characterize his potential. For man is *par excellence* the creature of growth. Man's distinguishing feature is his capacity to entertain, or even to be, an infinitely diverse set of states and contents of consciousness. For this reason, all knowledge is potentially available to everyone. And 'all knowledge' includes the capacity to modify oneself. Therefore every human being is omnipotent, *potentially*. Up until the Industrial Revolution the human capacity for infinite development remained merely a possibility, although it was one which was in evidence in the lives of the great saints and religious teachers. But with the advent of science the potential is revealed in a new guise. Science and technology have presented mankind with yet another chance to create the perfect species. (Christians might regard this as the fourth attempt, after Adam, Seth, and Jesus.) And as Theodore Roszak has pointed out with copious examples, the paramystical Aquarian consciousness is deeply committed to the belief that mankind is about to make a step forward in evolution, a growth into a new form of consciousness.

It is at this point that the deliberate ambiguity in the title of this section can be pointed out. 'The end of *Homo sapiens*' means both the *termination* and the *destiny* of mankind, and the question arising is whether indeed mankind must 'terminate', and if so, how. It is here that the Christian has a special contribution to make. It is also here that the possible tragic demise of our race must be recollected.

Christians who have tried to follow in their Master's footsteps on the Way know well that his crucifixion is part of that Way. They know that a man must die to himself before he can in truth be born again in spirit. When Jesus said, 'I am the Way, the Truth, and the Life', he must have meant that every human being had to share the defeat at Golgotha before it turned into eternal victory. Now as mankind is said to be in imminent danger of extinction, and by some hideous methods, it may well be that mankind *as a whole* must be crucified, even unto death, before coming into its inheritance. This is, at least, a conjecture for eschatology. It is especially relevant at this time when the planet Earth is becoming more and more one of a piece, McLuhan's 'global village', a 'whole-earth' seeking of the universal brotherhood of man. Might we not go down united, into the pit?

It would be foolish for Christians to neglect this possibility, for theirs is the only creed or ideology or philosophy which can make sense of mankind's present plight. They alone can say of suffering that it is a privilege, a sharing of the Cross of Calvary, and that suffering unto death is a glorious opportunity to be united with Christ; and they can say, with Teilhard de Chardin, that death itself is beneficent, the only way to grow beyond forms which have served their limited purpose. Christians alone can combine the optimistic and pessimistic tendencies of this era: they share the joy of the naive millenarian and Aquarian groups and movements, and, with them, look forward to the Second Coming, the New Age, the advent of *Homo christus*; but, with the serious and the worried, they look upon the possible extermination of the human race secure in the knowledge that it could be but a prelude to the resurrection of the species.

If the vision of human extinction is one part of the meaning of 'the end of *Homo sapiens*', the other part is the destiny of mankind, the nature of perfected man. In this connection the phrase 'the mystical destiny of mankind' is a helpful reminder that man's destiny is shown by Christ to be inevitably mystical in nature. But to preface the description of that destiny it is necessary to survey all contemporary or extant opinions concerning the future of mankind.

Visions of the future of man

This book is about the future, the future of the human race. Of course, it is hardly the first to tackle the subject. Many attempts have been made by writers of the most diverse backgrounds, writing at all periods of history. The prophetic dimension of the Bible, for example, shows how from time immemorial man has looked expectantly to the future. But the present generation is more conscious of the future than were any of its predecessors in recorded history. This is evident in, among other things, the appearance of the neonatal discipline which we call futurology.

The future has become a living dimension in mankind's consciousness, because he *knows* that it will be different from the past. In pre-industrial days, stasis was the hallmark of culture and society. But the advent of science and its causal agent, technology, has made *change* the one reliable factor. There are at present other reasons for the expectation of change: inflation is a prominent example. But it is *science* which guarantees the strangeness of the future. And in that expectant ambience many visions of the future have been presented to the world.

THE FUTURE OF MAN:
THE VISION OF SCIENCE AND SCIENCE FICTION

Atheistic humanists, usually writing under the inspiration of a vision of science, have foreseen a human future made glorious by the right application of science to human problems. Abraham Maslow, founder of humanistic psychology, was discussed in earlier chapters: his vision of eupsychian society, full of peak experiences for everyone, has much to recommend it, but the same criticism applies: to leave spirituality out altogether when discussing man's future and potential is to impoverish one's vision to the point of impotence. The same applies to Sir Julian Huxley, who was equally opposed to supernatural religion, and who, in his book *Religion without Revelation*, postulated a new religion of transhumanism or 'evolutionary humanism', although in fact he virtually re-defined spirituality as the transhuman faculty; and Maslow in effect did the same. Most of the great humanists are preaching about the immortal possibilities and inscrutable, sublime depths of human nature, and the closer they come along that route, the more relevant their contribution will be. H. G. Wells stood in this tradition, and he too foresaw world governments, perfected medicine, and the other attributes of scientific Utopia. Dystopias have also been envisaged by some authors – Aldous Huxley's *Brave New World* and George Orwell's *Nineteen Eighty-four* are classic depictions of the abuse of scientific power (and for that matter they illustrate the fallacy in the idea that science *per se* is good for man). But throughout history mankind has conceived visions of Utopia: the best-known examples include Plato's *Republic*, More's *Utopia* and Skinner's *Walden Two*, although there is a host of volumes which could also be included under this rubric, from Marx and Engels's *Communist Manifesto* to Buckminster Fuller's mystical architecture, from grandiose visions of one mankind to modest attempts to establish ideal small communities (this is an area in which the Church has been exemplary). But, apart from the last-mentioned, these visions can only be partial so long as they omit (a) morality, (b) spirituality, and (c) the 'supernatural' (in the theological sense).

More speculative Utopian visions came from the pens of the two greatest science-fiction writers, the English authors Olaf Stapledon and Arthur C. Clarke. The high calibre of their writings, and their relevance to mysticism, is partly explained by the fact that the science fiction which they wrote was for both simply speculative science and philosophy which, for the sake of convenience, they published as fiction. One of the results of this tactic is that both have made innovative contributions to what was earlier called science-mysticism. In fact, if there is ever a Bible of science-mysticism, they would be the St John and St Paul of it, for both have made their reputations by their controlled and purposive speculations as to the ultimate possibilities of science and technology in relation to man's needs and ultimately to human nature itself. Thus their writings constitute a part of what must become the classical canon of scientific-mystical Christianity, whose task is the actual scientific redesigning of mankind in conjunction with religion, to engender *Homo christus*.

Stapledon's *Last and First Men* (1930) was the first work, and remains by far the most important, to discuss in detail what would happen when mankind reached the point of being able to remake human nature through scientific means. He discusses several attempts at this, and we learn much. Some may complain that this is only fiction, and hence only marginally useful. But such a criticism displays a very poor grasp of scientific method. Science *is* fiction, it is fiction which has been put to the test. Certain events can be tested in the imagination – we all do it whenever we make plans – and Stapledon used in his books the method known to philosophers as the 'thought-experiment'.

One of the most spectacular of Stapledon's visions involved mankind as building giant brains to be their successors. Twelve feet across, these 'preposterous factories of mind' eventually ruled the world, but they found that near-infinite intelligence and knowledge was sterile and frustrating, for they 'lacked the bowels of mercy'. Stapledon's spiritual wisdom is evident in this parable; he is philosopher enough to know that man's intellect is only an instrument, not the man himself.

Arthur C. Clarke, a self-confessed devotee of Stapledon, has admitted to using Stapledon's ideas in his own novels, and he took the 'great brain' idea much further in his non-fiction book *Profiles of the Future* (1962). In the last chapter, which is called, significantly, 'The Obsolescence of Man', Clarke anticipated Christopher Evans's view of the machine as man's successor. But Clarke has been far more subtle, for while Evans sees machines as taking over from us on a separate line of evolution, Clarke sees mankind *evolving into* machines. The religious person who sees mankind as a purposeful part of God's creation naturally prefers Clarke's view.

The details of Clarke's theory need a little expanding. Clarke began by pointing out that it is in the integrity of a man's brain cells that his identity lies – at least, that is the belief of agnostics and atheists. He goes on from this premise to point out that if a man's organs and limbs and other parts of the body were replaced one by one by artificial counterparts, he would not be diminished but enhanced, and would remain the same person as long as his brain remained unaltered. The next point is that mankind could thereby attain godlike powers, for his brain could be linked to the most powerful and complex of man's machines. For example, he could enjoy as direct eyesight the electron microscope, the most powerful radio and optical astronomical telescopes; the fastest plane could be his very body, and his consciousness could be literally merged with that of another. And there would be no ageing; all would be non-biological except the brain, and the ageing of that would be perfectly controlled. And once neurophysiology was perfected, the brain itself would be replaced, gradually, first bit by bit and then increasingly until it was wholly replaced by a 'computer' version of the same personality. And at that point there would be no end to the power and opportunity of the computers, for they would spend a certain amount of their time improving themselves, and especially their intelligence, so that they would become more and more intelligent, until they had created a veritable chain reaction of superintelligent cognition. . . .

So much for science-mysticism when it is ungoverned by the sweet purposes of religion and spirituality; it is apparent how one-sided man would be without religion. Knowledge and power, these are the gods of science; but mysticism commandingly informs us that these are lesser gods; in this universe it is morality, service, and humility which reign.

The fallacy in Clarke's ideas about the obsolescence of man lies in its neglect of the spirit, the soul of man. Man is not a machine, not even potentially. No science could turn an embodied soul into a machine, for science, in its material aspect, is absolutely powerless on the spiritual planes. It is a sobering thought for science that if the entire weaponry of the world were detonated simultaneously, it would have no effect whatsoever on the supraphysical planes. Moreover, the mystic knows that the brain-body complex is not the real person at all; it is only an instrument with which his soul works on the lower planes. Clarke's fallacy lies in the idea that it is possible to go on indefinitely in improving a material body. But to the mystic this is like saying that a man can improve himself by buying bigger and bigger cars. The 'great brain' idea exactly corresponds to that belief. *Science* cannot improve the real man because it is powerless in the native country of the real man, the soul. Brain enhancement or brain damage simply improves or hinders the use of an instrument of the soul. Only morality and love, those unscientific impalpables, can move the soul.

However, it would be a tragic mistake to write off the Stapledon-Clarke vision, for it truly has enormous implications for the mystical destiny of man. The fact is that man *does have a body and a brain*, and the body is the temple of the spirit. Christianity, unlike Manichaeanism, does not preach that matter or the body is evil. Although some Christian authors sail close to that belief, it is generally held that the body is intrinsically good. But, since mysticism proclaims the perfectibility of man, and since as yet it is not widely believed that *Homo christus* must necessarily be discarnate, it follows that the physical body may be destined to be perfected by science, in which case the Stapledon-Clarke vision becomes relevant. This is, however, a big 'if'; it may well be that *Homo christus* will not have a *physical* body but a *resurrection* body. Whether or not this is the case will depend upon the answer to the question whether mankind will evolve into the new species by the route laid down in the New Testament – the death of all, the Second Coming, the judgement of all, and the resurrection of all those who have died in the course of human history – or by science. The former answer suggests a divine intervention of ultimate proportions, to tie up the fate of *Homo sapiens*; the latter suggests that man must find his own salvation, under Christ. If the latter is the case, we are faced with the most extraordinary task in our history: the design of our successors. Before undertaking directly so formidable and singular a task, it would be prudent to complete our survey of visions of the future of man.

One scientist who has not neglected the future of man's mind is John Taylor. In such books as *The Shape of Minds to Come* he has sketched the Stapledonian vision of superbrains, and in other books he has hinted at some mystical relationship which man may have with black holes. But he is a materialist with no conception of spirituality, and his ideas are subject to the same criticism as that levelled at other scientists: that he is leaving out of the account the only part of man that really matters. A scientist might retort that they are not speaking of matter but of *mind*, the truly human substance, but this too would be in error. Mind, like matter, is just another instrument of the spirit, and mind is not self-illuminate (as Patanjali compellingly proves in the *Yoga Sutras*); it is nothing more than a mirror or lens used by the higher self, the real man. And a supermind is impossible by definition, from the spiritual point of view, for while scientists may want to make knowledge and intelligence the basis of their intellectual currency, the mystic knows that love, which is an impossible mystery to the intellect, is the only real unit of human currency. As St Paul pointed out, when love is omitted all the accomplishments in the world are barren and useless.

Isaac Asimov is another scientist and science-fiction writer who has predicted scientific Utopias, but again without religious factors. The American psychologist Gardner Murphy, and the English author Gordon Rattray Taylor, are further exponents of the 'scientific Utopia' theme, and Edward de Bono seems to think that 'lateral thinking' can make man omnipotent and solve all his problems. But he neglects to say that, while 'lateral thinking' may propose, God, or the spiritual levels of being, will dispose. And not thinking, but love and righteousness, is the power: 'It is not necessary to think much, but to love much,' said St Teresa.

Erich von Däniken has something to say on man's future, though it is less voluminous than his utterances concerning the alien intervention in man's past. According to the end of *Chariots of the Gods?*, 'Man has a magnificent future ahead of him.' Elsewhere in this author's writings we learn that the magnificent future will apparently consist in colonizing the galaxy. Fascism and a lack of moral awareness are evident here, although von Däniken has alerted us to our wider responsibilities, and he has sharpened our science. This is more than can be said for some visionaries still revered by many – Nostradamus and Paracelsus. These sages have left us with utterances so cryptic, spawning interpretations so equivocal that they can contribute surprisingly little to a serious discussion of the future of man.

Studying the future has its pitfalls, as we always see with the perfect vision of hindsight. For example, Karl Marx, despite his atheism, apparently felt divinely inspired with the theory that has ultimately brought us to the brink of nuclear Armageddon. Marx predicted that communism would happen automatically in the western civilized world, but it has not, and almost certainly one can say that he was hopelessly wrong. This is the penalty, with an awful price which all mankind now struggles to pay, of trying to base opinions on secular, amoral intuition. One must reiterate that only in the light of spirituality can scientific or atheistic-communistic enterprises be sure of doing more good than harm.

The modern futurology has tried to be more insightful, but, so long as its prognostications remain in the mental, material realms, futurology is a waste of time. The future of man will depend largely, as it always has, on religious revelations, and the only way for futurology to succeed is by dedicating itself to God and then proceeding with the piety of St Thomas Aquinas. The real task of futurology is to assist mysticism in telling science how to perfect the material aspect of man, and in telling religion how to respond to the divine plan for human perfection. In science man tries to control the present; in religion, with its teleological mechanism – the summons from the Omega Point, the call of God from man's future – he learns to control that which is yet to come; and one day mysticism will teach him to perfect all that has been in the past.

THE FUTURE OF MAN: THE VISION OF MYSTICISM

Having completed the examination of non-religious (and in practice mostly scientifically inspired) visions of the future of man, it is agreeable now to turn to the testimony of thinkers of real spiritual stature, religious theorists who, presupposing the validity of the tenets of mysticism, have gone on to describe man's future and destiny in the light of not only the products of the little intellect and the coarse realities of the material plane, but also of the supramental, spiritual intuition from the higher self, the Christ within, and referring to supramental possibilities in man's evolution. These, the true mystics, know that even now man is an embodied soul, a spark of the divine nature, one with all, a god in exile, destined every last man to a triumphant realization of unity with God, 'lords of lightning, masters of the world, homeless, triumphant', certain at last to become superman, 'very God of very God'. As *Homo christus*, radiant, infinitely beautiful, courageous, and compassionate, they are the veritable incarnations of love and rectitude, perfect in body and mind, utterly fulfilled inhabitants of the New Jerusalem which is peopled by all men who have ever lived, are living, and will ever live. The city of nirvana and God-realization is at one with the very fabric of divinized time and space in the Christ-conquered universe, utterly free from pain, disease, suffering, strife and discord, war and jealousy, dislike, hate, remorse, despair and anguish, eternally occupied instead with the infinite varieties of love, unity, and beauty in an unending growth towards the infinitely receptive Deity.

We will begin our consideration of the mystics themselves with Hindu philosophers and western enthusiasts of Hinduism. All these thinkers agree that man's nature is essentially divine, and that his future will consist in an ever more glorious unfolding of his latent divinity, through self-culture (yoga and Buddhism). It is not only Hindu classical philosophy which presents this picture; it is adopted root and branch by theosophy (which claims to be the wisdom common to all religions) and indeed by most branches of occultism.

The Hindu metaphysic is concerned with two topics: the general nature of the universe (metaphysics, especially cosmology); and the nature and the role of man in the universe. These philosophers present a picture of a universe governed by law: the laws of evolution through morality, self-sacrifice, and love. This point must be stressed. The Hindu philosophy does not state that impersonal, 'scientific', mechanistic, material law governs the orderly universe: it reveals the astonishing picture of a *living universe governed by love*. This is the universal declaration of man's supreme research instrument, mysticism, and of course it receives its supreme incarnation – literally – in Christianity, in which it is uncompromisingly stated again and again that God *is* Love, and of course Christ is the uniquely pure incarnation of this attribute of Deity.

The Hindus further affirm that everything in the universe is constantly evolving towards greater self-realization, in the sense that they seek to realize their divine nature or Self, by removing the obstacles of egotistical concern with their *separate* self. Evolution towards self-realization is always in the direction of unity with all. God, who is the object of self-realization, is in all, both immanent and transcendent. All created matter and energy, whether or not we regard it as 'inanimate', evolves towards greater consciousness, self-understanding, altruism, and love; and the method of reincarnation, it is asserted, couples with the law of justice (karma) to help beings evolve. There is no 'punishment'; karma provides the best opportunities for growth. Suffering is the best karma, for it is the most efficacious instrument of spiritual growth. There is no death, for what we call death is just a change of form. Thus, since there is neither suffering nor death, evil is impossible, and is thus an illusion. The universe is the best of all possible universes. There is no limit to growth; it continues from the mineral to the vegetable to the animal to the human, and then to the superhuman, and to realms of consciousness beyond our understanding at present.

The nature of man reflects the nature of the universe, according to the occultist adaptation of Hinduism. This is expressed in the hermetic dictum, 'As above, so below', which refers to the theory that man (microcosm) contains in him every property of the universe (macrocosm), microcosmically expressed. This corresponds to the Christian vision that the Kingdom of God is in each man. Theosophists and Vedantists ascribe to man a number of components or elements or 'principles': as well as the body and lower mind they add the etheric double, the astral body, *prana* (the vital force), the higher mind, the Buddhi or spiritual intuition, the reincarnating ego, the causal body (container of memories of all previous lives), the atman or *purusha* (real self or God within), and the divine spark, the ray of Brahman, the individual's own sharing in God himself. Various combinations of these are known as the soul, spirit, individuality, personality, etc. Evolution consists, for humans, in achieving in the lower elements the perfect expression of the spirituality of the higher self. According to the Hindu-based philosophies, every human being is on the spiritual path, and will, sooner or later, in one life or another, achieve that goal, and become a god, a Master, an Adept, a Buddha, a Christ, a perfect man who will incarnate no more but will go on to a superhuman destiny in the supramental realms.

The authors who share this philosophy agree on the essentials, but there are differences between them. H. P. Blavatsky, writing with the greatest authority, has stated that our race will presently be transmuted into the sixth human race or root-race (we are part of the fifth, Atlantis was part of the fourth), and that will in turn eventually yield the seventh root-race, in which more and more men will become perfected men, Masters, Adepts. Alice Bailey, a disciple of Blavatsky, believed that in the twentieth century the entire 'hierarchy' of Masters would externalize itself in the material world, and, led by the Christ, would lead man into the new era of brotherhood. This vision is not entirely out of phase with the biblical predictions. Alice Bailey's disciple, Benjamin Creme, as we have previously had occasion to remark, believes that this has begun already, and that Christ is incarnate again. Creme does at least make unequivocal predictions about the immediate future of man, and *if* he is right, we are living in truly blessed times. Part of his teaching is that in this new era *every* human being will receive what is known in occultism as the first initiation, and this will instantly put an end to materialism and war and fear, since everyone will know his true, immortal, divine nature, and will know that he is literally one with his brother. Another occultist, Vera Stanley Alder, a visionary, has made similar prognostications. In her book *The Initiation of the World* she foresaw the opening of the Third, or Spiritual, Eye of all mankind, and the realization by everyone of his spiritual nature.

Attitudes to death will of course alter radically, since it is to be seen as an essentially beneficent institution. These authors go on to envisage a new world religion being disseminated by the Christ and his helpers; it will be a combination of Christianity, occultism, and Hinduism.

Sri Aurobindo, the great Indian yogi-scholar, published a series of accounts in which he showed in detail how the 'divine life on earth' will express itself, as the supramental consciousness, the spiritual faculty, or supermind, comes more and more to dominate the ordinary consciousness, thus ushering in the age of man's perfection and the *spiritual* Utopia which it engenders.

The great Annie Besant's many writings also contain visions of the future of man, such as *Building a Kosmos*, and her collaborator, C. W. Leadbeater, has devoted much space to the topic. He has even published a small book called *The Beginnings of the Sixth Root-race*, a clairvoyant study of a community of sixth-race people sometime in the future. Many other theosophically inclined authors, such as G. de Purucker, have described in moving and inspiring terms the great destiny of mankind if this theosophical-Hindu philosophy is correct.

CHRISTIAN MYSTICISM

The East has not been the only breeding-ground of religious visions of the future of man; Christianity also has an illustrious history in this respect. For the present discussion it is possible only to mention the two most important visions, but they suffice, since they are among the greatest of all human cultural products. They are the works of St John the Divine and Pierre Teilhard de Chardin. St John's is the most mystical of the Gospels, and it expounds a Christology which is most compatible with the christocentric argument of this book. And his Revelation is even more relevant, since it deals explicitly with the future of mankind in connection with the Christ. The last book of the Bible is its strangest, full of strange imagery, hermetic allusions, and recondite symbols. It has been interpreted in many ways over the last 2000 years. Many of the interpretations are mutually contradictory, and the work is still being searchingly analysed. Its images have been plundered by poets, novelists, and science-fiction writers; its announcements have inspired dramatists and even scientists as well as the religious to whom it was mostly addressed. It has been the rallying-cry of many millenarian sects; anyone believing the end of the world to be at hand has referred to it. Esotericists have had a field day with it, claiming it as the prime example of esoteric numerology, symbolism, and imagery. There is a colossal power in St John's vision; few can read it and be unaffected. Yet no one can say decisively just what it means. However, for our purposes the simplest exposition is sufficient. The Bible, which is the story of the creation and fall from grace of man, who was subsequently redeemed by God Incarnate, concludes with Revelation, whose message can be expressed, albeit in a simplified way, by the assertion that Jesus Christ will one day return (the 'Second Coming') to earth as King of all and everything; he will judge the living and the dead, and he will take the righteous with him into heaven, into the New Jerusalem which will begin at that moment, and will embody everything ever hoped for in heaven. History as we understand it will end, and God's purpose in man will be fulfilled. This too is consonant with the general argument of this book. St John's Revelation is set in the undated future, but it is almost certainly an allegory rather than a factual prediction, and as such should be interpreted broadly. However, it is not really consistent with the infinite care of Jesus for every lost sheep, that he would abandon even one lost soul. The idea of eternal damnation must be understood in its first-century context; had St John been educated in today's culture he would surely have refrained from predicting that the majority of the human race was doomed to eternal hell; such a belief directly contradicts St John's own insight that 'God is Love'. Moreover, as many sensitive non-Christians have realized, no one could enjoy eternal happiness while many of his brethren suffered. In Hindu parables the tale is told of a king who renounced heaven until he had saved the whole world with him, and in Buddhism, from which Christianity has much to learn in this matter, the idea of rescuing the suffering before accepting suffering for oneself is so intrinsic to the faith that it is enshrined in the highly crystallized concept of the *Bodhisattva*. This divine creature is a human being who has, in himself, attained to perfection after many lives but, although entitled to nirvana, refuses it and turns back to help the suffering world instead. Buddhist doctrine affirms that there have been many such, and there will continue to be such until all mankind is saved. This is certainly a more civilized religion than the Christianity of hellfire. Even non-religious people have pointed out that the principle of human brotherhood would never let them abandon even the dead; Stapledon envisages a future race of men trying to devise time-travel so that they can 'rescue the past', and Ernest Wood points out that even a moderately sensitive human being, let alone a God of Love, would baulk at condemning anyone to eternal punishment. Indeed, there is a consensus of human pity established throughout all recorded history that if God will not save all men they will have to undertake the task themselves. It would be a pleasingly ironical fact if this is indeed man's task for the future. When the era of human universal brotherhood dawns, all living men will work for each other, and it will be time for them to turn their attention to their predecessors to redeem them. This is no doubt the gist of St John's Revelation: the Christ who comes as King will surely raise the dead, but every last one will, sooner or later, follow him, the infinitely dutiful Shepherd, into the open gates of the New Jerusalem.

The last thinker to be mentioned in this catalogue is arguably the greatest of them all: Pierre Teilhard de Chardin, s.j., scientist, archaeologist, palaeontologist, and brilliant mystic, whose major works were suppressed by the Catholic censors until after his death (and we would, even then, never have seen them had he not had the wisdom to bequeath them to a friend who was able to publish without the approval of the Catholic authorities). Teilhard is now the object of a worldwide veneration and one of the most influential philosophers of this generation. Teilhard's achievement, which must be dramatically abbreviated for expression here, lies in two things. He had the courage to see that if Christ is who Christians claim he is, his domain must be cosmical, not merely terrestrial. Also, Teilhard was the thinker who, more than anyone else, was able to conceive of mankind as a whole, and as part of nature in which he is still evolving. Teilhard's great works, *The Phenomenon of Man*, *The Future of Man*, and a number of others, showed how the growth of man related to his spiritual growth as a species. In devising this theory he devised many new and now famous concepts, and the words to express them. His most famous idea is probably that which he called the *noosphere*, the mental atmosphere of our planet. In sum, his achievement was that, first of all, he brought Christianity into the Space Age and showed how it was believable even if extraterrestrial entities and cosmical perspectives reduce us to the scale of subatomic particles, for our Lord is the Redeemer of all worlds; and, secondly, he had the courage to see that mankind is *still evolving*. He was able to relate the future of man, as conceived scientifically from the viewpoint of biology, to the metaphysic of Christianity. Teilhard almost single-handedly reconciled science and Christianity, healing the wound that the previous hundred years of fighting between them had caused. Teilhard was a very great man, and in him we see one of the greatest examples in all recorded history of sheer intellectual brilliance combined with superlative open-mindedness, vision, flair, and courage, all tempered, inspired, and sustained by his unshakable strength of moral integrity and spiritual purpose. The annals of history record only one figure of comparable stature: Plato.

CONCLUSION AS TO THE FUTURE OF MAN

It is now necessary to present a brief synthesis of the views described in the preceding section. The following is the picture seen in the jigsaw which together they form.

Homo sapiens is near the end of his career. He has been a transitional creature, an amphibian, a short bridge between the subhuman ape and the superhuman Master who he is to become. It is not certain how *Homo sapiens* will die out – it may be instantly, through some catastrophe of his own making or a natural disaster (or perhaps, so interwoven are we with our planet, through some ecological disaster which is an inter-relation of the two), or it may be very slowly. Theosophists, employing superphysical research methods, report that the succeeding race will grow up amid *Homo sapiens* while the latter slowly dies out. But one thing is sure. Man has reached the point where he has consciously to help in designing his successor. This will be done in part by science and in part by spirituality, but the whole process is led by Jesus Christ, who represents the ideal, the prototype of the new man, who will therefore be called *Homo christus.* The universal mystic insight into the essentially spiritual nature of man is a guarantee that no materialist philosophy can play an important part in this greatest of all human projects.

It is possible to be more explicit about the task. Mankind has attained to, or arrived at, three points: to its redemption by Christ; to its near self-extermination; and to scientific power of indescribable dimension for self-improvement at the level of the species as well as the individual. It is clear that, as constituted, mankind cannot survive. It must change, and the two other facts unite in this task, which is the mission of mysticism. The Christ sets the pattern for the new species, and science, tempered by spirituality, brings it about. To an extent this work can be seen to have begun. The British Welfare State, for example, is inspired by spirituality and effected by science. The presence of trends in this direction supports the idea that the new race will emerge gradually. Theosophical doctrine declares that many hundreds of thousands of years will elapse before the new race is pure and dominant, but even after that length of time remnants of present-day mankind may be surviving.

The task of mysticism, therefore, is to be Christ's messenger to science in the design of the new race, *Homo christus.* So grand and exalted an endeavour demands its own chapter, appropriately enough the last in the book.

16

The Emergence of Homo Christus

The common features of science and spirituality

Christianity and science becoming as one? A seemingly preposterous, heretical idea, it will seem to many from both camps, for we have always been taught that such a rapprochement is absolutely impossible.

It is only natural that the idea of *science* expressing or effecting a *spiritual* reformation should be thought incoherent. But in fact the two *must* work together in this task: they are the yin and yang of man's nature, the two sides of his brain, and whereas hitherto they have been in frequent conflict, now, now that man is to be perfected, they must be united. The mission of mysticism is thus to build a bridge between man's spiritual and scientific centres, the two hemispheres of the brain. This may not be as difficult as it seems. Science and spirituality have much in common, and four shared properties should be mentioned. First, both are governed by law. And the law which governs spirit likewise governs science. Radical philosophers of science, notably Nicholas Maxwell, have pointed out that *de facto* science respects and bases itself upon the spiritual values, not only of truth, but also of harmony, beauty, and even love. Second, both science and spirit have limitless power. Hitherto they have differed in the realms in which their power has been expressed, but this differential specialization need not be maintained if they are united under mysticism. Third, spirituality and science are for the most part concerned with mankind, and science is, *de facto*, not a neutral, value-free enterprise at all, but a concealed homage to the God which it knows to be somewhere immanent in mankind. Fourth, both have the means to perfect mankind – each with its own methods and materials, each concentrating upon certain facets of human nature.

It might be argued that science will always be the junior partner of spirituality, but this cannot be decided until the mission of mysticism has shown more clearly the nature of the spiritual heart of science. It may be that science will no more confine itself to the electromagnetic spectrum but will express itself in spiritual fields. Spirituality, for its part, already reveals its operation in matter. The uniting influence of mysticism strongly suggests that where science and spirituality become united they will become indistinguishable.

A composite portrait of Homo christus, the new race

It is time to draw together the diverse strands of material which have herein been used to point to aspects of the nature of the new man. We shall consider *Homo christus* firstly at the level of the species and secondly at the level of the individual, and will conclude the book with a consideration of the programme for designing and creating the new species – that is, the mission of mysticism to particular terrestrial institutions.

In this consideration of the mission of mysticism to the human race it is necessary to point out that, as Christianity is for everyone, so eventual membership of the new race will be the right of everyone who has ever lived. The mystical perception of brotherhood will allow the exclusion of no one, and people will not be included because of their worthiness; nor will the 'unworthy' be excluded because of their unworthiness, for all are included by the unearned grace of God's love.

At the level of the species, it would be a mistake to insist dogmatically that there is an either/or distinction between *Homo sapiens* and *Homo christus*. The theosophical vision, of the latter very gradually replacing the former over hundreds of millennia, is the best guess, but it is also likely that there will be many gradations of race overlapping the pure examples of each. It is unlikely that genetic differentiation will cause a rapid segregation between the two, nor is it likely that until the distant future the two races would prove infertile in inter-racial marriages. On the other hand, it is impossible to predict with certainty what will be the effect of large numbers of people becoming more and more closely identified with Christ. It may well be that a sort of spiritual chain reaction would be caused by such an event: perhaps the effect of such 'Divinization' of mankind would be to burn up the outstanding karma of the rest of the race, thus taking all mankind instantaneously into its beyond. Such an event would be consistent with the mission of the Christ, and with God's unearned grace. It would also be reminiscent of another science-fiction novel by Arthur C. Clarke, *Childhood's End*, in which the human race undergoes precisely such an evolutionary chain reaction, and the new mankind becomes discarnate, vastly potent with energies of many kinds, and abandons earth for its cosmic destiny. But that new race consists only of the children; *Homo christus* contains everyone. It may well be that the meaning of Revelation's myth of the Last Judgement in some way refers to the spiritual chain reaction. Theosophical literature affirms that evolution is purposeful, and that man's growth into the spirit is part of the divine plan. But in view of the awesome power of the Christ, and the uncertain accuracy of superphysical research, it would be imprudent to do more than sketch the outline of the possible future.

At the level of the species, then, it is argued that *Homo sapiens* has begun to evolve into its successor, *Homo christus*; or the fifth root-race has begun to be replaced by the sixth root-race. This evolution is, in part, in response to the divine plan (which is another way of speaking of God's grace), in part due to science, and in part to mankind's will to evolve. But the greatest part is the example of Jesus Christ.

The new race which will, over perhaps a million years, evolve on this and other heavenly bodies will consist of men who more or less closely resemble Jesus. All men will be evolving towards his divine example, but they will differ greatly in their spiritual stature, for they all started at different times. The members of this race will, however, all have the basic Christ-attributes of love and compassion, moral perfection (to a variable degree), and supernatural control of nature. It may be asked what they will do. Their activities, so far as they are comprehensible at all to our unspiritual minds, would include the following. Like us, they will' have religion, but in them it will be a religion of universal mysticism, consisting not only of worship and intercession (but no petition) but mainly of mystical union with God. Indeed, in the later stages of the race everyone will be at the mystical stage of the unitive life, one with God the Father; and all will call him 'Abba', 'Father'. Gustav Mahler's vision of the whole universe beginning to sing will dominate their sublime art, but they will also have work to do. The work will be in three parts. First, the work of rescuing the past, devising time-travel and spiritual chronoengineering to eradicate from the past any hurt or suffering, fulfilling every wish left unsatisfied by the crude mechanism of the early human history. Thus they will at last bind into one brotherhood of perfect men all their brethren of the past, whose sacrifice went to make up the divine men of the future. True it is that to men these actions are impossible; but *Homo christus*, one with its Father, recalls that 'for God all things are possible'.

The second work of the new race will be evangelism and intercession for the rest of their known universe. This refers not only to extraterrestrial sentient creatures who may be suffering or ignorant, but also in a much wider sense to the allegedly inanimate objects, the heavenly bodies themselves, and all their constituents. The one life inheres in every atom, and the divine plan calls for every atom to awaken to full spiritual consciousness. The new race will have an important part to play in this programme.

The third part of the work of the race of *Homo christus* will be self-architecture. It is a duty for man to perfect himself, a duty laid down by Christ himself, and the ultimate perfection will always be beyond the present. It is a part of man's ongoing work to practise self-perfection as a species, and self-improvement through scientific and spiritual means will play a large part in his future.

The above remarks are suggested by Olaf Stapledon's visions of the nature of the most perfect human species. He also suggests that such a race will be universally telepathic, so that a racial mind will decide any major decisions, and every individual will be at least slightly acquainted with every other individual in the entire race. The plausibility of this notion is given support by the plethora of recent evidential proofs of the reality of parapsychological powers, with certain individuals such as Uri Geller showing powers of such force as to suggest that we are indeed at a turning-point in the evolution of the nature of human consciousness. Telepathy of the Stapledonian variety would also be the natural privilege of the universal brotherhood of man.

The members of *Homo christus* will, to a greater or lesser extent, all be far advanced on the spiritual path, and in the practices of the religions. Every one will be a master yogi, a Zen adept, and a near-perfect Buddhist. They will, more or less, enjoy near-perfect control over mind and body, and will have developed the yogic psychic powers (*siddhis*) accordingly. They will all, at the secular level, be near-perfect in self-knowledge; they will be 'self-actualized', and will be pursuing highly specialized professions which will be as heaven to each. There will be no illness except when deliberately accepted for spiritual purposes, not only for the individual's sake but for intercessory purposes: *Homo christus* will, as does Christ himself, shoulder the burden of other sufferers. Likewise there will be no politics, for the racial mind decides formerly 'political' matters, and no crime or civil unrest. For this is the race of Christs, in which 'God's will on earth' is truly and perfectly done. According to the spiritual development of each man, he will directly and most of the time be in contact with his higher self, and from its intuition he will take his decisions. All men will have 'cosmic consciousness', and will spend much of their time in *samadhi*, dwelling on the supramental realms; the most God-realized will abide there, thus becoming the forerunners of the next race, which will be truly and wholly superhuman and will not have material bodies at all. And every man will be an artist and a creator. In this race the Kingdom of God will at last reign. Every man will be constantly purposeful as he evolves to mortal perfection, yet his peace will be equally profound. The members of the race will, each with every other, have the love and rapport of our identical twins, and, such will be the oneness of the race, all will see that one of their most important tasks is character-building for the character of the whole race. This mystical destiny of mankind will, of course, be far more Utopian than any Utopia yet conceived by mankind.

There is in fact nothing sensational or far-fetched in these visions. They are implicit in the New Testament. This 'divinization' of mankind is the natural consequence of Christ-realization, for it must be remembered that in any human being the human whom we see is mostly the little ego, whereas the real person is the Christ within. Seen this way, the creation of *Homo christus* is all Christ's work, no more than the diversification of himself.

At the level of the individual it is natural to wonder whether differences and individuality will persist. We may be sure that they will; each person, according to the theosophists, is born on a different 'ray' of the seven primeval rays, and each has tendencies in connection with each of the other rays. The future men will all differ from one another, and they will each have unique work to do, calling for only their unique profile of talents and personality and temperament. Each person will obtain personal fulfilment, self-actualization and perfection by discovering and doing his work, which is also God's will for him. This will also result in the whole race producing what it can best create as a whole, for the jigsaw structure will again underlie the work of the species.

Men will differ, however, not only in their types but also in their spiritual advancement. Some will have reached the second initiation; others the fourth. Some will have attained to *dharma-megha-samadhi* and the beatific vision, others will more modestly have reached the *nirbija samadhi*. Some will be at the threshold of nirvana, others will just be deciphering the Voice of the Silence. All will be master of prayer and meditation, but some will be more masterly than others. There will be no jealousy or élitism arising out of these differences. The greater will guide the lesser, and the lesser will gladly accept guidance. And each will be blissfully contented with his lot, for he will know his divine destiny, and, having attained the nirvana of the soul, he knows that there is no hurry, that one place in time is as good as another, just as at the earlier initiation of the nirvana of the earth he realized that one place in space is as good as another, and that whatever happens to a man is the best for him.

In conclusion, individuality without separateness, uniqueness in brotherhood are the essence of the psychology of the new race.

Designing and creating the new race

DESIGNING

One of the most fundamental principles of occultism, considered as the mystical science of self-culture and self-realization leading to God-realization, is that man must cultivate himself or remain uncultivated. Because he is made in God's image, and has a share of the divine nature, a deep part of him is destined to initiate spiritual growth. This does not conflict with the Christian insight that all growth is through God's grace: the occultist accepts this as another expression of his awareness that he is already a very part of God, who acts as his inmost self and guide, revealing his presence in prayer and meditation. Thus mankind must not be bashful about designing its successor; for this is a case where it is literally true that God helps those who help themselves. Man is commanded by Christ to become perfect, and mysticism reveals the certainty that he will; but he must choose it for himself, and make it happen.

A second reason for the immediate design of *Homo christus* is that work designing man's successor has already begun in isolated factions all over the world, and now that the time is ripe the job must not be botched. Somehow all mankind must share in the project, which is to be the crowning achievement of *Homo sapiens*. This is not as far-fetched as it seems. The development of the 'whole-earth outlook' following the moon flights is a sign of the times; and it is significant that in 1875, when the Theosophical Society was formed, its first object was stated as the formation of a universal brotherhood of man. The pulse of mankind is quickening, and if humanity is coming into its inheritance of universal fraternity, all will be possible.

This leads to the question of who does the designing. The answer is everyone – but only when the universal brotherhood of man has become a reality. The project would be spoilt at the outset if tainted by fascist tendencies. It is all or none, and Stapledon's ideal of the racial mind must be made a reality. The next major question is the nature of the designing, the methods to be used. In this respect guidance must be taken from the occultist principle of stating from the beginning what exactly one wants, together with the scientific method of aim-oriented empiricism devised by the philosopher Nicholas Maxwell. This method requires all creative endeavours to spend a great deal of time discussing aims before embarking on research. Science, when practised this way, becomes incomparably more useful to mankind than the conventional 'standard empiricist' science which is concerned to discover 'truth' with 'pure science'. Maxwell shows that the very notion of 'pure science' is incoherent; science is a radically human activity, and all science is serving some more or less explicit human purpose. Thus the method of designing the new race will be aim-oriented occultism, but other important factors must be taken into consideration. First, the whole endeavour must be totally consecrated to God, and that consecration must be sustained by frequent meetings for prayer and meditation on the subject. Second, it must be borne in mind at all times that the purpose of the design programme is nothing other than the creation of a race of men approximating as closely as possible to Jesus Christ. But, third, an important reservation is necessary here: man is capable of designing and creating only in the physical and mental realms. He cannot affect the soul, only its setting. So, fourth, man must use the method of the gardener, not that of the sculptor, who chips away, or the builder, who adds. The soul of man is the seed within him, to flower as the Christ, and mankind's work is to design, not the Christ-nature which is already his, but the environment which will most perfectly conduce to the expression of the potential of the seed.

The next question is where the ideas for the design come from. In a sense, all come from God, the Holy Spirit, but the realms in which they express that Spirit are occultism (with its insistence on spiritual perfection as a realizable goal for man), science fiction (which, as the evolutionary conscience of mankind, is packed with relevant ideas about man and his environment and their development), science (which suggests our available resources), mystical religion (which contains all the ideas of how the awakened Christ-nature expresses itself in man), and from the human sciences (which contain our knowledge of human nature at the psychological and sociological levels). Special mention should be made of science fiction, which has a unique role of standing at the threshold of infinity: whenever man or his science reaches a point, science fiction goes beyond it to show that more is left to be done. It is the perpetual affront to the complacent, in this as in science.

CREATING THE NEW RACE: THE NEGATIVE WORK

Since mankind is such a long way from any kind of perfection other than that of his inmost nature, it is necessary for the mystical gardener to do a great deal of preliminary work before his plant can grow: there are masses of debris – psychological, sociological, and ecological – which must be cleared away before the soil can exert its nourishing powers on the Christ-seed. Of course, a more familiar way of describing this task is simply to say that man must be perfected and Utopia created. This, however, is a unique conception of Utopia in that it is designed not to impose human ways, but simply to let God's will express itself.

The work of preparation is focused mainly upon the satisfaction of the biological needs *and* the higher psychological and spiritual needs of everyone. It is for the most part the absence of these satisfactions which leads to unhappiness and strife, and when no man is lacking any of them there will be no motive for strife; and in any case, the developing whole-earth outlook and universal brotherhood will greatly reduce the jealousy and resentment which is the cause of so many wars. It is good to see and know that this brotherhood is developing; one can only pray that the trend continues. If that trend was extrapolated to the end of this century, the universal brotherhood would become a fact just as resources ran out: and the *united* mankind would survive even that seemingly disastrous calamity.

Among the obstacles to mysticism, possessions are always recognized as among the most troublesome. The sense of possessiveness builds on the sense of separateness. When the latter is shattered by the growth of the brotherhood, another cause of war will vanish, for all will spontaneously repudiate any ownership; all must thus one day tread the divine way of St Francis of Assisi in the practice of Christian communism and poverty. Similarly, any government would be a world government, but it would be empowered only very occasionally; for the rest, decentralized self-rule must be the norm, until Stapledonian racial telepathy occurs.

But the main thrust of this preparatory work must be the amelioration of pain and suffering. And first to go will be the fear of death, which stains black so many lives. With it will go the fear of hell, and pity for the 'lost souls of hell', for the growth of spiritual awareness will confirm the existing trend towards the certain knowledge that death is not the end, nor can it lead to 'hell'; rather, it is an essentially beneficent institution by which people refresh themselves and have the opportunity of seeing what they have achieved, what they have added to their immortal character, during the previous life. When this is all *knowledge*, the greatest grief of mankind will be forever allayed. Likewise, the pains of illness and misfortune will be seen for what they are – friends, reminders, pointers to the right path – and everyone will turn illness and misfortune to the spiritual purpose of growth. This understanding of what the eastern sages called karma will transform human life beyond recognition, for it will then be learned that what we call pain and pleasure are equally fruitful to our *happiness*, which is the deeper mood based in the soul. In fact, it would be no exaggeration to say that the mystical gardener's main task at this stage is the dissemination of certain knowledge, mystical experience of the soul, since that would be sufficient to put an instantaneous stop to strife. It is thus encouraging to hear from the millenarian theosophists that, in the new religion which is promised, all men will be given the first initiation, in which they will confront their immortal souls and understand the reality of karma, thus preventing them from further ill deeds.

This programme of spiritual initiation would also, needless to say, put an end to all those human 'problems' which have beset the human race since Adam; although extrahuman problems such as earthquakes would remain to test the united humanity.

The present mankind is, however, battered and bruised psychically, and the mystical gardener's work will include extensive psychotherapy for everyone, to bring the traumatized mind back to its pristine innocence. In this project the Maslovian humanistic psychology, with its emphasis on the joyful nature of the real man, will have a prominent part alongside the older psychotherapeutic methods. Indeed, the Maslovian outlook, with its promise of peak experiences and self-actualization for every man, will be one of the standards of united mankind, and the hundreds of techniques for self-actualization now developing at the hands of Maslow's successors will be the common property of everyone. General psychology will base itself on the spiritual psychology of Patanjali and St John of the Cross, and all will be aware of their divine potential; self-hate will be impossible.

In education the lessons learned will be love, brotherhood, morality, and spirituality; the master principle inculcated at school will be the imitation of Christ, for the whole species will be doing that. Art will burgeon to an even greater extent than is now evident, and self-knowledge leading to self-realization will be known by every schoolchild as the purpose of education (and indeed of all of life).

Inevitably in such a regime the spiritual powers of the supernormal, as displayed by the Christ (precognition, telepathy, miraculous healing, etc.), would become widespread, and more and more illnesses would be cured by faith and the Holy Spirit. Illnesses not thus cured would be accepted as serving an important purpose in the life of the sufferer.

Little need be said about politics, which is one of the biggest obstacles to spirituality, because the creation of the spiritual environment will ensure the generation of wise social institutions; and much of politics will become unnecessary, as it bases itself upon the premise of human separateness. The disappearance of jealousy and greed, resentment and fear will also perfect, *en passant*, the mass media, which at present are used almost wholly for purposes of commercial and political exploitation and control. The universal brotherhood of man will use the mass media for the purpose of love and unity: information will be given where it is needed, advertising abolished, consumer-viewing manipulation abolished.

It may be that man's terrestrial career is endangered by ecological occurrences; if so, part of the 'negative' work of preparation will entail the colonization of other heavenly bodies. This is definitely a possibility, as is told in the next section. Likewise, preparations are probably under way for the continuation of the human race in the event of a nuclear holocaust of global proportions. In both these matters the pages of science fiction will be found to be crammed with useful ideas at the level of the problem, project, programme, and paradigm. One of the most urgent preparatory tasks is in fact for a comprehensive content analysis of all extant science fiction to be undertaken by the designers of the new race.

CREATING THE NEW RACE: THE POSITIVE WORK

We can, for the sake of this last section, now presuppose a humanity which has been brought to relative perfection by the mystical gardener, the Holy Spirit. Our vision discerns a humanity which is united into a mystic brotherhood, and in which every member has passed the first initiation into the lesser mysteries of the immortal soul. The 'negative' preparations have achieved this, and the human race is united in its single purpose of creating a race of successors who will more nearly approximate to Christ himself. To design and create that race *is* the 'positive work' described in this section.

Let us consider, therefore, how this last race of *Homo sapiens*, so far beyond ourselves in spiritual stature, will go about the great work of designing and creating their successor. We have already pointed out the sources of ideas for the design stage; now we must survey the work as a whole, design and creation, and enumerate the resources which will be available for this divine project. They are, quite simply, art, science, religion, and personal relationships. Each of these four has its own profound mission.

Art is a joy beyond description to the awakened man. An earlier chapter pointed out that 'mystical aesthetics' must now develop in order to ensure that the true purpose of art be respected: for the real meaning of art is that every one of the aesthetic experiences which it engenders teaches something about the nature of the deeper recesses of the divine in human nature, and every such experience provides information about the design of *Homo christus*. As mystical aesthetics develops, there will be developed a special sub-science in which 'peak experiences' associated with art will be dissected phenomenologically so that the pure aesthetic experience can be separated from irrelevant emotional and cognitive accretions. And all creative art will more and more purely aim to add to this sum of mystical knowledge. No doubt every known variety of multi-media art, and countless as yet undiscovered ones, will contribute to the work.

Personal relationships will be an equally potent source of the advancement of the great work, for every relationship will have the character of mystical friendship, in which the friends will follow the mystical definition of a friend: 'A friend is a person whom one helps to *his* fulfilment and self-realization.' This Christian principle will lead to an invaluable succession of insights into the nature of *Homo christus*, and of course to the most perfect friendships imaginable to those concerned.

The new religion, whether it be Christian in essence or otherwise, will lead men to a near-constant apprehension of the divine in all and everything; after all, the real purpose of religion is nothing other than to bring men to God and to godly behaviour, and the new religion will do this to an extent far beyond even the imagination of existing religions.

But the last word of this section, as of the whole book, must go to science, for it is science which will, in the last analysis, have the actual responsibility of *creating*, under the Holy Spirit, the species whose construction is the ultimate mission of mysticism for ourselves.

This is a point at which a recapitulation is advisable. We have arrived at the final sub-section of the final chapter of a book which has tried to present a thesis in a cumulative way. The argument, which has interrelated science, spirituality, and the future of mankind, culminates in this section.

The starting-point of this book was the fact that, through the development of science and technology, mankind has ceased to be in the jurisdiction of natural selection. Man has the power to alter himself as radically as he chooses, and henceforward evolution is in his hands. This fact was coupled with the equally certain purport of the world's mystical literature, which is also concerned with the evolution of men and man. And Jesus Christ, the perfect man, the incarnate God, is the link between science and religion. He is to be the prototype of a race of *Homo sapiens* which will no longer suffer from spiritual incompleteness, or (as it is sometimes called) original sin. The mission of mysticism to mankind, therefore, is to lead *Homo sapiens* to the state in which it can use science and be led by spirit to create the race of Christs, the perfect race untainted by original sin. In this chapter it has been shown that the contemporary spiritual trend gives hope that a united mankind might appear in the foreseeable future, and it has in general terms been explained how the existing human race could, through mystical enlightenment, prepare itself for the great work of its career. Moreover, the basic design strategies were described. Now it is the actual creation, by science, that remains to be considered.

It can be assumed that existing science can easily be developed in ways that will potentiate it for this task. Medical science, for example, will doubtless eventually develop the means of combating, even preventing, all disease; physics will develop nuclear power in sufficient quantities for every person to use energy as required. These and many other possibilities have been sketched by Arthur C. Clarke in *Profiles of the Future*. But among his most important ideas are those mentioned earlier concerning the introduction of machines into man's nature and evolution, and the eventual assumption of the evolutionary leadership by machines alone. An analysis of this from the point of view of mysticism showed how it is impossible, because it neglects the spiritual dimension of man. But it is suggestive for the redesigning of mankind. So far as we know, human science could not prevent or destroy a soul, or anything on the spiritual planes. Thus, it would presumably have to rely on actual human babies or embryos for its work, which would have to be along the lines of genetic engineering and eugenics. The work of science, of course, is only to create perfected minds and bodies through which the soul may operate. Given that this is so, the preparatory work of science, in creating the ideal environment, should be sufficient, for the incarnate soul would then have every facility needed for its growth. But it is obvious that science is already developing the techniques with which to alter *in utero* the infant's characteristics, and it is only a matter of time before it will be possible to choose not only the sex of a baby, but also its colour, height, intelligence, and so on, and beyond that the development of behaviour genetics is providing psychologists with the opportunity of breeding for distinct behavioural traits such as aggression, curiosity, and extraversion. This prospect may horrify the religious person, who will think it unholy, but it is not, for the body and mind are material entities used by the soul, not the soul itself. And in any case, the religious critics of science must come to terms, the sooner the better, with the growing power of science to penetrate almost to the soul of man.

For the plain fact is that science is not going to go away if the devout ignore it. It is, for better or worse, a part of man's life, just as his body is a sacred temple of the Holy Spirit. It is always necessary for a mystic to come to terms with his body sooner or later, and it is necessary for mankind, not to stick its head in the sand, but to face the seemingly baffling question of the relation between the incredibly accelerating empire of science and the equally incredible, growing mystical consciousness. Somewhere in the confused no-man's land between science and spirituality there is now being born *mystical science*, or, as it may be called, *science-mysticism*, or mysticism of science. In its depths lies hidden the answer to the question of the nature of *Homo christus*. Science and spirituality can be likened to two identical triangles standing side by side. With the contemporary acceleration of each they have toppled towards one another, and at their joint apex man will pass through into the beyond which he cannot know until his whole species has been purified and made ready for that knowledge. We can only say that the one sure guide to that beyond remains the person of Jesus Christ, possessor of every human perfection, including many of which we are not even aware.

By two very different routes, man has come to the very brink of divinity; his science is more powerful than the greatest gods of the ancient Greeks; and he has Christ's mandate to seek divine perfection. But nonetheless he stands at the first major decision point in his evolution. He has the power to choose what he will become, and it is desperately important that he chooses wisely. And if he is to choose wisely, he must have an intimate understanding of every one of the resources which this book has shown to be at his fingertips.

There is no neat, simple answer to the question of the nature of *Homo christus*. We can only say that human superscience will have the task of creating one or more species which are patterned on Christ himself. As to further details, 'the rest is silence', for the truth about the matter is undoubtedly confined to the transintellectual, supramental realms, from which we hear only faint echoes and see 'through a glass darkly'. When we hear in full and see brightly we will know and comprehend, but then we will *be* that *Homo christus* whose urgent creation we are now compelled to undertake, spurred ceaselessly by the twin rowels of science and mysticism, bound to pursue unto death a vision of perfection whose very embodiment in the person of Jesus Christ perpetually astonishes and inspires us.

Index

Index